THE AMERICAN BAR ASSOCIATION

LEGAL

GUIDE

FOR

WOMEN

EFERENCE

D0062308

THE AMERICAN BAR ASSOCIATION

LEGAL GUIDE FOR WOMEN

RANDOM HOUSE REFERENCE
NEW YORK   TORONTO   LONDON   SYDNEY   AUCKLAND

The American Bar Association Legal Guide for Women

Copyright © 2004 by the American Bar Association

Please address inquiries about electronic licensing of reference products for
use on a network, in software, or on CD-ROM to the Subsidiary Rights
Department, Random House Reference, fax 212-572-6003.

This book is available for special discounts for bulk purchases for sales promotions
or premiums. Special editions, including personalized covers, excerpts of existing
books, and corporate imprints, can be created in large quantities for special needs.
For more information, write to Random House, Inc., Special Markets/Premium
Sales, 1745 Broadway, MD 6-2, New York, NY, 10019 or e-mail
specialmarkets@randomhouse.com

Visit the Random House Web site: www.randomhouse.com

Points of view or opinions in this publication do not necessarily represent the
official policies or positions of the American Bar Association.

This book is not a substitute for an attorney, nor does it attempt to answer
all questions about all the situations you may encounter.

Library of Congress Cataloging-in-Publication Data is available.

First Edition

PRINTED IN THE UNITED STATES OF AMERICA

0 9 8 7 6 5 4 3 2 1

ISBN: 0-375-72091-X

The American Bar Association

CONTENTS

FOREWORD

Robert A. Stein, *Executive Director*
American Bar Association

The American Bar Association is the nation's premier source of legal information. With more than 400,000 members, representing all specialties and every type of legal practice, the ABA is uniquely able to deliver accurate, up-to-date, unbiased legal information to its members, to the media, and to the general public. The ABA website—www.abanet.org—is an unrivaled database in the legal field.

Women face important legal issues throughout their lives—in school, at work, in their family lives, and after they retire. Lawyers frequently advise women about the law relating to numerous issues, from workplace discrimination to domestic violence.

This book provides you with the benefit of the ABA's network of hundreds of thousands of lawyers. *The ABA Legal Guide for Women* was written with the aid of ABA members from all over the country. Lawyers from the Section on Family Law, the Commission on Domestic Violence, the Commission on Women in the Profession, and many other entities within the ABA served as reviewers of the manuscript.

Our reviewers gave advice on the content of the book and went on to review draft chapters, providing clarifications, suggesting additional topics that would be helpful to readers, and polishing the manuscript to make it read even better. The reviewers brought a rich range of experience to the project, lending their expertise and experience to help present information about the law from a woman's perspective. For example, reviewers included women from the National Women's Law Center and other organizations that have litigated to advance women's rights; attorneys at the top of their profession; and professors of law from across the country.

Finally, the ABA's Standing Committee on Public Education provided oversight for this project. This committee and its excellent staff contribute the perspective of experts in communicating about the law.

Thanks to all of the lawyers who worked on this book, you can be sure that the information it includes is

- helpful
- accurate
- unbiased
- current
- written in a reader-friendly style that you can understand easily, and
- reflective of a national picture, since ABA members practice in all jurisdictions.

Public education and public service are two important goals of the American Bar Association. This book shows how the ABA takes an active role in providing the public with relevant and useful information.

The American Bar Association is the largest voluntary association in the world. Besides its commitment to public education, the ABA provides programs to assist lawyers and judges in their work and initiatives to improve the legal system for the public, including promoting fast, affordable alternatives to lawsuits, such as mediation, arbitration, conciliation, and small claims courts. Through ABA support for lawyer-referral programs and pro bono services (where lawyers donate their time), people like you have been able to find the best lawyer for their particular case and have received quality legal help within their budgets.

Robert A. Stein is the executive director of the American Bar Association. He was formerly dean of the University of Minnesota Law School.

INTRODUCTION

Alan S. Kopit, *Chair*
ABA Standing Committee on Public Education

Women have made significant strides in recent decades, in large part because of the protections afforded them by the law. Today, for example, women are finishing high school, graduating from college, and entering the workforce in record numbers. According to the U.S. Census Bureau, 89 percent of young women (aged twenty-four to thirty-five) have completed high school, compared to only 85 percent of men. Thirty-three percent of women in the same age group have completed college, compared to a mere 29 percent of their male counterparts. Women are now attending law schools and other professional schools in almost the same numbers as men.

Changes in the law have helped bring about this progress. Title IX, for example, prevents discrimination against women in schools and colleges, and Title VII prevents discrimination against women in the workplace. But in many instances, these laws are useful only if women know their rights, and the steps they can take to secure them. Many women who are victims of discrimination at school or at work do not even recognize that they have suffered discrimination, much less that it is against the law, and that there are steps they can take to stop it.

Of course, there are many areas of the law that have a particular impact on women that have nothing to do with discrimination. For example, the laws regulating rights in marriage, divorce, and child custody disputes are crafted in language that is gender-neutral. Nonetheless, these laws can affect women very differently from men, as a result of differences in women's working lives, earning capacity, and child care duties. The same holds true when it comes to laws that affect women later in life, when women are planning an estate or applying for Medicare. Finally, there are some areas of the law that are of direct relevance to women, such as laws relating to women's health issues (such as infertility, pregnancy, contraception, and abortion), and laws relating to violence against women.

It's all a bit daunting, isn't it? There are so many areas of the law affecting women in so many different ways, that a quick trip to the library to find out more seems almost impossible. That's where this book can help. It provides background information about all these areas of the law and more—it gives women information about their rights under the law, and suggests the pros and cons of various courses of action. It also gives details on websites to visit and numbers to call for more information.

ABOUT THE AUTHOR

Our principal author, Mary Phelan D'Isa, is a law professor and writer who has written on a wide range of subjects for the public, and teaches at Thomas M. Cooley Law School in Michigan. Her manuscript was reviewed and approved by experts on discrimination law, family law, health law, elder law and other areas, under the guidance of the ABA's Standing Committee on Public Education. Together, we've worked to provide you with easy-to-read information that will help you understand and use the law that affects your daily life, your plans for your children, and your future. Our goal is to provide you with information about the law that will help you spot problems before they become major—when they're easiest to handle. And don't worry, we explain the law in plain, direct language. You won't find legal jargon here—just concise, straightforward discussions of your options under the law.

HOW TO USE THIS BOOK

We've structured this book more or less chronologically, starting with the moment you walk through the schoolhouse doors, and ending with a look at the issues women face during retirement. The book is clearly organized so you can easily find the help you need at every stage.

Part One: Education Without Discrimination takes a close and detailed look at Title IX, the law that prohibits discrimination against women in schools and colleges. It explains when Title IX applies to you, what kinds of behavior constitute discrimination, and the steps that you can take if you think you're being discriminated against.

Part Two: Workplace Issues considers the kinds of legal issues women face in their working lives. Of course, this includes a look at discrimination (including sexual harassment), and what you can do if you're being discriminated against at work. But it also looks at some other workplace issues of particular interest to women—rights to parental leave and pregnancy leave, the legal issues relating to child care, and the legal side of working from home.

Part Three: Family approaches the law regulating marriage, divorce, child custody and child support from a woman's perspective, and gives you information about your rights that you can use. There's also a chapter on the rights of unmarried couples, which includes information on the kinds of steps you can take to ensure that you and your partner stay in control of legal issues relating to your health, property and finances.

Part Four: Health gives you some of the legal information you'll need to take charge of your health care, in four areas particularly important to women: infertility, contraception, pregnancy and childbirth, and abortion.

Part Five: Violence Against Women includes chapters on sexual assault and domestic violence. You can read about the state and federal laws that protect victims, what women can expect from police after a violent crime, and what happens if a perpetrator goes to trial. We'll also direct you to many other valuable sources of information, and to organizations that can offer you assistance.

Part Six: Money looks at two important financial topics for women: credit and government benefits. Find out more about how your credit works, and read on to learn whether you or your children could be eligible for government benefits.

Part Seven: Planning Ahead takes a look at the issues that women need to consider as they grow older and think about retirement. We cover pensions, medical issues, and Social Security, and of course, we also give you a thorough overview of the basic principles of planning your estate.

Our last chapter gives you websites, books, and other sources of useful information, many just the touch of a computer key or telephone keypad away.

WRITTEN WITH YOU IN MIND

We've made a special effort to make this book practical, by using situations and problems you are likely to encounter. Each chapter is clearly laid out, with a real-life starting situation that shows the practical ramifications of the subject.

Within chapters, brief special sidebars alert you to important points. Particular sidebars include:

- sidebars with this icon ▶, which generally give you practical tips that could be of benefit to you;
- sidebars with this icon ⓘ, which provide key additional information;
- sidebars with this icon ⚠, which generally warn you about a potential pitfall that you can navigate with the right information and help; and
- sidebars with this icon 🗐, which provide clear, plain English definitions to legal terms.

Another feature—"Ask a Lawyer"—highlights our experts responding to actual questions from people, giving legal information that may help you as you grapple with similar issues within your own family. This sidebar is denoted by the icon ❪❫.

At the end of each chapter, in a section entitled "The World at Your Fingertips," we advise you where to go for more information if you'd like to explore a topic further—usually to free or inexpensive materials that will fill your mind without emptying your wallet. The concluding section of each chapter—"Remember This"—highlights the most important points that the chapter has covered.

With this book, you'll be able to make informed decisions about a wide range of problems and opportunities. Armed with the knowledge and insights we provide, you can be confident that the decisions you make will be in your best interests.

Alan S. Kopit is a legal-affairs commentator who has appeared on national television for more than fifteen years. He is chair of the ABA's Standing Committee on Public Education and is an attorney in private practice with the firm of Hahn Loeser & Parks, LLP, in Cleveland, Ohio.

PART ONE

Education Without Discrimination

CHAPTER 1

Sex Discrimination at School: Education, Athletics, and Discrimination

The year was 1972. *Ms.* magazine debuted and Billie Jean King was named "Sportsperson of the Year"—the first woman to be so honored. The median household income was $9,697 and a postage stamp cost eight cents. In that year, Meg began her freshman year at Notre Dame, in the first class to admit women as undergraduate students.

Meg was the starting center for her high school girls' basketball team, but fencing was the only varsity sport offered for women at Notre Dame, so she didn't play any sport at college. Instead, she concentrated on her studies and hoped to become a trial attorney—despite the fact that women made up less than 6 percent of students enrolled in law schools. Congress passed Title IX on June 23, 1972, to ensure sex discrimination did not keep women from pursuing the educational opportunities available to men. Seven years later, Meg graduated from Notre Dame Law School.

Today, some thirty years after the passage of Title IX, a postage stamp costs thirty-seven cents and the median household income is $42,228. Meg no longer practices law, having given up a successful practice to spend more time raising her family. Today, women account for about half of all law school students, and the number of women playing competitive sports in college has increased fivefold in the past thirty years. Meg's daughter, Kate, who is also athletically gifted, is a senior in high school and is considering athletic scholarship offers from eight schools—something her mother never experienced. Notre Dame now boasts thirteen varsity sports for women—the same number of sports it offers male students—and the dean of its law school is a woman.

Is Title IX responsible for these dramatic gains for women?

Title IX prohibits sex-based discrimination under any educational program or activity that receives federal financial support. It was passed in 1972, as part of the Education Amendments to Higher Education Act of 1965. Its brief thirty-seven words read:

> No person in the United States shall, on the basis of sex, be excluded from participation in, be denied the benefits of, or be subject to discrimination under any education program or activity receiving federal financial assistance.

Many people assume that Title IX only requires equal opportunities for female athletes. In fact, it doesn't just cover sports—it applies to all aspects of education, from math class to band practice. The primary purpose of Title IX is to give all women and girls equal educational opportunities and benefits—and, in particular, to open doors to colleges and graduate schools. Before Title IX, many graduate schools had quotas on the number of women they would admit, and some schools set higher standards of admission for women than for men. Under Title IX, such practices are illegal.

This chapter will focus on the practical aspects of Title IX, including your rights under Title IX and ways you can protect and enforce those rights if you suffer sex discrimination in pursuing your education.

TITLE IX: BROAD AND BOLD

Title IX applies to any educational program or activity that receives any money from the federal government. This means that Title IX applies to

• public and private elementary schools, middle schools, and high schools that receive federal funds,

• vocational educational programs, school-to-work programs, and "tech prep" programs that receive federal funds,

• community colleges, state colleges and universities, and private colleges and universities that receive federal funds, and

- extern, intern, and fellowship programs at private companies or associations that are associated with or supervised by an educational institution that receives federal funds.

As you can see, Title IX is pretty broad. However, there are some exemptions. Religious institutions where religious tenets do not accommodate coeducational programs (e.g., Roman Catholic seminaries that prepare men for the priesthood) are exempted from Title IX. Boy Scout and Girl Scout programs are also exempt, as are sororities and fraternities. Title IX does not apply to military schools that train individuals for service in the U.S. military or merchant marines or to schools that have always been single sex. However, even if Title IX doesn't apply, discrimination may still be illegal in some schools. For exam-

(i) AN OFFICER AND A LADY

There are several colleges across the nation that are designed to train military officers, and all of them used to be exclusively male. However, the U.S. Military Academy (West Point), the U.S. Naval Academy (Annapolis), and the other colleges operated by the U.S. military have admitted women for more than twenty years. The two last holdouts were two state-supported military colleges: the Virginia Military Institute (VMI) and South Carolina's The Citadel. They finally went coeducational as a result of a Supreme Court decision in 1996.

The state of Virginia had established a separate, but very different, military training school using a preexisting program at Mary Baldwin College, a private women's liberal arts college in Staunton, Virginia. The Court held that establishing a separate leadership program for women at another institution did not meet the Fourteenth Amendment's requirement of "equal protection of the laws." Writing for a 7-1 Court in striking down this approach, Justice Ruth Bader Ginsburg said, "However well this plan serves Virginia's sons, it makes no provision for her daughters." The first female students were admitted to VMI in 1997.

ple, the U.S. Supreme Court decided in 1996 that women should be admitted to a single-sex state school, the Virginia Military Institute, under the Equal Protection Clause of the Constitution.

Originally, there was some question as to what it meant to receive federal funds under Title IX. Did the statute require funds to be given directly to a school? What if only one program in the school received funds? Was that sufficient for Title IX to apply to the whole school? In 1988, Congress amended the law to make it clear that if any part of an educational institution receives federal money, Title IX covers all of the institution's programs and activities. This amendment opened the door for discrimination charges against athletic programs, which rarely receive federal funds directly. It made it clear that Title IX applied to off-campus extracurricular programs and activities, such as playing in the school band off campus. The National Women's Law Center and others have successfully argued that Title IX also applies to state high school athletic associations. Even though the associations themselves may not receive federal funds, they exercise controlling authority over the athletics programs of schools that do receive federal funds. Similar arguments can be made when schools assign control of programs to private contractors, such as when failing schools hire private companies to run them.

DISCRIMINATION UNDER TITLE IX

There are two types of discrimination under Title IX. **Disparate treatment** discrimination occurs whenever you are treated differently because of your sex. This might occur, for example, if you and other girls are assigned to home economics classes and boys are assigned to shop class, or if a teacher gives males pamphlets about careers in construction, but does not give the same information to females. It is also discriminatory for a teacher or supervisor to pay little attention to you and other females in the class, but give the males help and advice. There might be disparate treatment discrimination in athletics if a high school athletics program schedules girls in a nontraditional or less popular season, while the boys play in a traditional season.

Disparate impact is a more subtle form of discrimination that occurs where actions that appear to be gender neutral actually affect one sex more than the other. For example, there may be disparate impact discrimination if your school has a rule that "students with long hair cannot conduct chemistry experiments." Such a rule appears to be gender neutral because it applies to all students, but in fact it applies to more female students than male, because more females have long hair. The school might be able to justify the policy if it can show a "substantial legitimate justification" for the rule. For example, it might argue that such a policy is necessary for safety reasons. Female students might argue in turn that safety could be protected to the same extent if students with long hair were required to keep it tied back during experiments. Similarly, a rule that students can only play tuba in the school marching band "if a student can carry a tuba for one hour" might be discriminatory. The rule appears to be gender neutral because it ostensibly applies to all students, but in fact it is likely to apply to more female students than male students, because female students are less likely to have the physical strength and stamina required to carry the instrument for so long.

TITLE IX'S ROLE IN ATHLETICS

Title IX has been especially beneficial to women athletes. The number of female college athletes has increased more than five-fold since Title IX was enacted—in 1972, fewer than 32,000 women participated in college sports, and in 2002, the number of female athletes was about 160,000. But while more than 50 percent of the students at Division I colleges are women, they receive only about 41 percent of the opportunities to play sports, 43 percent of the athletic scholarship dollars, and 32 percent of the dollars spent to recruit new athletes.

( ) ASK A LAWYER

Q. *I complained to my school that the girls are training in the traditionally
female careers and the boys in the traditionally male careers, but they
say that this is just the result of the choices students make. Is that a
fair defense under the law? Is there any requirement that schools
have to enroll a given percentage of girls in some classes?*

A. In vocational or career and technical high schools, it is not uncommon
for girls to be clustered in traditionally female programs such as cos-
metology, health care, and child care while the boys are enrolled in traditionally male programs such as construction, aviation, and plumbing.
These patterns of enrollment have consequences for, among other
things, the wages boys and girls can earn when they complete their
programs. Often, these patterns are not the result of choices made by
the students. Sometimes, sex segregation in vocational programs is
due to guidance counselors who steer students toward training programs that are traditional for their gender. Or girls might drop out of
male-dominated courses due to sexual harassment from a teacher or
peers. In both examples, the school is discriminating against girls on
the basis of sex, which is not permissible under the law.

   While there is no requirement under the law that schools achieve
a certain percentage of male or female students in particular vocational training programs, girls have the right to receive information in a
nonbiased manner about all vocational training programs offered by a
school and the right to recruitment practices that are free from sex
stereotypes. Girls must receive equal treatment in the classroom and
must have equal access to upper-level math and science courses. If
you suspect your school is discriminating against girls, tell a parent or
someone you trust and investigate the school's procedure for filing a
complaint of sex discrimination. If your school refuses to fix the problem, file a complaint with the U.S. Department of Education's Office
for Civil Rights or consult a lawyer.

—Answer by Ellen Eardley, Fellow
National Women's Law Center, Washington, D.C.

Q. At my school, women make up more than 55 percent of the student body, yet men's sports get almost two-thirds of the athletic budget. How is this possible under Title IX? What can we do to get more funding for women's sports?

A. While Title IX does not require schools to spend the same amount of money on men's and women's sports, it does require schools to treat male and female athletes equally overall. So the question is, when comparing the whole men's sports program to the whole women's sports program, are male and female athletes treated equally? To make this comparison, you have to look beyond any difference in money spent on the men's versus the women's program to see if more money means better athletic benefits and services. For example, a difference in the amount of money a school spends on men's versus women's uniforms may not be discriminatory if the uniforms are of equal quality but the men's just cost more than the women's. But if the school spends more on men's uniforms because they are new and of good quality, whereas the women's are old and of poor quality, then the school is discriminating against the women.

The fact that the athletic budget is so skewed toward men's sports at your school may suggest a Title IX problem. Here are some things you can do to get more funding for women's sports: raise the issue with the athletic director or principal, talk to the booster clubs for girls' sports to see if they can help, file a complaint with your school's Title IX coordinator (every school or school district is supposed to have one), file a complaint with your local Office for Civil Rights, or file a lawsuit. If you choose to file a lawsuit, you will need specific examples of how male athletes receive superior benefits and services and you will need to show that the lower amount of money spent on women's sports reflects discriminatory treatment.

—Answer by Neena Chaudhry, Senior Counsel
National Women's Law Center, Washington, D.C.

Q. *The boys' basketball team at my school gets to practice in the new gym every afternoon; the girls' team has to practice in the old gym, which is smaller and colder. I think this is unfair and I made a complaint to my school about it. Next thing I know I was dropped from the team. I'm sure this is "retaliation." Can I make a complaint about this? To whom should I complain?*

A. You are correct in believing that the treatment of your team is unfair. It is also unlawful under Title IX, which requires that boys' and girls' teams receive equal opportunities to use practice facilities. The teams should take turns using the new gym. It also violates Title IX for your school to retaliate against you for complaining about the discrimination. Therefore, you should file a complaint with your school's Title IX coordinator. You can also talk about the matter with someone who has authority over the person to whom you originally complained.

The school must investigate your complaint and have you reinstated on the team if it agrees that you were retaliated against. It should also end the discriminatory treatment of the girls' team and make sure that no one else is retaliated against.

If your school is not responsive to your complaints, you can complain to the Office of Civil Rights of the U.S. Department of Education, or, as a last resort, file a lawsuit.

—Answer by Dina Lassow, Senior Counsel
National Women's Law Center, Washington, D.C.

Q. *I'm pregnant, but I don't want that to end my education. Does the law require any special help for pregnant students or new mothers? What can I do to continue my education after I have the baby?*

A. Title IX prohibits discrimination based on pregnancy and parental or marital status. So, for example, it requires the educational institution to provide you with an excused medical leave of absence for a period deemed reasonable by your doctor. The institution cannot require a doctor's certification verifying your ability to continue participation, unless it requires such a certification for all students under the attention of a physician. In addition, the institution must provide separate programs for you if you want them (although it cannot require you to take separate programs), and any separate programs must be comparable to the instructional programs provided to other students.

—Answer by Neena Chaudhry, Senior Counsel
National Women's Law Center, Washington, D.C.

The Title IX athletics policies responsible for the progress of women and girls in sports have been controversial, facing repeated legal challenges by critics who claim the policies are hurting certain men's sports. Specifically, some have argued that Title IX imposes quotas because it requires schools to provide women with equal participation opportunities that they don't want, thereby forcing schools to cut men's teams. The fundamental premise of these critics' arguments is the stereotype that women are inherently less interested in sports than are men. Every federal appellate court to consider these arguments has rejected them and upheld Title IX's athletics policies.

A plain reading of the Title IX policy at issue demonstrates that it neither imposes quotas nor requires (or encourages) schools to cut men's teams. To prove it is providing males and females equal opportunities to play sports under Title IX, a school must satisfy any one part of the following three-part test:

• Demonstrate that its percentage of female athletes is nearly the same as its percentage of female undergraduate students
• Show that it has a history and continuing practice of increasing opportunities for women
• Prove that it is fully accommodating the athletic interests and abilities of its female students

Proponents of women's sports note that while women's participation opportunities have increased since Title IX was passed, men's opportunities have also increased. And just as some women's teams have been cut, so, too, have some men's teams, in response to changing interests and abilities, budgetary factors, or other choices by schools. Moreover, a government study shows that women's opportunities do not come at the expense of men's opportunities. According to a 2001 study by the General Accounting Office, from 1992 to 2000 72 percent of colleges and universities added teams for women without cutting any men's teams.

In 2002, the Department of Education established a commission to look into this issue and make recommendations about whether Title IX's athletics policies should be changed. In the face of a national outpouring of support for Title IX, the Commission on Opportunities in Athletics reported in 2003 that Title IX was working well on the whole, but nevertheless submitted recommendations to the Department of Education that would substantially weaken the three-part test. In July 2003, the Department of Education reaffirmed the validity of Title IX's three-part test and reiterated that dropping men's sports to comply with the test was disfavored.

ENFORCING TITLE IX

If you have suffered sex discrimination, there are three possible ways in which you can pursue a claim under Title IX. You can
- complain to your educational institution,
- file a complaint with the Office for Civil Rights (OCR) of the U.S. Department of Education, or
- commence a lawsuit.

You can pursue any one of these options, or all three if you wish. Most people start with the internal grievance procedure, then complain to the OCR if that fails, and then file a federal lawsuit if OCR drops the ball.

Complain to the Educational Institution

Under the law, all educational institutions are required to designate at least one employee to be a Title IX coordinator. The institution must tell you the coordinator's name, office address, and telephone number. It must also distribute its written policy against sex discrimination and its grievance procedure for making complaints. If you don't know how to contact the coordinator, check with the administration of your school—the dean or the principal should be able to tell you whom to contact. If you are discriminated against at your school, you should find out who the Title IX coordinator is and make a written complaint.

The law does not require that you pursue the school's internal grievance procedure first or at all, but this is usually the cheapest, quickest, and most direct way to resolve your claim. You do not usually need to hire a lawyer to follow this procedure, unless there are special circumstances (e.g., if you are part of a larger class of students who have similar claims). You might want to consult a lawyer if you feel uncomfortable confronting the school.

Here are a few tips: check your school's policy and make sure you complain within the time period specified; make sure that your complaint conveys all the crucial details—who was discriminated against, when, by whom, and how; and be sure to indicate how the school may contact you for further information. If you can, keep a detailed record or diary of everything related to your complaint, as well as a copy of anything in writing that you receive or send. If you speak to someone in person or over the phone, make sure you record the time and date, his or her name and position, what was said, and any promises the person made. Finally, you should send copies of your written complaint to everyone who may be responsible for enforcement: the Title IX coordinator at the school, the principal, the superintendent of schools, and the school board. Giving notice to all of these parties may be important if you subsequently need to prove liability in a lawsuit.

Each school's procedures will vary, but OCR regulations require that schools and other institutions provide for "prompt and equitable resolution of complaints." The length of the complaint process will depend on the nature of the complaint, but it should be a matter of a few months at the most, and it should, in some fashion, give you the opportunity for a fair hearing. If you complain to your school and it does not respond within a reasonable period of time, or if you are dissatisfied with the resolution it reaches, you may file a complaint with the OCR or sue your school in court, assuming that you act within the applicable time limits.

File a Complaint with the OCR

If making a complaint through the school's internal procedures would be futile because the discrimination is so pervasive, or if you filed a complaint through your school's internal procedures and are not satisfied with the result, then you may want to file a complaint with the OCR.

Anyone who believes that Title IX has been violated can file an OCR complaint. You do not have to be the victim of the discrimination to complain. You can complain if you are a student who suffered discrimination, the parent of a student who suffered discrimination, a witness to discrimination, or a representative of a group of students who suffered discrimination.

You should make your complaint to the OCR in writing. You can send in a complaint by e-mail or fax, but if you take that route, OCR officials will ask you to mail in a signed copy as well. The OCR won't accept anonymous complaints, but it will try to keep your identity confidential. It may have to disclose your identity in the course of investigating your complaint.

Your written complaint should include the same kind of information as your complaint to the school. In as much detail as possible, you should explain who was discriminated against, in what way, and by whom. Your complaint should detail when the discrimination took place, state who was harmed (this might be different from the person who was discriminated against), and identify who can be contacted for more information. Be sure to give the OCR a list of witnesses who will corroborate your facts. If you have already been through your school's grievance procedure, you should also indicate the reasons you were dissatisfied with its decision. You need to be sure to sign and date your complaint and let the department know where you can be reached by phone and mail. The OCR will only look into the issues you raise in your complaint, so it is important to make your complaint as detailed as possible and include all information that might be relevant.

Within seven days, the OCR will acknowledge receipt of your complaint. The agency will then review your complaint to see whether Title IX applies to your educational institution or program and may get back to you and ask you for more information. Within thirty days, it will contact you by phone or mail to let you know whether it will investigate your complaint.

There are several reasons why the OCR might not proceed with an investigation of your complaint. It may not proceed if the allegation has already been decided elsewhere, unless you are dissatisfied with the results of that hearing and you filed within sixty days after the completion of that separate action. It will not investigate if a decision on the same or a similar allegation is pending elsewhere. The OCR also will not act if the discrimination took place too long ago—usually more than 180 days before you file with it. However, in practice discrimination is usually ongoing and the time limit does not apply.

If the OCR does choose to investigate, its goal is to reach an appropriate resolution and resolve the complaint within 180 days. Be warned: There is always a backlog of complaints at the OCR, and the goal of 180 days is honored mainly in the breach.

The OCR can take several actions to reach an appropriate resolution:

• The OCR might set up meetings between you and your school to explore the issues and work out mutually satisfactory solutions.

• The school might offer to take action to solve the problem, in which case the OCR will ask it to sign an agreement and will then (in theory) monitor the situation to see that the action is taken. Be aware that the OCR has been criticized for negotiating weak deals with schools.

• The OCR can conduct a fact-finding investigation—collecting data, interviewing witnesses, evaluating evidence, and making findings and conclusions. If the OCR finds a civil rights problem, it can ask the school to comply with Title IX voluntarily. The complainant is usually left out of this kind of negotiating process and often only learns of it after a resolution has been reached. The OCR has the power to terminate a school's federal funding for noncompliance, but in fact the Department of

Education has never withheld federal funds for a Title IX violation. In most cases, the mere threat of such withholding is enough to induce the school to comply.

- The OCR may also refer a case in which it cannot get voluntary compliance to the Department of Justice for court action. This kind of action is extremely rare.

The OCR can also initiate its own review of a school. In fact, there are too many covered schools and other educational institutions for the OCR to monitor individually, so it rarely conducts compliance reviews on its own initiative. This means that you need to take the lead: If you suspect your rights under Title IX are being violated, then you need to make a complaint to get the OCR involved. Many schools do not comply with Title IX because so few students complain.

 ## HOW YOU CAN HELP THE OCR WITH YOUR COMPLAINT

You can assist the OCR while it is reviewing your complaint by doing the following:

- Join all the people who have suffered from the alleged discrimination. For example, if five other girls were excluded from the same shop class, join all of them in the same complaint.

- List all witnesses who have information about the discrimination and ask the OCR to contact them.

- Promptly respond to all communications from the department.

- Call the regional OCR office and get the name and phone number of the investigator assigned to your complaint.

- Remember that by being a cooperative, interested complainant, you may receive better attention.

- Consider asking your congressperson to write a letter to the regional office to facilitate your complaint. To find information on your senator or representative, visit www.senate.gov or www.house.gov.

If you are dissatisfied with the OCR's actions, you still have the right to sue the school or other educational institution. This option is discussed in the next section.

File a Lawsuit

Before the Supreme Court's 1979 decision in *Cannon v. University of Chicago*, courts were split over whether women had the right to bring a Title IX lawsuit on their own behalf. Then, Geraldine Cannon, who was denied admission to medical schools at two private universities, filed her own civil rights suit charging the schools with discriminating against her on the basis of sex. The lower federal courts dismissed her claims, but the Supreme Court reversed and held that she did have the right under Title IX to file a private lawsuit against the universities.

If you have pursued your school's internal procedures and have made a complaint to the OCR without success, you may wish to consider a private lawsuit. Most cases are filed in a federal court, but this is not required. If you do file in a state court, however, the school or other educational institution will most likely try to remove the case to a federal court.

Lawsuits allow you to attain lasting and enforceable change by forcing institutions to change discriminatory policies. You can seek compensation in the form of money damages, but the usual relief is injunctive. An **injunction** is a court order that orders a party to take certain action. For example, in a case in which a school scheduled girls' volleyball in a nontraditional season, a court might order the school to start scheduling girls' volleyball during the traditional fall season.

Of course, lawsuits take time, which can be an issue for students—a court cannot give a student the opportunity to compete in a competition that took place years ago. Moreover, if you graduate before the lawsuit is resolved, a court might toss out your case if the issue you're litigating will no longer have any effect on you. To prevent this from happening, you should file a **class action**. This is a lawsuit in which you sue not only on your own behalf, but also on the behalf of others who have sustained similar injuries or losses. If you bring a class action, then you can ensure that current and future students can obtain relief even if you graduate while the lawsuit is still in progress.

Lawsuits definitely require a lawyer who specializes in discrimination law and can be costly. They are the last resort for most people. Your lawsuit must be filed within applicable limitation periods, which your lawyer will be able to check for you.

Retaliation

Many people fear that their school will retaliate against them if they complain about discrimination. The law prohibits schools from intimidating, harassing, or discriminating against you because you made a complaint or filed a lawsuit.

Unfortunately, this law is not much of a deterrent and retaliation occurs all the time, although the chances of retaliation decrease if you gather the support of a whole team or ask a group of classmates to complain. Retaliation may take many forms. For example, it is retaliation if

- a school fires a coach who complains that her team is not getting fair treatment,
- a coach does not let a complaining student compete, or
- a teacher gives a complaining student a bad grade.

If you can show that you suffered adverse action because you complained about discrimination, your school may be liable.

TITLE IX: OVER THREE DECADES LATER

Title IX has had and is having a significant impact on the way we run every aspect of our educational institutions, but the statistics clearly show that women have not yet achieved equity in education. Proponents of Title IX say we've come a long way, but we still have a long way to go.

The National Coalition for Women and Girls in Education published a report card on the progress of Title IX in 2002, the statute's thirtieth anniversary. The report gave progress under

(i) OTHER REMEDIES FOR DISCRIMINATION AT SCHOOL

Title IX is not the only law that protects you from sex discrimination at a school; however, it is probably the broadest because of its far-reaching scope. If you are contemplating a lawsuit to assert your rights, you should seek the help of a lawyer. A lawyer will be able to suggest some alternatives to Title IX that may be worth pursuing in your particular situation. Subject to some limitations, claims for sex discrimination at a school may also be pursued through the following laws:

- The Equal Protection Clause of the Fourteenth Amendment to the U.S. Constitution (which applies to sex discrimination by state actors). This is almost always pleaded with Title IX in legal complaints. It only applies to state actors such as public schools, not to private schools.

- The Public Health Service Act (a federal law that is limited to sex discrimination against students in the health profession).

- Title II of the 1976 Amendments to the Vocational Education Act of 1963 (a federal law that addresses sex discrimination in vocational schools).

- Title IV of the 1964 Civil Rights Act (a federal law that allows the attorney general to sue public schools and colleges for sexually discriminatory policies).

- The Equal Educational Opportunities Act of 1974 (a federal law that prohibits discrimination against children in public schools on the basis of race, color, sex, or national origin).

Your lawyer might also be able to make an argument under state and local civil rights laws. Some states' laws relating to sex discrimination in education and or public accommodation are stronger than Title IX.

Title IX an overall C average. The best grade given—a B—went to "access to higher education" (in recognition of encouraging gains in the number of women enrolled in college), while the lowest grade—a D—went to "career education" (as many as 90 percent of students enrolled in programs traditional for their gender). "Athletics" received a C+ (encouraging gains for women's sports, but budgets still disproportionately support men's sports). The report expressed concerns about many issues, among them the failure of women to be adequately represented in technology programs and career programs leading to higher wages. The report called for better data collection about women in education, more research into problem areas, and stronger enforcement of existing laws and regulations.

THE WORLD AT YOUR FINGERTIPS

• To find an OCR enforcement office in your region, check out the "Contact OCR" page of the U.S. Department of Education's website at http://wdcrobcolp01.ed.gov/CFAPPS/OCR/contactus.cfm. You may contact the OCR directly by phone (1-800-421-3481) or e-mail (ocr@ed.gov), and you may even file a complaint online at www.ed.gov/ocr/complaintprocess.html.

• The Department of Education website provides a wide range of resources on Title IX—you can find department rulings, regulations, official publications, and links to other Title IX materials at www.ed.gov/index.jsp.

• The Women's Educational Equity Act Resource Center provides an exhaustive list of links to Title IX web sources. Click on the "Links" button at www.edc.org/WomensEquity.

• The National Coalition for Women and Girls in Education is a nonprofit organization devoted to improving educational opportunities for girls and women. Its website contains a number of publications on Title IX, including the report card on Title IX referred to earlier, at www.ncwge.org.

• The American Association of University Women is a good source for information on gender equity in education at www.aauw.org.

• The National Women's Law Center provides more information on Title IX and athletics (and on other areas, including sexual harassment and career and technical education) at www.nwlc.org. The site also includes a publication called "Check It Out" that can help you to determine whether your school is complying with Title IX in the area of athletics at www.nwlc.org/pdf/checkitout.pdf.

• The Women's Sports Foundation website includes reports and statistics on Title IX and athletics at www.womenssports-foundation.org.

REMEMBER THIS

• Title IX is more than an equal-opportunity athletics law: it applies to every aspect of every educational program or activity that receives federal funds.

• If your school is discriminating against you, then it may be engaging in illegal conduct under Title IX. Don't wait for the school to change its policies or for the OCR to enforce Title IX; take action and make a complaint.

• If you have suffered sex discrimination under any educational program, you can pursue one or more of the following options:
  • follow the program's internal grievance procedures,
  • file an administrative complaint with the OCR, or
  • file a private lawsuit in state or federal court.

• Remember to keep a careful eye on time limits, keep copies of all correspondence, and make inquiries about the progress of your case. If you show your school or the OCR that you won't lose interest and walk away, you're more likely to see results.

CHAPTER 2

Sexual Harassment in Schools: Recognize Harassment and Stop It—Fast

Bonnie is a college student who really enjoys college—or at least she did until now. One of her professors, she thinks, is showing the wrong kind of interest in her. He's finding excuses to talk to her after class, introducing personal topics, and generally acting too friendly and even flirtatious. All this is making her very uncomfortable. She doesn't even want to come to class anymore—but, short of dropping the course, what can she do about it?

You can be a victim of sexual harassment regardless of your gender, race, or age. A 2001 study by the American Association of University Women found that most students, male and female, experience some form of sexual harassment during their years at school. However, all students' experiences are not equivalent. Girls are more likely than boys to experience harassment and are likely to experience it more frequently.

Sexual harassment can be devastating for victims. It can threaten their physical and emotional well-being, influence how well they do in school, and make it difficult for them to achieve their educational and career goals. Despite this, many people don't take sexual harassment seriously or don't understand what it is. They think that victims should just ignore the harassment or go about their lives and put it behind them. But studies and case reports show that sexual harassment makes victims feel humiliated, scared, confused, and angry.

This chapter will look at sexual harassment from a legal perspective and show you the steps that you can take if you are a victim of sexual harassment in school.

SEXUAL HARASSMENT AND TITLE IX

The law defines **sexual harassment** as any unwanted sexual advance; request for sexual favors; or visual, verbal, or physical conduct of a sexual nature. Sexual harassment is a form of sex discrimination under Title IX. As explained in chapter 1, Title IX prohibits gender-based discrimination under any educational program or activity that receives federal financial support. Thus, sexual harassment is illegal in all public and private schools and in other educational programs that receive federal funds.

Title IX protects both male and female students from sexual harassment committed by a school employee, another student, or a third person. For example, one federal court found sexual harassment where a college professor repeatedly opened his class by referring to one of his students as "Monica" and asking about her weekend with "Bill"—though she had a different name and bore little resemblance to the infamous intern. The federal court found that "a reasonable jury could find that the Monica statements were more than mere joking comments or occasional vulgar banter, but were sexually charged and designed by [the professor] to convey certain images about the student." Some cases involve physical harassment. For example, a student at Virginia Commonwealth University established sexual harassment when her professor spanked her after she failed to get an acceptable score on a makeup exam.

Title IX even protects students from sexual harassment in circumstances where the perpetrator and the victim are members of the same sex. For example, in a case in which a group of female students taunted another female student about engaging in sexual activity, the Office for Civil Rights (OCR) found that such comments could amount to illegal sexual harassment under Title IX.

Title IX provides that you have a right to complain about harassment to your school or to the OCR. You can also commence a lawsuit against your school for failing to prevent the

(i) TITLE IX AND THE FIRST AMENDMENT RIGHT OF FREE SPEECH

Students and teachers in public schools have a right to free speech under the First Amendment, which applies in the classroom as well as in all other educational programs and activities. But threats and intimidation are not part of free speech. The OCR suggests in its guidelines on sexual harassment that threatening and intimidating actions targeted at a particular student or group of students are not protected under the First Amendment and that the school must take prompt action to stop such conduct and prevent it from recurring.

---

harassment and seek damages or an injunction from a court. But it is important to understand that you cannot bring a lawsuit under Title IX against the individual who harassed you. If the harassment involved physical or sexual assault, you may be able to bring a criminal or civil suit against the harasser (see chapter 15, "Sexual Assault," for more information).

THE DIFFERENT TYPES OF SEXUAL HARASSMENT UNDER TITLE IX

Like workplace sexual harassment (which is discussed in chapter 3), sexual harassment in schools can be divided into two categories: quid pro quo and hostile environment.

Quid pro quo is a Latin term meaning "something for something." This form of sexual harassment often involves an abuse of power, and it occurs when a teacher or some other school employee causes you to believe that you must submit to unwelcome sexual conduct before getting something of value or that you will suffer adverse consequences for refusing to submit. Quid pro quo sexual harassment does not have to take the form of intercourse. Any sexually charged conduct—from a request for a date to a demand for sex—can qualify, if it is coupled with a threat or promise of official action. The harasser—who could be a teacher, a janitor, a coach, or any other person who is employed by the school and has authority over you—might ask you to submit to sexual harassment in exchange for

- permission to participate in a school program,
- a good grade,
- a scholarship, or
- a good recommendation.

In each case, the key is that the sexual conduct of the harasser is linked to something of value. For example, it is quid pro quo sexual harassment if a teacher threatens you with a bad grade unless you agree to go to dinner at his place. It does not matter whether you agree to go or not, or whether you get a good or bad grade. Either way, if your teacher implies that your grade hinges on your acquiescence, then your teacher's conduct is unlawful quid pro quo sexual harassment under Title IX.

Hostile environment sexual harassment at school occurs when a teacher's, costudent's, or even visiting outsider's unwelcome sexually harassing conduct is so severe, pervasive, and objectively offensive, and so undermines and detracts from your educational experience, that you are effectively denied equal access to an institution's educational resources and opportunities. It might be hostile environment harassment if you cannot pay attention in class because a classmate stares at your breasts during class and constantly makes lewd comments to you. The harassment has to be so bad that it is difficult or unpleasant for you to do regular school activities, such as play on a sports team, walk down school hallways, or pay attention during class.

The following kinds of actions can result in hostile environment harassment:

- sexual advances,
- touching of a sexual nature,
- telling sexually offensive jokes,
- making comments about a student's clothing or body,
- standing or rubbing against a person,

- making suggestive gestures or noises,
- sexually touching oneself or someone else, or
- talking about sexual activity in front of others.

One incident of sexual harassment may constitute quid pro quo harassment, but it usually takes a series of incidents to create a hostile environment. A hostile environment can occur even where the harassment is not targeted specifically at the individual who complains. For example, where a student or group of students regularly direct sexual comments toward a particular student, a hostile environment may be created not only for the targeted student, but also for others who witness the conduct.

Students date each other during high school and college, and obviously not all sexual banter between students is harassment. For example, according to the OCR guidelines, a comment by one student to another student that she has a nice figure will not, by itself, amount to sexual harassment. Similarly,

---

ⓘ IS IT HARASSMENT OR FLIRTATION?

Sexual Harassment . . .	Flirting . . .
feels bad	feels good
is one-sided	is reciprocal
feels unattractive	feels attractive
is degrading	is a compliment
feels powerless	feels in control
might include negative touching	might include positive touching
is unwanted	is wanted
feels invasive	feels open
feels demeaning	is flattering
makes you sad or angry	makes you happy

Source: Feminist Majority Foundation at www.feminist.org

---

a request for a date or a gift of flowers, even if unwelcome, would not create a hostile environment. However, where it is clear that the conduct is unwelcome, then repeated requests for dates or attempts to make contact could create a hostile environment.

Of course, not all physical conduct is sexual in nature. For example, sexual harassment is probably not involved if your high school coach hugs you when you make a goal, if your teacher gives you a consoling hug when you are injured, or if you demonstrate a sports move that requires you to have contact with another student. In one case, the OCR found that a teacher's actions in patting a student on the arm, shoulder, and back and in restraining the student when he was out of control did not amount to illegal conduct of a sexual nature under Title IX.

(i) TITLE IX AND LESBIAN STUDENTS

Title IX does not specifically prohibit discrimination on the basis of sexual orientation. However, Title IX might protect you if you are a lesbian if you are harassed because of your sex or because of your failure to conform to gender stereotypes, and good lawyers will argue this. But the harassment must clearly be based on your "sex" and not on your "sexual orientation." For example, it is probably not sexual harassment if a group of students heckles you with comments based on your sexual orientation (e.g., if a group of students tells you "lesbians are not welcome at this table in the cafeteria"). On the other hand, harassing conduct directed toward you because of your sex may create a sexually hostile environment and, therefore, may be prohibited by Title IX (e.g., if a group of male students makes you a target of its sexual or other harassment).

If you're a lesbian and you think you've been harassed, you might also be protected by other federal and state laws. For example, one gay student used federal equal protection law to challenge public school officials' failure to take action against antigay abuse in his school. He was awarded nearly a million dollars.

MAKING A COMPLAINT TO YOUR SCHOOL

As explained in chapter 1, Title IX requires your school to have a written policy against sex discrimination and to notify employees and students (and parents of elementary and secondary school students) of the policy. Experts believe that the best way to prevent sexual harassment is to distribute these policies widely, so that everyone knows what constitutes sex discrimination and how such allegations are handled at the school. These policies should identify the person or group who should receive complaints about sexual harassment. This may be the Title IX coordinator, the principal, or even the school board.

If you are being sexually harassed, the first step you should take is to make a complaint to the appropriate person at your school. If you don't know whom to complain to, you could ask your principal, teacher, or guidance counselor or ask for a copy of the school's written policy against sex discrimination. Once your school is made aware of an allegation of sexual harassment, it should respond promptly and effectively, not only to stop any ongoing harassment, but also to put measures in place to prevent harassment in the future.

WHAT CAN I DO IF I AM SEXUALLY HARASSED?

Sexual conduct is unwelcome if you don't invite it and view it as undesirable. Just because you didn't immediately object doesn't mean that you welcomed it. Perhaps you didn't resist out of fear, or perhaps you willingly participated in similar conduct at an earlier time and now you find it unwelcome.

If the person harassing you is in a position of authority over you, then the issue of consent is automatically suspect. Any sexual conduct between an adult school employee and an elementary student will be considered nonconsensual; in cases with secondary students, there will be a strong presumption that it is not consensual.

If you are harassed at school, you should do the following:

• Tell the harasser that you don't like what he or she is doing and that you want him or her to stop.

• Tell someone about it who you trust and who has been designated to handle such issues in your school. If you feel you are being ignored, be persistent.

• Remind yourself that sexual harassment is wrong and illegal and that it should be stopped.

• Keep a journal of your experiences. Such a journal could provide valuable evidence of harassment if you bring a lawsuit against your school.

COMPLAINTS AND LAWSUITS

If your school does not deal adequately with your allegations of sexual harassment or if the person who is harassing you is in a position of power in the school and has the potential to derail your complaint, then you should consider taking further action. You can file a complaint with the OCR or you can file a lawsuit against the school. Chapter 1 details the steps you need to take to make a complaint to the OCR. If you think you may want to commence a lawsuit, then you should consult with a lawyer.

If you make a complaint or commence a lawsuit, the OCR or the court will look at the "constellation of surrounding circumstances, expectations, and relationships" when considering whether you have been a victim of sexual harassment. This test means that incidents of sexual harassment that would not be illegal alone may create an illegal hostile environment when considered in combination with other similar incidents. For example, if you are taunted by one or more young men about your body, the OCR may find that a hostile environment has been created if the conduct has gone on for some time or takes place throughout your school, or if you are taunted by a number of students. The more severe the conduct, the less need there is to show a series of incidents to demonstrate a hostile environment—particularly if the harassment is physical (e.g., attempts to touch your breasts, genital area, or buttocks). In fact, the OCR guidelines make it clear that a single or isolated incident of sexual harassment may, if sufficiently severe, create a hostile environment.

The OCR or a court may also consider
- the degree to which the conduct affected your education,
- the type, frequency, and duration of the conduct,
- the alleged harasser's identity (sex and age) and the relationship between the alleged harasser and you,
- the size of your school, the location of the incidents, and the subject(s) of the harassment,
- the number of individuals involved,
- the context in which the harassment occurred, and
- other sex discrimination or sexual harassment incidents at your school.

The U.S. Supreme Court held in 1999 that a school could be liable for money damages under Title IX for sexual harassment committed by its staff or students. However, the Court stated that to recover monetary damages, a student must show that an official who had authority to address the alleged harassment had actual knowledge of the harassment. It is not enough for an administrator to have enough information to infer that a teacher harassed a student. This requirement of "actual knowledge" means that it is extremely important that you complain to the person or group the school designates to receive sexual harassment complaints, which could be the Title IX coordinator, the school principal, or the school board. The school will only be liable for money damages if you complain to the appropriate person and that person fails to take reasonable action to deal with the harassment or was deliberately indifferent to known acts of harassment. You may be able to show that your school was "deliberately indifferent" if it failed to discipline your harasser or failed to take appropriate steps to protect you.

The standards for obtaining injunctive or equitable relief

(e.g., an injunction ordering the school to enforce sexual-harassment policies) or for administrative enforcement are not as strict. If an employee of the school harasses someone while he or she is carrying out the responsibilities delegated to him or her by the school, then the school is strictly liable. For example, if a teacher harasses a student while teaching, then the school is automatically liable, even if the school did not know about the teacher's harassment. If an employee of the school harasses a person, but the harassment does not take place within the course of the employee's daily responsibilities, then the school is only liable if it knew or should have known of the harassment.

THE WORLD AT YOUR FINGERTIPS

• The OCR guidelines, which provide many examples of sexual harassment, are available at www.ed.gov/legislation/FedRegister/other/1996-4/100496c.html.

• The American Association of University Women published a landmark report on sexual harassment in schools in 1993. That report was revisited in a 2001 publication, *Hostile Hallways*, and contains important statistics and insights into the prevalence of sexual harassment in schools.

You can read *Hostile Hallways* at www.aauw.org/member_center/publications/HostileHallways/hostilehallways.pdf.

• Nan Stein of the Wellesley Centers for Women has written several reports on sexual harassment in schools, focusing on ways in which it can be prevented. You can find an interview with Stein in which she discusses sexual harassment in schools at www.edletter.org/past/issues/2000-jf/stein.shtml.

• Your school can seek technical assistance in preventing sexual harassment by contacting an equity assistance center. There are ten equity assistance centers across the nation, several of which have staff who consult with or provide training to schools in the area of sexual harassment. Visit www.equitycenters.org for more information.

REMEMBER THIS

• Sexual harassment is an illegal form of sex discrimination under Title IX.

• Quid pro quo harassment occurs when a harasser is in a position of authority over you and subjects you to sexual harassment.

• Hostile environment harassment occurs when harassing conduct (by a teacher, student, or visitor to the school) is so pervasive and persistent that it creates an intimidating or offensive environment or affects your performance at school.

• You don't have to accept sexual harassment. Your school should have policies on sexual harassment that give you a simple way to complain about the harassment. If the school's response is not satisfactory, you can file suit in court or complain to the OCR.

• If you do complain to your school about harassment, make sure you complain to the person designated to deal with it or to someone who has authority over the harasser. You may not be entitled to receive money damages from your school in a lawsuit if you do not complain to the designated person.

PART TWO

Workplace Issues

CHAPTER 3

Sex Discrimination at Work: Making Your Rights Work for You

Keesha has a doctorate in chemistry. Her boyfriend, Stephen, has a doctorate in chemistry, too. But while Stephen has risen through the ranks at the laboratory where they've both worked for the last five years and is managing a staff of three people, Keesha has stayed in pretty much the same position, doing routine work. Keesha's colleagues have told her that it's not her fault that she hasn't been promoted, but that women just don't make good research leaders. Besides, in a few years she'll leave to get married and have children, right?

Despite Keesha's belief that her gender is not relevant to her ability to do her job well, she is paid less than colleagues with similar qualifications, is overlooked for promotions, and has assumptions made about her private life.

Women have always worked, both inside and outside the home. However, countless women in the paid labor market have faced discrimination and harassment and have not always been paid fair wages. In January 2004, more than 68 million women were working, and they comprised about 46 percent of the U.S. labor force. U.S. Bureau of Labor statistics show that the women's labor force is growing faster than the men's, and that by 2008 women will make up about 48 percent of the paid labor force. But on average, women earn only seventy-five cents to every dollar earned by men and hold the majority of low-wage jobs.

Women are still underrepresented in upper management positions—only six of the Fortune 500 companies have female chief executive officers. The "glass ceiling" is a well-worn metaphor for the workplace barriers that prevent women and minorities from getting top jobs in corporate America. The idea is that a glass ceiling exists between workers and top management and allows the workers to see through to the upper-management world above them. At first, most workers do not even notice the barrier; however, as soon as they try to work their way up the corporate ladder, they bump into the ceiling and are prevented from rising up. The glass ceiling was the subject of much debate in the 1980s, when many women suffered discrimination and had to fight to make it to the top. Over twenty years later, women are still discriminated against, but are able to take advantage of federal and state antidiscrimination laws as they battle their way to the top.

The most comprehensive and powerful federal law that prohibits sex discrimination in employment is Title VII, which was passed as part of the Civil Rights Act of 1964. State and local governments also have the authority to pass laws protecting you from discrimination in the workplace. Many state laws give female employees more and broader protections than federal laws and apply to small companies that may not be covered by federal laws.

TITLE VII

When the civil rights bill was originally introduced before Congress, Title VII prohibited discrimination in employment based on an employee's "race, color, creed, or national origin." A coalition of white southern conservatives opposed the civil rights bill altogether and thought that including a provision banning discrimination on the basis of sex would help torpedo the bill. Fortunately, their plan backfired, and the whole bill, including the prohibition against sex discrimination, was passed in 1964.

Title VII prohibits employment discrimination based on an employee's race, color, religion, sex, or national origin. It applies whether you are an employee or a job applicant and protects you from being discriminated against because of your gender in any term, condition, or privilege of employment, including hiring,

⚠ THE HOSTILE BOSS

Unfortunately, there's no law that stops your boss from being a jerk. According to lawyers, many people think they can complain about being in a "hostile work environment" because their manager is making life difficult in the office by issuing demands and impossible deadlines. But merely having a curmudgeon as a boss does not provide the basis for a discrimination lawsuit. Title VII is only triggered when there is discrimination in your workplace.

firing, promotion, layoff, compensation, benefits, job assignments, training, and tenure. Title VII applies to all employers that employ fifteen or more individuals. It also applies to labor unions, state and local governments, and the federal government. Title VII protects you whether you are a full-time, part-time, or temporary employee.

WHAT IS DISCRIMINATION?

The law groups employment discrimination under Title VII into two distinct categories:
1. Disparate treatment
2. Disparate impact

Disparate treatment employment discrimination occurs when an employer treats you differently from other employees because of your sex—for example, if an employer will not hire you because you are a woman. The question is whether the employer discriminated against you because of your sex or did not give you the job for some other reason. Typically, in such cases the employee alleges that the treatment was discriminatory and the employer responds that it had a legitimate, nondiscriminatory basis. For example, an employer would not be discriminating on the basis of sex if it hired a male applicant because he had three years more experience than the female applicant or because he had an advanced degree or spoke more foreign languages than she did.

One type of disparate treatment discrimination is **facial discrimination**, which occurs when an employer has a policy that is explicitly based on sex (e.g., "only males need apply"). Unless the employer can defend the policy by showing that an employee's sex is a **bona fide occupational qualification** (**BFOQ**), then such intentional discrimination is illegal. A permissible BFOQ might exist where a film company insists on hir-

 **MIXED MOTIVE CASES**

In some cases, an employer's actions may be partly motivated by sex discrimination and partly by a legitimate, nondiscriminatory reason. In such cases, the employer's actions are unlawful. In the 1989 landmark mixed-motive case *Price Waterhouse v. Hopkins*, the Supreme Court held that once a plaintiff has shown that sex discrimination affected an employer's decision, the burden shifts to the employer to show that it would have reached the same result if it had relied solely on legitimate, nondiscriminatory factors.

In this case, Anne Hopkins, an associate accountant up for partnership, took her employer to court after she was not promoted. According to the partners making the hiring decision, Hopkins did not make partner because of her aggressiveness and lack of interpersonal skills. However, one of the hiring partners actually advised her that if she wanted to improve her chances, she should "walk more femininely, talk more femininely, wear make-up, have her hair styled, and wear jewelry."

Under the Civil Rights Act of 1991, which is now incorporated into Title VII, an employer will be liable for a violation of Title VII if discrimination was a motivating factor for a decision, even if there were other factors in play as well. If an employer shows that it would have made the same decision anyway, it can avoid damages liability, but the court may still be able to issue an injunction.

ing a male actor to play Antony and a female actor to play Cleopatra, or a modeling agency books only female models to model wedding gowns or women's hosiery. However, stereotypes or generalizations based on average gender differences are not BFOQs. For example, an airline cannot refuse to hire female pilots because of a generalization that women are shorter and will not be able to reach the pedals. Fortunately, facial discrimination cases are much less common than they used to be.

Disparate impact employment discrimination occurs when a policy that appears to be neutral has the effect of discriminating against women as a group. For example, an employer may decide to hire only applicants who do not have custody of preschool-age children. On its face, the employer's decision is not discriminatory—it applies to both male and female applicants. However, this policy disproportionately screens out women applicants as compared to male applicants because more women are custodial parents. This policy, therefore, would have a discriminatory effect, or **disparate impact**, on women. If there is a disparate impact, the policy is unlawful unless an employer can prove that the discriminatory policy is required by **business necessity** and is significantly related to the requirements of the job. Even if the employer can meet the business necessity standard, the employee will still have the opportunity to show that there is an alternative employment practice with less disparate impact that will serve the employer's goal.

Female applicants for firefighter positions have successfully alleged disparate impact in several cases, in which they challenged fire departments' physical strength and agility tests. The women showed that the requirements were set too high—at levels requiring strength and ability that was more than necessary to ensure qualified recruits—and that qualified women were being unnecessarily excluded. In these cases, the women did not need to show that the fire departments were trying to exclude them: it was enough to show that the policies had a disparate impact on them as women. Since the policies weren't sufficiently job related (too much strength was required), there was illegal discrimination.

(i) SEXUAL ORIENTATION AND EMPLOYMENT DISCRIMINATION

State and local governments are increasingly passing laws that prohibit discrimination based on sexual orientation. So far, about a dozen states and numerous local jurisdictions prohibit employment discrimination based on gender identity, characteristics, or expression—you can find a summary of state, city, and county laws that prohibit discrimination at www.lambdalegal.org/cgi-bin/iowa/documents/record?record=217.

Some victims of workplace harassment based on their sexual orientation have also been successful in bringing their lawsuits under Title VII, where they have been able to show discrimination based on sex.

There are no federal laws that prohibit employment discrimination based on sexual orientation. They have been proposed, but none have passed. The **Employment Non-Discrimination Act** is a federal bill that, if enacted, would prohibit job discrimination based on sexual orientation. As currently drafted, the act would cover "perceived" sexual orientation, so it would protect employees who are perceived as gay or lesbian— even if the perception is erroneous.

Sexual Harassment Discrimination

Sexual harassment is a form of employment discrimination. Unwelcome sexual advances, requests for sexual favors, and other verbal or physical conduct of a sexual nature constitute sexual harassment when such conduct affects your employment, interferes with your work performance, or creates an intimidating, hostile, or offensive work environment. The courts will look to the "constellation of surrounding circumstances, expectations and relationships" when deciding whether sexual harassment has occurred. It is unlawful for a man or a woman to harass a woman.

Quid pro quo sexual harassment occurs when your employer or someone in the superior chain of command makes a job or a job benefit (e.g., working hours, raises, or transfers) conditional on your participation in sexual activity. It also occurs when you suffer adverse consequences (e.g., worse job shifts, demotion, or termination) for refusing to submit to a sexual advance. The term "quid pro quo" is a little out of date (the Supreme Court now asks whether harassment has resulted in a "tangible employment action"), but it is still commonly used. Such harassment often involves abuse of power by an employer, although it also involves improper and unwelcome sexual conduct. For such harassment to be the basis of a lawsuit, the harassment does not have be explicit: it is enough if harassment can be implied from the harasser's words or conduct. For example, your boss need not make your request to take your vacation during the last two weeks of August dependent on whether or not you have sex with him. If you discuss your vacation plans with your boss and shortly thereafter he propositions you for sex, a court may find implicit quid pro quo sexual harassment.

Hostile work environment sexual harassment occurs when your employer creates, condones, or allows an intimidating, hostile, or offensive work environment to continue. A hostile work environment exists when the work environment becomes "polluted" with unwelcome sexual words or conduct. If you want to sue your employer for hostile work environment sexual harassment, you will need to prove:

1. That you were subjected to a work environment in which there were sexual advances, requests for sexual favors, or other verbal or physical conduct of a sexual nature by your employer, manager, supervisor, coworkers, or customers;

2. That you did not welcome the conduct; and

3. That the conduct was sufficiently severe or pervasive to alter the condition of your employment and create a hostile working environment for you.

In deciding whether there is a hostile environment, a court will consider whether the conduct was physical or verbal, or both; the frequency of the conduct; whether the conduct was patently offensive; whether the alleged harasser was a coworker or a supervisor; whether the conduct was directed at more than one person; and whether the conduct was welcome or unwelcome.

Your employer may have a defense to a charge of hostile work environment harassment if you have not suffered any adverse employment action (such as discharge, demotion, or an undesirable job assignment), and the employer can prove the following elements:

• That the employer exercised reasonable care to prevent or promptly correct any sexually harassing behavior; and

( ) ASK A LAWYER

Q. If the guys I work with occasionally make unwelcome sexist jokes and comments, but do nothing more, is this sexual harassment?

A. Courts will look at the "totality of the circumstances" in order to determine whether unlawful sexual harassment occurred. The more severe the conduct, the less frequently it has to occur; the less severe the conduct, the more frequently it has to occur.

A stray remark alone usually does not constitute harassment. But inappropriate jokes in the workplace can constitute hostile environment sexual harassment if they are unwelcome, severe, or pervasive enough to create an environment that a reasonable person would find hostile or abusive, and if that environment is subjectively perceived by the alleged victim to be hostile or abusive. The key here is that the courts will use both an objective and subjective standard. The conduct must be perceived by a reasonable objective person to be severe, pervasive, hostile, and abusive, and the alleged victim must subjectively perceive the conduct in the same manner. There is no "bright-line" test to determine if the conduct is severe and pervasive enough to constitute a hostile environment.

—Answer by Lerisa Heroldt
Associate, Alston Hunt Floyd & Ing, Honolulu, Hawaii

• That you failed to take advantage of any preventative or cor-
rective opportunities provided by the employer, such as those set
out in an employment manual or personnel policy. In many
cases, this requirement places an obligation on employees to
take some action in response to sexual harassment (as discussed
on page 45).

It is sometimes difficult for an employee to tell when someone crosses the line from merely inappropriate or annoying conduct into unlawful sexual harassment. If you're being harassed
and you're not sure whether the behavior amounts to unlawful
harassment, then consult with an attorney or contact the Equal
Employment Opportunity Commission (EEOC) or a state or
local agency for more guidance.

Pregnancy Discrimination

In 1978, in direct response to a Supreme Court case that held
that discrimination on the basis of pregnancy was not sex discrimination under Title VII, Congress amended Title VII to
make clear that discrimination on the basis of pregnancy is a
form of sex discrimination. Since the Pregnancy Discrimination
Act (PDA) is part of Title VII, it also applies to all private
employers who employ fifteen or more individuals and to the
state and federal government.

Title VII makes clear that an employer cannot refuse to hire
you because you are pregnant or plan to become pregnant; nor
can an employer refuse to hire you because coworkers, clients,
or customers have a bias against pregnant women. If you are
affected by pregnancy or childbirth, an employer cannot treat
you differently from any other employee who is similarly able or
temporarily unable to work. If pregnancy does interfere with
your ability to do your job, then your employer must make light
duties or similar arrangements available to you if such arrangements are offered to other workers who have similar duties or
positions and who are temporarily disabled because of a medical condition. As long as you can perform the major functions

(i) SOME DIFFERENCES BETWEEN FEDERAL AND STATE WORKPLACE DISCRIMINATION LAW

Federal laws prohibit workplace discrimination on the basis of:

- Race
- Color
- Sex
- Pregnancy
- National origin
- Religion
- Age
- Disability

State and local government discrimination laws often prohibit discrimination on the same bases as the federal laws, and may include additional prohibitions on the basis of:

- Smoker/nonsmoker status
- Marital status
- Sexual orientation
- Weight (which may be a disability in some circumstances)
- Political affiliation
- Arrest or conviction records
- English-speaking proficiency
- Submission to polygraph, HIV, drug, or alcohol tests
- HIV status
- Sickle cell traits
- Family responsibility
- Parenthood
- Personal appearance
- Public-assistance status

- Unfavorable military discharge
- Being a victim of domestic abuse
- Citizenship status

of the job, you cannot be discriminated against because you are pregnant. If you take leave after the birth of your child for medical reasons, your employer must hold your job open during your medical leave for the same amount of time your employer would hold a job open for another employee on sick or disability leave. Many employers are also covered by the Family and Medical Leave Act (discussed in chapter 4), which gives you certain rights to unpaid leave following the birth or adoption of a child. The PDA also has implications for the provision of contraception under the health plans offered by employers (see chapter 13, "Pregnancy and Childbirth," for more details).

THE AGE DISCRIMINATION IN EMPLOYMENT ACT

The federal Age Discrimination in Employment Act (ADEA) was passed in 1967 and protects anyone who is forty years of age or older from employment discrimination based on age. Although ADEA is gender neutral, it is of particular interest and application to women because youthful appearance is given disproportionate weight in many jobs held by women. Think about the last time you saw a crop of over-forty female receptionists or news anchors.

These protections apply whether you are an employee or a job applicant, and they protect you from being discriminated against because of your age in any aspect of employment, including hiring, firing, promotion, layoff, compensation, benefits, job assignments, training, and tenure. ADEA applies to all private employers with twenty or more employees and, like Title VII, it includes state and private-sector employers as well as the federal government.

The federal law means that
- if you are at least forty years old, you cannot be forced to retire from your job when you reach a certain age,
- you do not have to accept a job with less responsibility or less pay just because you turn sixty-five, and
- you cannot be denied training or promotion opportunities just because of your age.

In addition, the federal law prevents employers from using age as a factor in hiring, firing, layoff, demotion, working conditions and hours, and compensation and benefits. Some state and local laws bar discrimination on the basis of any age, not only discrimination against those over forty.

ADEA does not prevent employers from offering early retirement incentive programs to employees over forty. These plans are legal if they are voluntary and they comply with other federal laws; they can provide you with substantial benefits if you are willing to retire early. However, giving up your job early may have great disadvantages for you, both economically and personally. If possible, you should review your options with a financial planning advisor. You should also be aware that if you accept an offer of early retirement, your employer may ask you to sign a waiver of your rights under applicable age discrimination laws, including your right to sue your employer. Your waiver will be legal if it is "knowingly and voluntarily" made and if your employer follows specific procedures in the law by giving you extensive notice, disclosing information, and providing you sufficient time to make your decision. You may want to consult an attorney before signing such a waiver.

THE EQUAL PAY ACT

The Equal Pay Act was passed in 1963, one year before Title VII. This act applies to virtually all employers, including the federal government, and prohibits employers from paying men and women different amounts for equal work. Equal work does not necessarily mean identical work—it can be characterized as what the courts call "substantially equal." To decide if two jobs are substantially equal, a court will look at the skill, effort, responsibility, and working conditions required for each position. If all four of these factors are equivalent, then the jobs most likely require equal pay rates.

If you are being paid less than your male colleagues for equal work, then you can bring a lawsuit against your employer in court. You do not need to bring a charge before the EEOC before you commence a lawsuit. The time limit for commencing a lawsuit is usually two years.

STEPS YOU CAN TAKE IF YOU ARE BEING DISCRIMINATED AGAINST

If you are being discriminated against at your job because of your sex (which includes sexual harassment), there are several steps that you can take:

1. Confront the person discriminating against you and ask him or her to change his or her behavior.

2. Complain to your employer.

3. File a charge with the EEOC (or a state or local agency).

4. File a private lawsuit (after you receive a "right to sue" letter from the EEOC, as explained later in this chapter).

Of course, there is one other option: You can walk away from the discrimination by leaving your job. There are some advantages to this: You will not have to deal with the stress and emotional challenge of a making a complaint—a process that can take years—and you can get another job and get on with your life. On the other hand, if you don't complain your employer will go unpunished and may continue to discriminate against other women.

Confront the Person Discriminating against You

If you are being discriminated against at work, one of the first things you can and should do is tell the person discriminating against you to stop. Sometimes, coworkers and supervisors are simply unaware that they are discriminating against women. There is a good chance that if you confront the person who is discriminating against you, then the discriminatory behavior will change. This is especially true if the discrimination you are experiencing is at a relatively low level—for example, if other employees tell dirty jokes, or if there are offensive cartoons or pornographic pictures posted in the office break room.

If the person discriminating against you ignores you or you are not comfortable being face to face with him, write a note or letter to him demanding that the behavior stop. Save a copy and make sure to keep a written journal or notes of everything you do—including whom you spoke to, who saw or heard you, and how you felt when you were discriminated against. There is no substitute for a good paper trail. If the behavior doesn't stop, you shouldn't stop your efforts to end it. Your next step should be to complain to a higher-level manager or to human resources.

Complain to Your Employer

It is important that you bring discrimination in your workplace to the attention of a manager or supervisor, who acts as the agent of the employer in the workplace. Your employer may be unaware that its policies have the effect of discriminating against you and other women, and may be willing to make changes if you request them. If an employee is discriminating against you, your employer may be able to deal with the behavior internally.

If you are suffering discrimination in the form of sexual harassment, it is even more important to complain to your employer. As discussed earlier (see page 40), if your company has an internal grievance procedure for complaining about sexual harassment and you fail to follow it, then your employer has a defense to your harassment complaint, and your lawsuit may be unsuccessful. Even if your employer does not have a formal policy, your best bet is still to make a complaint to your supervisor, the human resources department, or a manager or other

(i) WHAT HAPPENS WHEN MY DISCRIMINATION CLAIM IS COVERED BY BOTH STATE AND FEDERAL LAW?

If you have been discriminated against in violation of your state's law, you can file a claim with your state fair employment agency. The EEOC refers to these state and local agencies as Fair Employment Practices Agencies (FEPAs), and through "work sharing agreements," the EEOC and the FEPAs protect your rights under all applicable laws and avoid overlap by following two practices:

- If you file a charge with a FEPA and the issue is also covered by federal law, the FEPA will file your charge with the EEOC to protect your federal rights. You don't need to file with the EEOC yourself. This is called "dual filing." In such cases, the charge will usually be kept by the FEPA for handling.

- If you file a charge with the EEOC and the issue is also covered by state or local law, you can check a box on the EEOC forms to indicate that you'd like the EEOC to dual file the charge with the state or local FEPA. The EEOC will sometimes handle the charge itself, but will often farm out a case to a local or state agency.

higher-up in the company. The fact that your employer does not have a policy may count against it in a subsequent lawsuit.

Filing Your Charge with the EEOC

The EEOC is the independent federal agency that enforces Title VII and the other principal federal statutes that prohibit employment discrimination. The primary role of the EEOC is to investigate complaints about discrimination in the workplace.

If you believe that you have been discriminated against at work under a federal law because you are a woman, you may file a **charge**, or complaint, with the EEOC. You'll need to fill out a form giving information about the discrimination you suffered, including dates, times, and witnesses, and a statement as to why you believe the discrimination is based on your sex. Your later private lawsuit may even be constrained or limited to what you included in your complaint to the EEOC. For this reason, it's important to make your complaint as thorough as possible. You may file your charge by mail or in person at the nearest EEOC office. Anonymous complaints will not be accepted; however, any individual, organization, or agency may file on your behalf in order to protect your identity. Despite these protections, if you make a complaint, it is likely that your employer will either figure out, or will have to be told of, your identity for due process reasons.

You do not need a lawyer to file a claim of discrimination with the EEOC. The EEOC will help you complete the necessary forms to start your complaint, and you may bring a relative, friend, or coworker with you. The agency may wish to interview you outside the presence of a coworker who is aware of or involved in the situation about which you are complaining.

The first thing that will happen when you file a charge with the EEOC is that the agency will notify your employer that a charge has been filed against it. After that, the following may occur:

• The EEOC will investigate your claim to determine if there is **reasonable cause** to believe that discrimination has occurred. Your charge may be assigned for priority handling if the initial facts support a violation (although realistically this rarely occurs) or for follow-up investigation.

• The EEOC may make written requests for additional information, interview witnesses, review documents, and visit your workplace.

• Your charge may be settled at any stage of the investigation if you and your employer express an interest in doing this. Your charge may also be selected for the EEOC's mediation program if you and your employer consent. Mediation, if offered by any agency (federal, state, or local), may be worth pursuing as it is virtually always the quickest way for a charge to be dealt with. If mediation is unsuccessful, your claim will be returned for further investigation.

• The EEOC has the authority to litigate on your behalf if there is reasonable cause to believe you have been a victim of discrimination.

• Your charge may be dismissed at any time if, in the EEOC's best judgment, further processing or investigation will not establish that you were illegally discriminated against.

• When the EEOC completes its investigation of your charge, it will send you and your employer a letter. The letter will state whether the EEOC found reasonable cause to believe the law was violated and will inform you that you have ninety days after receiving the letter to file a lawsuit. This is called a **right-to-sue letter**. Even if you think you'll probably file a lawsuit, you still need to file a claim with the EEOC first, because you need a right-to-sue letter before you can begin a lawsuit in court.

When you file a charge, you commence a long, slow process, and the EEOC has a long backlog of complaints. There is nothing wrong with telephoning the investigator to find out the progress of your charge. As is so often the case, the squeaky wheel gets the oil.

The most important thing to remember about filing an employment discrimination charge is that there are specific time

▶ **PURSUE YOUR RIGHT TO SUE**

Be warned—there is a huge backlog at the EEOC, and its investigations can take more than six months. You may want to consider asking for a right-to-sue letter after the EEOC has had the complaint for 180 days, even if it has not finished investigating your claim. This letter enables you to file a lawsuit in state or federal court. If you plan to sue on your own anyway and you want to do it quickly, it is worth getting this right-to-sue letter without waiting for the EEOC to complete its full investigation.

limits for filing and you must stick to them to protect your rights. The time limits for filing vary, depending on what law you allege was violated and whether your state's laws also prohibit this behavior. For example, Title VII claims and ADEA claims must be filed with the EEOC within 180 days of the discrimination, but you may have more time to file with a state or local agency if it has an agreement with the EEOC. Of course, in many cases discrimination is ongoing. In the case of such "continuing violations," the time limit is extended back to cover actions that would otherwise be time-barred, as long as at least one incident occurred within the relevant time limit.

Further Legal Action

You must file a lawsuit in state or federal court within ninety days after you receive the right-to-sue letter from the EEOC. You may file a lawsuit even if the EEOC has not found reasonable cause to believe the law was violated (although such a finding may be an indication that you do not have a strong case). If you elect to sue your employer, then it is advisable to hire an attorney to navigate the complex substantive and procedural rules that will govern your case. Because there is only a short time between the EEOC's issuance of a right-to-sue letter and the time when a lawsuit must be filed, you should have a lawyer lined up before the EEOC closes your case.

If you win or settle a lawsuit, you may be entitled to several types of relief. A court might issue an **injunction**, which is a court order requiring a party to do or refrain from doing something. For example, if the discrimination meant you were not hired for a job, then a court might order an employer to hire you. If you were not promoted because of discrimination, then you might be promoted. And if you were fired because of discrimination, then you might be reinstated.

You may also receive **back pay**, which is money to compensate you for any pay that you lost because of the unlawful discrimination. This may be pay that you lost because you were fired, because you were not promoted, or because you were not paid overtime. Back pay can be awarded for the period beginnig on the day that the unlawful discrimination occurred and ending on the day the judgment is entered. Back pay can also include payments for benefits lost during that same time period, including payments that an employer would have made to your pension fund. The statute limits eligibility for back pay to a maximum period of two years before the EEOC charge was filed, and back pay is capped at $300,000 for large companies, and less for small companies. You may also receive **front pay**, which is compensation for the period between the date of the judgment and the date of reinstatement. If a court orders an employer to reinstate you, and an appropriate position is not immediately available, the employer must pay front-pay damages to you until such a position becomes available. In cases in which reinstatement is not a viable option because of continuing hostility between you and your employer, or where you have psychological injuries as a result of the discrimination, courts have ordered front pay in lieu of reinstatement. Front-pay awards can be large, because they are not subject to a statutory cap. You may also be eligible for compensatory and punitive damages, which are awarded by a court when the discrimination was intentional. Such damages under Title VII are capped at $300,000.

If your claim is based on disparate impact, then the court may only award you back pay and attorney's fees and put you in the position you would have been in had there been no discrimination (which is called **make-whole relief**). It may also grant injunctive relief.

Retaliation

In addition to prohibiting employment discrimination on the basis of sex, Title VII and other federal and state employment laws also prohibit your employer from retaliating against you because you allege discrimination. Retaliation is prohibited whether you complained formally or informally to your employer, a coworker, or an outside agency or filed a legal action.

ⓘ FEDERAL EMPLOYEES AND EMPLOYMENT DISCRIMINATION

If you are a federal employee, then the federal antidiscrimination laws apply to you, but you have to follow different procedures. For example, every federal agency has an Equal Employment Opportunity (EEO) counselor whose job is to try to resolve discrimination complaints. If you are discriminated against, you must contact your agency's EEO counselor within forty-five days of the alleged discrimination. The counselor will investigate your complaint and try to resolve it informally. If no resolution is reached, then the counselor will notify you that you have fifteen days to file a formal discrimination complaint with your agency and will tell you how to file it. Once you have filed a formal complaint, the agency will investigate your complaint. If you are not satisfied with the investigation, you must, within fifteen days, either request a hearing on the complaint or an immediate decision from the head of the agency without a hearing. An independent administrative law judge from the EEOC will conduct the hearing and issue the decision. This decision is then sent to the head of your agency, who may accept, modify, or reject it.

After your agency head's decision, you have three options: accept the decision, file an appeal with the Office of Federal Operations of the EEOC, or file a lawsuit within ninety days. If you seek an EEOC appeal, the EEOC has 180 days to review your file and issue its decision. If you are not satisfied with the EEOC decision, you may file a lawsuit within ninety days of receiving that decision.

Retaliation is any adverse action your employer takes against you because you have made a complaint about discrimination. You are being retaliated against if, after you have made a complaint about discrimination, you are:

- Demoted
- Disciplined
- Fired

- Passed over for promotion
- Given negative evaluation
- Given a change in your job assignment (e.g., in your tasks, duties, hours, or shifts)
- Passed over for one or more bonuses
- Given a salary reduction
- Given an unjustified negative job reference
- Subjected to hostile behavior or attitudes

To bring a successful retaliation claim, you must establish that you have suffered adverse action as a result of your complaint about discrimination and not for any other unrelated reason. You can make a complaint to the EEOC about retaliation or bring a lawsuit. Retaliation is often a big issue in discrimination cases, and it is not uncommon for a woman alleging Title VII sex discrimination to lose her case on her initial claim, but win on her separate claim of retaliation.

THE WORLD AT YOUR FINGERTIPS

- You can find more information about Title VII and the other laws enforced by the EEOC at www.eeoc.gov. To find your nearest EEOC office, call 1-800-669-4000 (voice) or 1-800-669-6820 (TTY).
- To learn about state discrimination laws, contact your state's department of labor or fair employment office. To learn more about local discrimination laws, contact your city or county clerk's office.
- State and local bar associations often have referral services to lawyers who can help you with a discrimination case. Often, an attorney will hold a brief consultation at a minimal fee. You can find a link to your state or local bar association at http://www.abanet.org/barserv/stlobar.html.
- The website for the Harassment Hotline provides a wealth of information about sexual harassment and includes a comprehensive state-by-state review of each state's laws on sexual

harassment at www.end-harassment.com. It can also be contacted at 1-949-643-8489.

• Equal Rights Advocates provides valuable information on the rights and economic opportunities of girls and women at www.equalrights.org. The organization also provides women with free legal advice on discrimination and harassment over the phone at 1-800-839-4ERA.

• To help end wage inequities, the National Committee on Pay Equity (NCPE) coordinates an annual Equal Pay Day, celebrated on a Tuesday each year. Tuesday is the day when women's wages symbolically "catch up" to men's wages from the previous week. For more information about Equal Pay Day, visit the NCPE's website at www.pay-equity.org.

• Women Work! The National Network for Women's Employment provides publications and information for women about employment, health, and other issues at www.womenwork.org./resources/individual.htm.

• The AFL-CIO has a website devoted to working women. It includes information on the legal issues that working women face and a survey on the priorities of working women at www.aflcio.org/issuespolitics/women.

• You can find an in-depth policy analysis of some of the issues that affect women in the workplace at the website of the Institute for Women's Policy Research at www.iwpr.org.

• Detailed information on making a complaint about discrimination or harassment, from the personal perspective of a woman who has done just that, is available at the website of 9to5, National Association of Working Women at www.sexharassment.net.

REMEMBER THIS

• You have the right under federal law not to be discriminated against at work just because you are a woman. Sex discrimination includes sexual harassment.

• State and local laws are often broader than federal law and may even apply to small employers.

• The PDA, which is part of Title VII, contains specific protections from discrimination for pregnant women.

• The ADEA bars discrimination on the basis of your age, if you are over forty. Many state and local laws bar discrimination on the basis of any age.

• If you suffer discrimination or harassment at work, there are several ways in which you can seek redress. Make a complaint to your employer or to the EEOC, and if things don't change, consider bringing a lawsuit against your employer. You can help change the culture of your workplace and seek compensation for yourself.

• Consult your local EEOC or state labor office to make sure you follow the appropriate procedures within the appropriate time limits to protect your rights.

CHAPTER 4

Family-Friendly Laws and Policies: Pregnancy Leave, Maternity Leave, and Working from Home

Stephanie works as a graphic designer for a small company with four employees. She is delighted when she finds out that she is pregnant and decides she wants to work for as much of her pregnancy as possible and take three months off from work after the birth of her baby. Then she plans to return to work, although she hopes to be able to spend three days per week in the office and two days per week working from home so that she can save on child care costs.

Many women assume that they are automatically entitled to leave when they are pregnant or after they give birth. The good news is that there are several state and federal laws that prevent discrimination against pregnant women and guarantee unpaid maternity leave. The bad news is that these laws don't apply to all employers. There are two important federal laws in this area: the Family Medical Leave Act and the Pregnancy Discrimination Act, which is part of Title VII. This chapter will explain how the Family Medical Leave Act works and will help you determine whether you are entitled to leave. It will also take a look at some of the legal issues surrounding more informal family-friendly policies offered by some employers, such as telecommuting.

THE FAMILY MEDICAL LEAVE ACT

The Family Medical Leave Act (FMLA) was the first law signed by President Bill Clinton, just sixteen days into his first presidency

📄 MATERNITY LEAVE VERSUS PREGNANCY LEAVE

Pregnancy leave and maternity leave are not the same. **Pregnancy leave** is medical leave for a pregnancy-related disability. A pregnancy-related disability is any condition caused by your pregnancy that renders you unable to perform the functions of your job. Pregnancy leave includes leave you take when you are unable to work while you are pregnant, as you get ready to deliver, or as you recuperate from delivery.

Maternity leave is now often referred to by the gender-neutral moniker **parental leave**, which reflects the fact that under the Family Medical Leave Act both the mother and the father are entitled to unpaid leave to look after a child. Maternity leave is the child care period that starts after your disability from the pregnancy and birth has ended. Maternity leave is not medical leave; it is leave to care for your child after birth.

in 1993. It was a watered-down version of previous bills, with shorter leave periods and fewer covered workers, but some commentators predicted that women would nevertheless suffer more discrimination because employers would refuse to hire women of childbearing age. Others hailed the FMLA as a victory for families and workers and argued that family leave would no longer be stigmatized as a women's issue and as a drain on the workplace.

This federal law entitles you (whether you are male or female, married or single, gay or straight, a parent or childless) to up to twelve weeks of unpaid, job-protected leave per year. If you take leave under the FMLA, your employer must continue to pay for your health insurance and allow you to return to your job (or an equivalent one) when your leave is over.

You can take your twelve weeks of leave as **parental leave**, within twelve months after you give birth or adopt a child. You can begin the leave before the child arrives, if necessary for pre-natal care or preparations for the child. And if you need to take leave to adopt a child, you may be able to use parental leave anytime during or after the adoption process—for example, if you need to travel to a foreign country to bring your child home.

The FMLA also entitles you to up to twelve weeks of **medical leave** per year. You're entitled to a total of twelve weeks of leave each year—so you can take twelve weeks of parental leave, or twelve weeks of medical leave, or six weeks of each. You can take a medical leave if you have a **serious health condition**, which is defined as any illness, injury, impairment, or physical or mental condition that involves

• inpatient care at a hospital, or

• continuing care by a health care provider, and incapacitation for more than three days.

You can also take leave if you need to care for an immediate family member with a serious health condition. An "immediate family member" under the FMLA is defined as a

• child (including an adopted child),

• parent (including any person who cared for you when you were a child—no biological relationship is required, but in-laws are not included), or

• spouse (same-sex domestic partners are not currently included).

Pregnancy-related conditions can also be "serious health conditions" under the FMLA. In fact, they are treated slightly differently from other serious health conditions. If you suffer any incapacity due to pregnancy, you do not need to show proof of continuing treatment or inpatient care—prenatal care and conditions associated with pregnancy, childbirth, or recovery from childbirth are deemed to be serious health conditions for the purposes of the FMLA. As a practical matter, this means that if your doctor says that a period of leave is medically necessary due to pregnancy or childbirth and you meet other qualifying conditions, you will be able to take leave under the FMLA, without having to show that your condition merits hospitalization. Some courts have held that a pregnant woman who suffers from severe morning sickness can take leave, regardless of whether the woman receives medical treatment.

The FMLA also allows you some flexibility in taking your leave: you can take your twelve weeks a month, a week, or a day at a time—or even a few hours a day—up to a cap of 480 hours (for full-time employees). This latter type of **intermittent leave** may be a good option if you want to keep on working while you are also caring for a sick family member, if you need daily medical treatment, or if you have morning sickness during your pregnancy. Intermittent leave may also be a good option if you simply can't afford to take twelve weeks of unpaid leave from work and would like to spread the leave—and the pay cut—over a longer period of time. Of course, you will have to work out the type of leave you take (unless it is for a serious medical condition) with your employer.

Unfortunately, not all working women are entitled to benefits under the FMLA. The act does apply to all public agencies (city, county, state, and federal government)—regardless of size. But in the private sector, it only applies to employers who have fifty or more full- or part-time employees within a seventy-five-mile radius. And even if you work for an employer who is covered by the FMLA, you must still be able to show that you have been employed there for at least twelve months and have worked at least 1,250 hours to qualify for leave. Moreover, you may not be entitled to FMLA leave if you are among the top 10 percent of income earners at your company.

ⓘ SICK LEAVE FOR GAY AND LESBIAN EMPLOYEES

Employers must grant FMLA leave to gay and lesbian employees to care for qualifying "immediate family members." Thus, if a gay or lesbian couple adopts a baby and both or either of them work for covered employers, they are entitled to parental leave regardless of their gay or lesbian status—though they will not automatically be entitled to FMLA leave to care for each other. Chapter 7, "Unmarried Couples," provides more information on other legal issues that affect same-sex couples.

Recent statistics show that 41 million Americans are not covered under the FMLA for one of the above reasons. This means that about 40 percent of the private-sector workforce nationwide is not entitled to FMLA leave. If you are not covered by the FMLA, then it is worth checking your company's policies—many employers provide family leave even when federal law does not require them to do so. It is also worth contacting your state's department of labor to find out whether you might be entitled to leave under state laws or programs.

If you want to take leave under the FMLA, you must give your employer thirty days' notice. If you need to take leave because of an emergency or if you can't predict how long you'll need to take leave, then you need to give your employer whatever notice is practicable. If you don't give your employer timely notice, your leave may be delayed. Your employer may ask you to provide medical certification and may even ask you to seek a second opinion (at your employer's expense). Your employer—not you—is responsible for designating whether your use of any paid leave benefits will also count as your FMLA leave. Your employer may require you to use your accrued paid leave to cover some or all of your FMLA leave.

If you believe your employer has violated the FMLA, then you should talk to your human resources department to see if you can resolve the issue. If you cannot resolve your claim satisfactorily, then you should consider making a complaint to the Wage and Hour Division of the Department of Labor's Employment Standards Administration. The Department of Labor may bring an action in court to compel your employer to comply, but this is unlikely. You may also bring your own private lawsuit against your employer for alleged violations. Unlike Title VII cases, discussed in chapter 3, you do not have to file with the Equal Employment Opportunity Commission (EEOC) first or wait for a right-to-sue letter to bring a lawsuit on your own behalf. However, you must file your lawsuit within two years of the alleged violation—or within three years if your employer's violation was "willful" (deliberate). If you do file a lawsuit, your damages will be similar to those you may get for other employment law violations (which are discussed in chapter 3) and include back pay, attorney's fees, and injunctive relief (e.g., the court can order your employer to give you leave or reinstate you).

Most employment laws impose liability for violations on your employer. For the purposes of Title VII, discussed in chapter 3, your employer is "a person engaged in an industry affecting commerce." This means that if you are discriminated against by your supervisor under Title VII, you can't sue him or her directly—you can only sue the company. The FMLA is a bit different. "Employer" is defined broadly to include "any person who acts, directly or indirectly, in the interest of an employer." Courts have increasingly been allowing supervisor liability for violations of the act. Thus, if your complaint is with your manager or supervisor under the FMLA, you may be able to impose personal liability on him or her for violating some of your federally protected employment rights. Of course, an individual is unlikely to have the deep pockets of an employer, so you may make a strategic decision to sue your employer if you are pursuing money damages.

THE PREGNANCY DISCRIMINATION ACT

As discussed in chapter 3, the Pregnancy Discrimination Act stipulates that employers of fifteen or more employees may not treat women affected by pregnancy, childbirth, or related medical conditions differently from any other employees who are similarly able or temporarily unable to work. This means that your employer's own policies may require it to give you leave: Your employer must give leave to pregnant women who are unable to work if it gives leave to employees who are unable to work for other reasons.

A common example is that of disability leave. If an employer offers paid leave to workers who are temporarily disabled and unable to work for medical reasons, then it must also offer paid leave to employees with a pregnancy-related disability. Most obstetricians will certify that a woman is disabled for six weeks after a normal vaginal delivery and eight weeks after an uncomplicated cesarean delivery.

STATE LAWS

Many states have specific laws covering pregnancy leave and maternity leave. For example, Hawaii's laws on pregnancy leave apply to all employers with more than one employee; in Iowa and New York, the laws apply to employers with more than four employees. The law in California applies to employers of five or

---

( ) ASK A LAWYER

Q. My employer doesn't give any kind of pregnancy or maternity leave, and federal and state law doesn't help. Is there any argument I can make, to my employer or to a court, that might force my employer to provide this kind of leave?

A. You can make an argument if the employer has a policy of allowing time off for other kinds of medical or personal situations. For example, if the employer has a written policy that allows employees to take time off to recover from a heart attack or an auto accident, then you can argue that it is pregnancy discrimination not to allow a similar amount of leave for pregnancy or maternity. Even if it is not a written policy, you may have a legitimate argument if your employer has allowed this in practice. You can talk to a lawyer who specializes in employment law about what options you may have under state or federal law and whether there is any other theory of law that may apply to your particular situation. Most lawyers are willing to talk to you for a reasonable fee, or sometimes for free, for a one-time visit.

—Answer by Irene Jackson
Attorney, Mediator, and Arbitrator, Irving, Texas

more people and requires employers to give leave for up to four months—even if an employer's disability policy for other disabled employees provides for less leave. In Puerto Rico, pregnant employees are entitled to a "rest period" that includes four weeks before and four weeks after childbirth. The U.S. Chamber of Commerce website has short summaries of the leave available in many states at www.uschamber.com/sb/P05/P05_4402.asp.

The FMLA expressly provides that states are free to require additional or expanded protection for employees—and if your employer meets the criteria for both state and federal laws, then your employer must comply with both. This does not mean that you get double the leave time, but it does mean that your employer will have to follow the law—state or federal—that grants you the greatest benefits.

FAMILY-FRIENDLY EMPLOYMENT POLICIES

Unsurprisingly, there is no single, broad federal law that requires employers to provide women with alternative work schedules or part-time work on demand. However, some employers offer flexible work hours, part-time work, or the option of working from home to employees, often in a bid to attract highly qualified women. As with all employment decisions, an employer cannot discriminate between employees on the basis of race, color, sex, national origin, religion, disability, or age when granting flexible work options.

Many women take the option of part-time work. Of course, if you work part time you'll take home less pay each week than a full-time employee. Fair enough. But what you may not realize is that working part time can mean that you do not qualify for health benefits and will receive reduced pension contributions. If you work full time and are thinking of moving to a part-time position, talk to your employer about what effect this will have on your benefits. The money you lose by giving up health insurance may cost you even more than your pay cut.

A particularly favored option for women seeking flexibility in their work is telecommuting. You are not telecommuting if you are self-employed or take work home without getting extra pay (we all fall into this category!). But if you receive pay for work done at an alternate site—which may be your home or a special telecommuting space away from your main office—then you are a telecommuter. If you telecommute, you probably do so one to three days a week, and you probably use your home computer and the Internet or e-mail to do your work. A survey conducted by Telecommute America in 2001 reveals that more women than men telecommute and that they are most likely to be between the ages of thirty-five and forty-nine, which is also when they are likely to have young children at home. This poll also shows that the majority of telecommuters are satisfied with their work styles. Of course, not all jobs are suited to telecommuting—it may only be an option for you if your job involves professional, knowledge-related tasks.

If your employer allows telecommuting, chances are good that you will be subject to the terms of a company telecommuting policy or telecommuter agreement. This should set out the

(i) WHY WOULD MY UNION OPPOSE TELECOMMUTING?

If you are a working woman with children in child care, telecommuting may help when you can't find or can't afford full-time child care. Telecommuting may allow you to accommodate your child's school and activity schedules more easily and without missing work or taking time off. More important, it gives you the chance to bring home a paycheck or benefits or both—and still be available for your family.

So why would your union object? Some unions have objected in the past for two reasons: (1) work from home is difficult to regulate and has the potential to become "sweatshop labor" and (2) as a telecommuter, you become isolated from your coworkers, which makes it harder for your union to organize and conduct collective bargaining.

terms of your telecommuting and state that your telecommuting should not affect your benefits, bonuses, or chances of promotion. You may also need to investigate some of the following legal issues. These issues may also apply to you if you are self-employed and work from home.

Insurance

Your home insurance policy will not necessarily cover your home office. You'll have to read your policy to be sure. Often, the policies exclude business use. You can probably upgrade yours to cover the increased risks caused by the business, and you'll have to pay a little more for it. If you use your car in your work, you may also need to pay extra in automobile insurance.

Workers' Compensation

Even if you work at home, your employer will still need to pay workers' compensation insurance contributions on your behalf. This means that if you are injured at your home while you are working (e.g., if you suffer carpal tunnel syndrome), then you may be eligible for money to pay for medical expenses and to replace income lost as a result of injuries or illnesses that arise out of employment. There must be a causal connection between your injury and an employment requirement.

Occupational Safety and Health Laws

The federal Occupational Safety and Health Administration (OSHA) has issued a directive stating that it will not inspect home offices for violations of federal safety and health rules and it does not expect employers to do so either. The directive also states that an employer is not liable for the safety of conditions at an employee's home office. If you complain to OSHA about your home office, it may informally let your employer know about the home office condition, but it will not follow up with you or your employer. However, to avoid possible workers' compensation actions, many employers do provide telecom-muters with ergonomic furniture and advice about home office setup.

Taxes

Depending on how much work you do at home, you may be liable for state and local income taxes for any money paid to you for your work at home. The good news is that you may be able to claim some income tax deductions for nonreimbursed business expenses incurred for your home office.

Computers

Even if you're working at home, your employer can access records of the websites that you visit and the e-mails that you send, just as if you were working in the office. Employers remain concerned about protecting proprietary information, preventing harassment, and ensuring that company time is devoted to company work. Breaching any of these employment policies remains cause for disciplinary action, even if you are working from the comfort of your home office. It's also important to remember that your

---

(i) TELECOMMUTING FOR FEDERAL EMPLOYEES

There are a couple of federal laws that relate to telecommuting. Public Law 106-346 §359 applies only to federal executive agencies and requires such agencies to establish policies "under which eligible employees . . . may participate in telecommuting to the maximum extent possible without diminished employee performance." The National Air Safety and Telecommuting Act and the Small Business Telecommuting Act also propose pilot programs aimed at encouraging employers to offer telecommuting options to their employees.

---

employer probably owns the software on your computer, and you do not have an automatic right to use it for nonwork purposes.

THE WORLD AT YOUR FINGERTIPS

• The website of the Department of Labor provides detailed information and FAQs about the FMLA at www.dol.gov/dol/allcfr/ESA/Title_29/Part_825/toc.htm. There are also links to state departments of labor where you can find out more about relevant laws in your state.

• The National Partnership for Women and Families, which drafted the FMLA in the 1980s, provides information on the FMLA and state labor laws at www.nationalpartnership.org.

• You can find a good overview of the law relating to telecommuting at the website of Gesmer Updegrove, a law firm, at www.lgu.com/publications/employnon/13.shtml. Another good site for some basic information is www.telework-connection.com/legal.htm.

REMEMBER THIS

• The FMLA and the Pregnancy Discrimination Act may protect your job if you have to take time off for medical reasons while you are pregnant or after delivery. There may also be relevant laws in your state.

• The FMLA may also entitle you and your spouse to leave if either of you needs to take time off to care for yourself, your child, or a seriously ill immediate family member.

• If you are not eligible for leave under the FMLA, you may be eligible for parental leave or medical leave under state statutes—check with your state's department of labor.

• Even if an employer is required to give you job-protected leave, the leave does not necessarily have to be paid.

• No state or federal laws require your employer to give you part-time work or the opportunity to work from home. However, employee demands are making these options more common.

CHAPTER 5

Dependent Care: Child Care and Elder Care Issues

The days and nights of Sonia Johnson are full. Every morning she has breakfast with her son, Robert, and her husband, Jack, and races out the door to work from 8.30 a.m. to 5.00 p.m. On her way home, she picks up Robert from child care and drops him at home so Jack can cook him dinner. Then she drives across town to her mother's house. Her mother is eighty years old and has osteoporosis. Sonia brings her groceries, takes care of small domestic jobs, and cooks her evening meal every night. After they've eaten and Sonia has helped her mother get ready for bed, Sonia heads home. Robert is asleep, Jack is tired, and Sonia's long day has only just finished. Sonia is performing the ultimate balancing act: the working wife, mom, and daughter caught between two generations.

Ask any working mother or daughter what she needs as much as a good job with fair pay, and she'll probably tell you dependable, affordable, quality care—be it for her children or her parents. This chapter briefly looks at the available alternatives for dependent child and elder care and highlights some pertinent legal issues.

CHILD CARE

The most narrow definition of "child care" describes the care given from nine to five in a child care center to preschool-age children. But as any working mother knows, child care is also needed for infants and older school-age children; it is needed before and after school and during school breaks for holidays and summers, and when a child is too sick to go to school.

According to the AFL–CIO, every day nearly 24 million school-age children need care during out-of-school hours.

Before you sign up for any care, you must first assess your needs, your budget, and your willing and able friends, family members, and neighbors. No one size fits all—and no one child care option will solve all of your needs. Work schedules, family finances, logistics, and availability all play a role in selecting any alternative. One or more of the following options might be right for you.

Child Care Centers

Child care centers provide care to children in groups. All states require centers to be licensed; however, the requirements for a license vary from state to state. Licensing does not guarantee quality (and such laws have been criticized for making it easier to license your child care provider than your dog), but it does require minimum health and safety features as well as training standards for your child's individual providers at the center. All state training standards are different—staff might be required to have credentials in early childhood education and child development and be proficient in first aid. In addition, state-licensed centers are inspected once a year.

The pros and cons of such centers depend greatly on what your needs are. Many parents choose child care centers because they like the larger groups and the variety of individual providers and attendees they supply. They also find comfort in knowing that the centers are licensed by the state and, in all but extreme circumstances, are open and available when they are needed by Monday-to-Friday, nine-to-five workers, which is 7 a.m. to 6 or 7 p.m. in most centers. Drawbacks include higher costs than other alternatives—although many centers do offer discounts for siblings—and the potential for double costs when your child is sick and ineligible for care at the center. They are also not always an option for special needs or disabled children, because they are not approved for such care or because they are not set up to provide the special care your child needs.

☊ ASK A LAWYER

Q. I've been paying our babysitter in cash since she was sixteen. Five years on, she collects our son after school five days a week, for which we pay her $100 per week. Do I really need to deduct Social Security and fill out all those other forms? What could happen if I don't do this?

A. It sounds like they babysitter has been your employee and you should have been deducting Social Security and withholding income taxes for her for some, if not all, of those years. You should talk to an accountant to find out how much you actually owe and the best way to approach the Internal Revenue Service (IRS) to get the situation taken care of. You may also need to talk to a tax lawyer, but often an accountant who practices before the IRS can handle the whole matter for you, and may charge less than a tax lawyer. Don't wait, it will only get worse if you let it go on and do not deal with it.

—Answer by Irene Jackson
Attorney, Mediator, and Arbitrator, Irving, Texas

Care in an Individual's Home

Child care in a provider's home is a popular alternative to a child care center. Most states require some sort of certification for providers who care for more than four children, although laws vary by state. Some states have voluntary regulations for providers caring for fewer than four children. State regulations range from minimum health and safety rules, to requirements that providers undergo criminal background checks and training. Some states inspect providers every year, while other states conduct only random inspections. Almost every state has some sort of regulation for any provider—live-in or live-out—who receives child care subsidy payments, which are discussed later in this chapter. Some centers may also be accredited with the National Association for Family Child Care. Accreditation requires some experience and training. You can search for accredited providers at www.nafcc.org/accred/brochure.html.

This type of care is usually preferable if you want to give your child a more homelike environment with a smaller group than that at a center. Convenience and the personal reputation of the individual provider are often determinative, but this choice is often also favored because it is generally less expensive than a center and, in some cases, more flexible. However, like a child care center, individual providers may also choose not to care for your sick or contagious child.

In-Home Child Care

In-home child care givers include live-in nannies and au pairs as well as live-out nannies and housekeepers. Such care arrangements are not generally regulated by state law, but a few states regulate nanny placement agencies. Some agencies and carers may receive federal subsidies (discussed later in this chapter), in which case the state may require criminal background/child abuse and neglect checks, as well as some minimal training.

Some parents feel that in-home care is safer and that they can have more control over the care their children receive if they employ the caregiver. For many families, in-home care is more convenient and flexible than other kinds of care, and where there are several children it is not significantly more expensive than other alternatives. However, if you employ an in-home caregiver directly, you should be aware of the employment issues you may encounter, which may entail some additional work on your part (see the "Nannies, Nurses, and Housekeepers: Being the Boss and Hiring In-Home Helpers" sidebar below).

Kith-and-Kin Caregivers

"Kith-and-kin" caregivers are relatives, friends, and neighbors who care for your children. These caregivers are rarely regulated by state law, although some states require criminal background

NANNIES, NURSES, AND HOUSEKEEPERS: BEING THE BOSS AND HIRING IN-HOME HELPERS

When you hire someone to work in your home, you should make sure you are well informed about all the relevant employment law issues. The first step is to determine whether the worker is an employee or an independent contractor.

Generally, an independent contractor is paid on a "per job basis" rather than receiving a regular wage, and is free to accept or decline assignments. For example, if you use a temp agency to provide occasional babysitting services, it is likely that the worker will be considered an employee of the temp agency and work as an independent contractor for you. There are many factors to consider in determining whether a person is truly an independent contractor, which you can find on the website www.toolkit.cch.com/text/P07_1115.asp, the Business Owner's Toolkit.

On the other hand, an employee is paid a salary and the employer controls and directs the employee's work and hours. A full-time child care worker who lives in your home is likely to be an employee. Employers have several obligations to employees and are subject to state and federal laws. Employers must

- withhold Social Security and state income taxes and pay a matching share of Social Security taxes as well as unemployment insurance payments for any employee whose wages exceed $1,400 in any year (workers under age eighteen are exempt unless the employer provides their primary source of income),

- report and pay withholding taxes and payroll taxes on their personal income tax return,

- keep a record of the name, address, and Social Security number for each household worker, as well as a record of what each worker is paid, and

- provide employees with an end-of-the-year W-2 earnings statement and file a copy with the Social Security Administration and state and local taxing authorities.

If you employ someone, you may also want to consider purchasing workers' compensation insurance, which will cover the cost of workers' compensation benefits if your employee is injured at work. It is also important to remember that it is against the law to employ someone who is not eligible to work in the United States. Once you've decided to hire someone, you should ask for documents verifying that the employee is able to work. (Under the law, you cannot ask for such documentation until you've hired someone.)

For more information, go to the Social Security information page for household workers at www.ssa.gov/pubs/10021.html (or you can call 1-800-772-1213 for answers to your household worker questions).

checks and minimal health and safety training if they are receiving federal subsidy payments. They are often the most convenient and affordable alternative for many working families.

THE COST OF CHILD CARE

"Can I afford to work?" It sounds like an odd question, but for many women, there is a choice between working and making just enough to cover child care costs, and staying at home and surviving on public assistance. For some, it is a question of whether the time and effort spent away from the family is worth the monetary gain of employment. Not only is good child care hard to find, it is also hard to afford. Add to that the fact that most child care workers are underpaid women, and you see the flip side of the coin: it is also hard to provide quality child care.

There are many different kinds of assistance available to help defray the cost of child care. Some women are fortunate enough to work for an employer who provides subsidized child care or offers child care as a benefit. Or you may qualify for one of the following programs:

Federal government subsidies for child care are adminis-

tered by the Child Care and Development Fund and are distributed by the states. Each state sets its own guidelines for how the
funds will be distributed—most states fund child care for low-
income families through a voucher system. If you apply for benefits and are eligible, then the state will send vouchers (which
are kind of like coupons for child care) directly to a child care
provider, and you will not have to pay for the care. In most
states, to be eligible for subsidies your children must be under
the age of thirteen and must live with a parent who is working or
attending job training or an educational program. The level of
assistance you will receive will vary, depending on where you live
and the kind of care you need. Your state may pay higher rates if
your provider is accredited or offers hard-to-find care, such as
weekend and evening hours, or infant care; it may pay less if
your provider is not licensed. You may also be asked to contribute to the cost of child care on a sliding-fee basis. Again, this
will be set at your local agency, and your contribution will be
based on your family size, income, and other factors.

You can apply for child care vouchers at your state's local
Child Care Resource and Referral agency. Additional information is available at the Child Care Bureau website at www.
acf.hhs.gov/programs/ccb/index.htm. For a state-by-state list of
contact offices as well as other helpful child care information for
each state, check the National Child Care Information Center
website at www.nccic.org. In addition, there may be available
funds or assistance through a local city or township agency.
Check local listings for social service agencies or call Child Care
Aware toll-free at 1-800-424-2246 to find out more.

Private scholarships or assistance may also be available
from individual providers or programs—especially those offered
by nonprofit community groups such as the YMCA, United Way,
or religious congregations. Assistance may be in the form of
scholarships or tuition assistance. Some assistance is also distributed according to sliding scales that consider your household
size, family income, and extenuating circumstances (including
medical or housing costs, disabilities, and so on).

Several different tax breaks may also be available to you, depending on your circumstances. You may be eligible for three different types of **tax credits** under the IRS federal tax code:

1. Child and Dependent Care Tax Credits, which allow credit for up to 30 percent of a family's child care expenses

2. Child Tax Credits, which mean you can reduce the taxes you owe by up to $1,000 for each dependent child under age seventeen by filing Form 8812, "Additional Child Tax Credit"

3. Earned Income Tax Credits, which allow a tax credit to low-income persons

To claim any of these tax credits on your annual return at the end of the year, you must have receipts or proof of your child care payments. If you are eligible for all three credits, you may be able to claim all of them—so if you jump through all the hoops you can save a lot of money. It's also worth checking your state law—over half the states offer child and dependent care tax credits. Of course, if you spend more on child care than you owe in taxes, you will receive a limited benefit.

Dependent Care Assistance Programs (DCAPs) provide another kind of tax break for which you may be eligible. DCAPs allow employers to offer qualified employees up to $5,000 a year in tax-free child and dependent care benefits. Most commonly, an employer establishes a DCAP as a salary-reduction plan: employees are permitted to set aside up to $5,000 from their annual salaries to cover their employment-related child and dependent care expenses. In effect, the employee receives tax-free child care.

It takes effort and advance planning on your part to participate in a DCAP. Your child care provider must supply a federal ID number, and you often have to prepay the care provider and then give periodic receipts to your employer for reimbursement during the year. You also have to decide at the start of the year how much you want to put into your account. If you do not use it all for child care, you cannot get a refund on what is leftover at the end of the year. Thus, it is often referred to as a "use-it-or-lose-it" tax benefit.

ⓘ HOME ALONE?

There are no state or federal laws regulating when a child is old enough to be left home alone or to care for younger siblings or other children. Some states have guidelines that are distributed through child protective services agencies and administered at the state or county level. For example, the guidelines in Fairfax County, Virginia, require that any child left alone must feel comfortable being left alone and must have a safety plan worked out ahead of time. The guidelines also provide that

- no child under age seven should ever be left alone for any amount of time,
- a child of eight to ten years should be left alone for no more than one-and-a-half hours and only during daylight and early evening hours,
- a child of eleven to twelve years should be left alone for no more than three hours, but not late at night or in circumstances requiring inappropriate responsibility,
- a child of thirteen to fifteen years may be left alone, but not overnight, and
- a child of sixteen to seventeen years may be left alone, in some cases, for up to two consecutive nights.

There are also guidelines about babysitting. To learn more about the guidelines for your state, contact the National Clearinghouse on Child Abuse and Neglect Information at 1-800-394-3366.

ELDER CARE

For the first time in U.S. history, the average married couple has more living parents than children. The responsibility for parents' care most often falls on women (generally on the oldest daughter). In fact, three out of every four caregivers are female. And because women are the fastest growing segment of the work-force, competing time demands force them to juggle multiple roles. This group of caregivers, caught between the demands of their children and their parents, is sometimes referred to as the **sandwich generation**.

If you have elderly parents, there are many legal issues that you are likely to confront, and it is vital to talk with your parents and plan for every possibility well in advance. A good starting point, and one of the most useful legal documents for you to have, is a durable power of attorney. A **power of attorney** is writ-ten authorization to act on another's behalf for whatever pur-pose is designated, so you can pay bills and take on his or her other financial matters; a **durable power of attorney** continues to be valid during or after any incapacity of the person on whose behalf the power was created. It is important to talk to your loved ones about setting up a durable power of attorney. You should also discuss a **durable power of attorney for health care** so you can make decisions about your loved one's health care in an emergency. One tip: A power of attorney is no longer in effect once a person dies—which means, for example, that a bank won't let you withdraw money out of your mother's bank account after her death. Chapter 19 provides more information about these documents. You will also need to make sure that your parent or loved one has an up-to-date estate plan and that you know who the executor is (you can find more information about estate planning in chapter 20).

If your parents are frail and need actual care, then you are likely to face a host of other issues. Caring for a disabled or dependent relative or friend has been compared to caring for a child—and it can cost as much or more. You may be eligible for some relief in the form of Child and Dependent Care Tax Cred-its and Dependent Care Assistance Programs, discussed earlier in this chapter, which can be applied to the costs of care for your dependent parents. But the cost of care for the elderly is high, and most families are unlikely to be able to afford full-time care, even with the tax credits. If your parents are in good shape now, you're planning for their future, and your parents have a large amount of assets they'd like to protect (over $100,000), then you may want to think about purchasing long-term care insurance. Such insurance may cover assisted-living facilities, adult day care, respite care, and other long-term care services. If you start paying for this insurance early, then the premiums are relatively low. Look out for policies with a ninety-day exclusion period—if your parents pay for the first ninety days of care, then premiums can be up to 30 percent lower.

Medicaid will also pay for long-term care and some kinds of at-home nursing care (see chapter 19, "Issues for Senior Women," for more information about eligibility). One point worth noting: There is no legal obligation for you to pay for your parents' care—only a spouse may be held legally responsible for helping pay the cost of nursing home care. Children sometimes feel pressured to help pay for a parent's nursing home care because of the shortage of nursing home beds, especially Medicaid-covered beds. Some nursing homes give admission preference to private-pay patients over Medicaid patients because private-pay rates are higher than the amount that Medicaid pays. While admission priority for private-pay patients is admissible in some states, it is illegal in others.

If you do not have insurance for long-term and nursing care and you cannot afford to pay for someone to help you care for your parents, then you may find yourself providing a lot of the care yourself. You may spend time providing direct care—cooking meals, helping around the house, and so on—and doing administrative work, paying bills, filing insurance claims, and filling out Medicare forms. It is important for you and your sanity to spread the burden and ease the pressure. There are many organizations that may be able to help you care for a loved one.

The first place to start is your local Area Agency on Aging (AAA). Every area of the country is served by either an AAA or a state unit on aging. These agencies help local communities develop services specifically for older residents and channel funds provided under the Older Americans Act, which is the main federal law that provides funding for services to the elderly. AAAs will be able to give you information on local charities, organizations, support groups, and churches with programs and information to help you. For example, your AAA might be able to help you locate elder day care and respite care to enable you to take a break from caring for your parents. Your AAA can also give you information on national programs for which your loved ones might be eligible, like Meals on Wheels.

Don't forget that your parent or loved one probably has friends who can also help with care. Make a list of your parent's or loved one's network of friends—old colleagues, acquaintances from church, bowling buddies, and so on. These people might be able to do some shopping or cleaning for your loved one, or you might be able to call on them for help when you need it.

In an emergency, you may be able to take leave from work to provide care to your parents. The Family Medical Leave Act (FMLA) entitles you to take up to twelve weeks of unpaid leave a year to care for a family member with a serious medical condition. The FMLA does not apply to all employees—refer to chapter 4 to see whether you are eligible. If you are not eligible, you may still be entitled to leave under state or local laws.

THE WORLD AT YOUR FINGERTIPS

• The Department of Health and Human Services' Administration for Children and Families hosts a National Child Care Information Center. This is a comprehensive A-to-Z forum for child care issues, complete with FAQs, information sheets, and links at www.nccic.org.

• The Child Care Aware website at www.childcareaware.org provides sample child care agreements, which function as simple contracts and help clarify what you should expect from your caregiver. The site also includes checklists that you should consider when selecting a child care provider.

• You can find more information about the tax breaks available for child care and elder care by accessing a free, detailed, and annually updated booklet through the National Women's Law Center website at www.nwlc.org/pdf/

CreditWhereCreditIsDue2004.pdf. The booklet is thorough and can help you work out whether you qualify for any or all of the credits and benefits.

• Most AAAs have written materials that describe resources in the community. Some have brochures that identify common problems that the elderly might face, with resources and ways to solve the particular problem. You can call the Eldercare Locator at 1-800-677-1116 to find the contact details for your local AAA or visit the website at http://www.eldercare.gov/Eldercare/Public/Home.asp.

• The National Family Caregivers Association is a grassroots organization for caregivers and provides information, FAQs, and links to other useful websites at www.nfcacares.org.

• The site of the American Bar Association's Commission on Law and Aging contains information on dealing with the legal aspects of planning for incapacity by means of durable and medical powers of attorney, living wills, and trusts at www.abanet.org/elderly.

REMEMBER THIS

• Women comprise about half of the U.S. workforce today and are responsible for most of the child care.

• There are several forms of child care available to working mothers, but they can be expensive.

• Relief from the high costs of child care can come in the form of tax credits. You are often allowed to use more than one credit.

• If you have elderly parents or loved ones, you can save time and heartache through discussion and advance planning. Remember that there are many good sources of information and support out there—contact your local AAA for more information on resources in your community.

PART THREE

Family

CHAPTER 6

Marriage: Your Rights, Your Responsibilities, and the Law

Tim and Sophie are young, in love, and have decided to get married. Sophie has already thought about the dress, asked her sister to be a bridesmaid, and planned a guest list. Tim's friends are planning his bachelor party, and Sophie's friends have booked a cruise so that they can all celebrate her last days as a single woman.

But there's more to marriage than a dress and a party. Tim and Sophie might want to think about the legal implications of their marriage. How will it affect the property they own now and the property they hope to acquire? Will Sophie become responsible for Tim's debts? Will they owe more in taxes because they are married?

The moment you say "I do," your relationship acquires a legal status. You might have rights to your spouse's property and future income (and your spouse might have rights to your property), you may be responsible for each other's debts, and you may be subject to different tax rates from single people. Understanding your legal rights before you enter into marriage will give you more control over your future and perhaps help you avoid financial losses and other legal troubles.

WHAT IS MARRIAGE?

Marriage is both a private bond between two people and an important social institution. We speak of marriage as being a contract, but the rights and obligations of spouses are defined by law, and marriage can change your legal status.

The requirements for marriage are simple, although they vary from state to state. In general, a couple wishing to marry must obtain a license in the state in which they choose to be married. Licenses are often administered through the office of the county clerk, city clerk, or clerk of court. The associated fee is usually low.

You can be married in a religious or a civil ceremony. Civil ceremonies are usually conducted by judges. In some states, county clerks or other government officials may conduct civil

---

(i) SAME-SEX MARRIAGE

The traditional view—and legal definition—of marriage is restricted to unions between a man and a woman. But in 2004, a decision by a Massachusetts court extended the right to marry in that state to same-sex couples. A number of cities across the country began issuing marriage licenses and performing marriage ceremonies for gay and lesbian couples shortly thereafter. All of the provinces of Canada and certain European countries extend the right to civil marriage to gay and lesbian couples.

If you live in a jurisdiction that allows same-sex marriage and you choose to marry another woman, you will be afforded all of the same rights and responsibilities as opposite-sex couples under state law. If you live in a state that does not recognize same-sex marriage, but travel to, for example, Canada or Massachusetts to marry your same-sex partner, then your home state may not recognize your marriage as valid. Indeed, many states have passed laws to this effect. It remains to be seen how the federal government will treat such marriages for purposes of federal income tax, employee benefits, Social Security, and other federal laws that are contingent on marital status. A federal law passed in 1996 called the Defense of Marriage Act purports to restrict the definition of civil marriage for purposes of federal law to unions between a man and a woman. (You can find information about divorce issues relating to same-sex marriage in chapter 8.)

---

ceremonies. Religious ceremonies are usually conducted by authorized religious officials, such as ministers, priests, or rabbis. Native American ceremonies may be presided over by a tribal chief or other designated official. Contrary to popular legend, ship captains are not automatically empowered to perform marriage ceremonies. States generally do not require that certain words be used in a marriage ceremony, but the person or persons conducting the ceremony should indicate that the two individuals agree to be married.

A BRIEF HISTORY OF MARRIAGE

In ancient Greece and Rome, marriage was often arranged by families without consulting the prospective husband or wife. Men could take a wife and a concubine, and if the wife gave her consent, the concubine's children could be appointed as heirs. Greek society commanded that the wife be faithful to her husband, to ensure that her children were legitimate.

Love and marriage did not necessarily go together in the Western world until the twelfth century, when the troubadours are credited with creating the first notions of romance. At the beginning of the thirteenth century, the Catholic Church got involved and decreed that marriage was a sacrament that required consent. In the 1500s, governments started to exert some control over the legality of marriage, and in 1753 the English Parliament passed a law requiring marriage licenses and regulating when and where marriage ceremonies could take place. Marriage had evolved from a cultural custom to a legal contract.

In England and the United States, men got the better end of the bargain when they married: At the moment of marriage, a man became the owner of his wife's personal property, and he had what was called "tenancy by marital right" in his wife's land, which gave him the rights to any rents or profits from any land his wife owned at the time of the marriage or that she acquired during marriage. Moreover, because husbands and wives were considered one legal person (i.e., the husband), a wife could not contract with her husband or with anyone else.

Fast forward to the late nineteenth and early twentieth centuries, when women obtained much-needed reform of marriage, including the right of married women to make contracts, to control their own earnings, and to manage their own property. The sexual revolution of the 1960s and 1970s and the invention of the contraceptive pill helped to weaken the link between sex and marriage, and we no longer assume that marriage and procreation are inevitably related. Greater protections against sex discrimination in the workplace enacted during this time also helped weaken the link between money and marriage.

Today, women in the United States are waiting longer to get married, often citing the desire to get a college education and begin a career. Women are more economically independent than in the past, and social attitudes toward sex outside of marriage are more tolerant. In 2000, American women married for the first time at an average age of twenty-six, an all-time high. The percentage of never-married women and men between the ages of thirty and thirty-four is more than triple the percentage of never-married single people in this age group just thirty years ago. However, the majority of women do marry eventually. By the age of forty, more than 80 percent of women will have married at least once.

PROPERTY OWNERSHIP IN MARRIAGE

Even the ancient Egyptians recognized a woman's right to inherit, control, and dispose of property in her own name. Thousands of years later, we've finally caught up with them. Today, a woman retains title to property and all ownership rights in property she owned before marriage. She also holds title and rights in all separate property she acquires after marriage. And, of course, spouses may also own property together during their marriage.

(i) WOMEN AND SAME-SEX UNIONS: A LESSER-KNOWN HISTORICAL PERSPECTIVE

At various times in history, most societies have recognized same-sex unions, and some have even sanctioned same-sex marriages. They were recorded in popular Roman culture and literature, and there is evidence of same-sex unions and marriages in Native American, African, and Asian cultures.

Same-sex unions between women were at one time viewed differently from same-sex relationships between men because sex was defined only as intercourse and, without a penis, intercourse, per se, could not take place between women.

These relationships flourished from the Renaissance onward and, according to William Eskridge, "genuinely took off as a social phenomenon in the eighteenth century, when women's needs for intellectual and emotional respect far outstripped the ability of socialized males to meet those needs and when many women had the economic means to be independent of men. For many women, these female friendships generated a great deal more emotional intensity than they could find in marriage."

By the nineteenth century, women's expanded opportunities and control over their personal relationships allowed these unions to proliferate. With a nod to the lives of a female couple in Henry James's 1885 novel, *The Bostonians*, the term "Boston marriage" was used to describe a long-term monogamous relationship between two otherwise-unmarried women. Boston marriages were not legally sanctioned, but they were popular among well-educated, professional women.

Some female unions did result in legal marriages, but only through the phenomenon of "passing," when a woman dressed in men's clothing, to the extent that she could pass for a man in several aspects of life—including numerous physical exams in one notorious incident. Several passing women further crossed traditional gender lines by joining the

armed forces. It is estimated that some four hundred women passed as
men to serve in the Union Army during the Civil War.

Source: William N. Eskridge, "A History of Same Sex Marriage," 79 *Va. L.
Rev.* 1419 (Oct. 1993).

Title-Based Property States

States vary in how they allocate ownership between spouses in a
marriage. In **title-based (separate) property states**, the marital
status of a couple does not affect its ownership of property. In
other words, what was hers is still hers, what was his is still his,
and each spouse will own all that he or she earns or acquires
during the marriage. Forty-one states have separate (individual)
ownership systems.

Spouses in separate-property states generally own property
together under one of the following forms of co-ownership:

Joint tenancy is a form of ownership that exists when two or
more people own property that includes a right of survivorship.
This means that each person has the right to possess the property, and if one partner dies, the survivor automatically becomes
the sole owner. Any two or more people—not just spouses—may
own property as joint tenants. The interests are divisible, which
means that a creditor may claim one partner's interest in the
joint tenancy property.

Tenancy by the entirety is allowed in less than half of the
states. It is a form of co-ownership of property by spouses,
which, like joint tenancy, includes a right of survivorship. However, the interests are not divisible, which means that a creditor
of one spouse/debtor may not seize the property for payment of
debts. Each party usually must consent to the sale of the property. As in joint tenancy, divorce may result in a division of the
property, in which one spouse becomes the sole owner, or in a
sale, in which the proceeds are divided between the spouses.

Tenancy in common is a form of co-ownership that gives
each person control over his or her share of the property, and the
shares need not be equal. The law does not limit tenancy in

common to spouses. A tenancy in common does not automatically provide a right of survivorship—when one owner dies, that share passes to the heirs named in her will.

If you live in a separate-property state and divorce, disposition of your property depends on the court. You and your spouse might take from the marriage exactly what you each put in. Or a court might divide the property somewhat differently. Chapter 8 contains more information about the way in which property is divided.

Community Property States

There are nine community property states: Arizona, California, Idaho, Louisiana, Nevada, New Mexico, Texas, Washington, and Wisconsin; and one community property territory: Puerto Rico. A tenth state, Alaska, allows married couples to voluntarily enter into "community property agreements or trusts." In community property states, both spouses own property and income acquired during the marriage fifty-fifty. This might include all wages earned during the marriage, a house bought with marital funds, and cars and personal property. Even if one spouse has title to the property, the property may still be community property. For example, if a woman buys a car, is the only driver, and holds title to the car, the car may still be marital property if any part of the payment for the car came from marital funds.

The law in community property states still allows each spouse to own some property separately. Although definitions vary by state, **separate property** generally includes
- property owned before the marriage,
- property a spouse acquires through inheritance or a gift,
- property a spouse acquires as personal injury damages,
- property a spouse acquires after the couple is legally separated, and
- property or proceeds gained from the sale of separate property sold during a marriage.

Your spouse may also voluntarily give up his rights in any of your property.

(i) CHANGING NAMES

A woman's name changes only if she wants it changed. In the past, a woman would often change her last name to her husband's name when she married. Now, society recognizes your right to take your spouse's name, keep your original name, or use both names. Some people use one name socially and another for professional and legal purposes. The general rule is that if you use a chosen name honestly and consistently, then it will be recognized as your true name. The important thing is to use only one name for all official purposes.

If you are changing your name, you should notify the appropriate government agencies, including the Internal Revenue Service, the Social Security Administration, the Passport Agency (within the U.S. State Department), the post office, state tax agencies, the driver's license bureau, and the voter registration bureau. You should also notify any professional organizations or commercial businesses with whom you have a relationship, including professional licensing agencies, professional societies, unions, the mortgage company, the landlord, banks or credit unions, charge card companies, the telephone company, other utilities, magazines, newspapers, doctors, dentists, and schools and colleges that you attend or attended.

In some community property states (e.g., California), community property is divided equally between spouses in a divorce; in other states, the courts are allowed to fine-tune property divisions depending on what is "equitable." Chapter 8 contains more information.

PREMARITAL AND POSTMARITAL AGREEMENTS

Premarital and postmarital agreements change the division of marital property from what state law would otherwise provide.

The difference between these two different types of agreements is when they are entered into: **premarital**, **prenuptial** ("prenup"), or **antenuptial agreements** are entered into *before* a couple marries; **postmarital** or **postnuptial agreements** are entered into *after* a marriage has taken place but before it ends.

The stereotype of the rich man and the young, gold-digging bride as the sole candidates for premarital agreements went out in the 1980s. Today, women have more education, more career opportunities, more money, more businesses, more political clout, more marital property, and more child support rights than ever before. Women are generally held to the same legal standards as men—especially when it comes to their rights and responsibilities in marriage. So, love notwithstanding, there are many legitimate reasons why men *and women* choose to enter into such agreements. For example, premarital agreements

- help to clarify the parties' expectations and rights for the future,
- allay fears and minimize uncertainties about how a divorce court might divide the couple's property if the marriage fails,
- protect each spouse's premarriage assets,
- avoid the loss of a family business in the event of death or divorce,
- ensure, in second or third marriages, that certain assets will be passed on to the children or grandchildren of a previous marriage,
- help to shield one spouse from the bad credit rating of the other, as long as the parties keep their separate property separate and inform creditors of their agreement to keep their assets and debts separate.

Premarital agreements may also be used in marriages where a woman sacrifices or puts her career on hold to put her spouse through school or support him while he pursues his career goals. The agreement can ensure that the wife who sacrifices or postpones her career will be adequately compensated if the couple divorces. Finally, remember that the rights and obligations of spouses differ from state to state. If a couple moves to another state, the spouses' relationship may change even without their knowing it.

So what does it take to create a valid premarital agreement? The validity and enforcement of such agreements are matters of state law. Generally, premarital agreements must be in writing and signed by the parties. Beyond that, courts are concerned with fairness and will consider several factors in deciding whether an agreement is enforceable:

• whether the parties fully disclosed their income, debts, and assets to each other,

• whether any party waiving rights did so with full knowledge,

• whether the parties had ample time to consider the agreement before the wedding (divorce lawyers cite an "invitation-mailing rule" that says if you want the agreement to be valid, make sure it is negotiated and signed before the wedding invitations are mailed),

• whether the parties were represented by different lawyers or had the opportunity to be represented by different lawyers (a lawyer is not legally required to represent either party; however, having separate lawyers helps to create a balanced, negotiated agreement that both parties understand), and

• whether the parties entered into the agreement voluntarily and free of any fraud, duress, coercion, or mistake of fact.

Premarital agreements most often contemplate the parties' rights upon divorce or death. They may also deal with issues of property—for example, the right of either party to mortgage, sell, or otherwise dispose of and control certain property and the ownership of the benefits to a life insurance policy or pension. They often include agreements that each party make a will or create a trust to carry out the intent of the premarital agreement (see chapter 20, "Estate Planning," for more information on wills and trusts).

Importantly, premarital agreements are neither binding nor enforceable regarding issues of child custody or child support; courts have the sole power to decide these issues according to the best interests of the child. However, you can state your intentions and some judges may find such a provision useful. More information on child custody and visitation is available in chapter 9.

In the negotiation of many premarital agreements, the amount of spousal support must be fair and just. State laws are not uniform here, and none of them sets specific amounts of support that must be provided. Some states require subsistence levels (enough to keep a spouse off welfare), but most states will look at many factors, including the duration of the marriage, and may require a higher level.

The legal standard used by many courts in determining appropriate spousal support is **unconscionability**. "Unconscionability" refers to agreements that are unusually harsh and unfair. Some courts define an unconscionable agreement as one that no sensible person would offer and that no sensible person who was not under duress or delusion would accept. This is a subjective standard, and courts have interpreted it in different ways. An unconscionable agreement will not be enforced. To promote fairness and avoid unconscionability, many premarital agreements will have an **escalator clause** or a **phase-in provision** that increases the amount of assets or support given to the less wealthy spouse based on the length of the marriage or if there is an increase in the wealthier party's assets or income after the agreement is made.

Postmarital agreements are less common than premarital agreements, and the law is less settled concerning their validity and enforcement. They generally have the same goal as premarital agreements—to protect assets or income upon death or divorce—but they are usually first contemplated after a period of marital conflict or a significant financial change. The criteria that apply to premarital agreements—fairness, full disclosure of debts and assets, and absence of duress—also govern postmarital agreements. However, since the parties are already married, they may be held to a higher standard of fairness when it comes to financial issues.

LIABILITY FOR SPOUSAL DEBTS

Property can be divided between two or more people; unfortunately, debt can be divided between spouses as well. Depending on the nature of the debt and where you reside, you may be responsible for your spouse's debts.

( ) ASK A LAWYER

Q. My fiancé wants me to sign a prenuptial agreement. This seems totally unromantic to me and contrary to everything marriage should be. Could there be any reason for him to do this that doesn't make me doubt him? Could he have a reason that I could accept?

A. Strangely, or perhaps not so strangely, where marriage customs provide for arranged marriages rather than marriages on the romantic model, the resulting unions are often more stable. Parents and matchmakers see to it that things are set up properly. Marriage is an important commitment and should not be entered into with rosy and unrealistic expectations. Rather than ask why he wants a prenup, maybe you should ask why you didn't think of it?

There are many reasons for a prenuptial contract, especially if there is a family business, outstanding debts, or existing children from an earlier marriage. You shouldn't want a husband who is willing to abandon his responsibilities . . . you could be next.

Instead of getting angry or worried about a marriage agreement, worry about the terms. If what he is proposing is a marriage of "what's mine is mine and what's yours is mine," cancel the chapel pronto. If he is just trying to work everything out for both of your benefits, that is great. Why not sit down and ask what terms *you* would like to govern your marriage and see if he and you are not only in love but also compatible?

Whatever you do, be sure to have a lawyer look at any prenuptial agreement. Don't talk to his lawyer; get a lawyer of your own choosing. Your local bar association will be happy to refer you to someone whom you can afford.

—Answer by Marilyn Ireland
Professor, California Western School of Law,
San Diego, California

Q. For thousands of years, marriage has been between a man and a woman. Now, we hear about marriage between two men or two women. How is this legally possible?

A. People know that marriage is an important stabilizing institution in society, so they make the mistake of assuming that the legal definition of marriage has been static over a long period of time. This is just not true. Just in the United States, marriage laws are a lot different today than they were not long ago. What's more, marriage laws differ from one state to another. There are different age requirements in different states as well as different rules about cousins who want to marry. And property and support laws differ from the West and Southwest to the East Coast and Midwest.

Marriage law, like all law, changes to accommodate social realities. Can you imagine how few marriages there would be today if a woman had to become a ward of her husband upon marriage? No professional woman would agree to give up her property, earnings, and legal identity today. She probably would just "live with" the guy instead.

This does not mean that any change to the legal definition of marriage is a good change, just that any proposed change should be judged based on something other than mistaken assumptions that marriage at all places and times has been subject to a single and unchanging definition. When marriages were mostly between young people who were starting a family, one definition was appropriate. Now that many people, be they senior citizens or same-sex couples, are marrying not to procreate but for companionship, it is time to ask not "Why gay marriage?" but rather "Why not?"

—Answer by Marilyn Ireland
Professor, California Western School of Law,
San Diego, California

> Q. *I got married in a small religious ceremony in Mexico. The United States will recognize my marriage, won't it?*
>
> A. Foreign marriages that are only performed in a church are not recognized in the United States. For a marriage to be recognized here, the parties must have registered their marriage with that state's authorities. In predominantly Catholic countries, like Mexico, people often have only a church ceremony and don't bother getting registered. As a result, that marriage is not recognized as being valid in the United States.
>
> —Answer by Lydia Brashear Tiede
> Attorney, San Diego, California

If both you and your spouse cosign for a debt, then both of you will be responsible for paying it—regardless of who incurs it. For example, if you both apply for a charge card and you both sign the application and promise to pay the charge bills, both of you will be responsible for paying the entire balance, even if only one of you made a purchase and even if one of you disapproved. The same principle applies if you and your spouse cosign a mortgage for your home. You are each liable to the mortgage company, even if one of you no longer lives in the home.

You may also be responsible for your spouse's debts even when you do not cosign, if the debt can be considered a **family expense**. Some states have enacted family expense laws that make both spouses liable for expenses incurred for the benefit of the family, even when one spouse did not sign or approve of the expense in advance. Other states impose the family expense obligation by common law (i.e., without a statute). Thus, if your spouse charges groceries at a local store or takes your children to the doctor for care, you could be liable because these expenses benefit the family.

On the other hand, don't expect your spouse to be liable for that off-road vehicle that you bought for yourself and won't let him use, and you should not be liable if your spouse goes nuts on a shopping spree at the mall. You will normally only be liable for your spouse's debts if you cosign for the loan. The major exception is if you live in a community property state, in which case each spouse is liable for debts incurred by the other spouse. If your spouse has debts that he cannot pay, then a creditor could take marital property to satisfy the debt and could even garnish a portion of your wages.

Debts incurred during marriage must be distinguished from debts incurred before marriage. Generally, each spouse is not liable for the debts the other spouse brings to the marriage, even in community property states. These debts are the responsibility of the spouse who incurred them before the marriage. However, in many states, including some that are not community property, certain premarriage debts such as child support may be collected against the marital property of a new marriage. These provisions put the marital property of second wives at risk. For example, if a man is $15,000 behind in support payments to children of his first marriage, remarries, and owns a house in joint tenancy with his second wife, the couple's house may be taken by a court to pay off the child support debt. Or if you and your spouse both put your wages into a joint checking account and file joint tax returns, the amount of support due to a child of your spouse's first marriage may be assessed against your joint income. If you are a second or third wife and you are worried about prior spouses or creditors placing a claim on assets of your marriage, you should keep your property separate in your own name and never commingle it or own it in joint tenancy with your spouse. Unless you are very careful not to pay taxes or mortgage bills from a joint checking account, some judges could consider the entire property to be commingled and no longer separate. It is much more difficult, of course, to keep property separate in community property states.

LIABILITY FOR TAXES

If both spouses' names and signatures appear on a state or federal income tax return, then both are liable for the taxes. The

( ) ASK A LAWYER

Q. The guy I'm going to marry is perfect in every way—except that he owes tons of money for college loans. Is there any way I could be on the hook for what he owes?

A. If these debts were incurred before the marriage, are in his name only, and you have never cosigned for them, then you should not be responsible for them. Be careful, however, because if in the future these loans are refinanced, more money is borrowed, they are collateralized with marital assets, or if you cosign for a new loan that merges into the preexisting one, you could have some liability.

—Answer by Sharon L. Corbitt
Sneed Lang, P.C., Tulsa, Oklahoma

Q. My husband is trying to borrow money to start a business. The bank wants me to cosign the loan. What does this mean?

A. Banks often want spouses to join in a loan. This gives the bank twice as much assurance that the loan will be paid, particularly if you are working. Please understand, however, that if you do cosign this loan, then you are just as liable for the debt as your husband, even if you are not actively involved in the business. You should make the decision on whether to cosign this note based on the risk involved in the venture and the history of success (or nonsuccess) of your husband's business. If you do not feel comfortable with signing the note, then perhaps placing an asset as collateral in lieu of your signature is an alternative.

—Answer by Sharon L. Corbitt
Sneed Lang, P.C., Tulsa, Oklahoma

Q. People used to talk about "common-law" marriages. What does that mean? Can you be married in this way without knowing it? Is it like regular marriage?

A. Not all states recognize common-law marriages, and even in those that do, the requirements vary from state to state as to what is necessary to establish a common-law marriage. In states that recognize common-law marriage, it is indeed like a regular marriage in all respects, except that there is not a legal ceremony with the requisite license. There may or may not be some sort of informal ceremony. In general, if persons present themselves as husband and wife (e.g., introduce each other as spouses) and perform acts consistent with being married (e.g., listing each other as spouses on health or life insurance policies, making wills listing each other as spouses, and filing joint taxes as married persons), then they will be considered married by common law if common-law marriages are recognized in their jurisdiction.

—Answer by Sharon L. Corbitt
Sneed Lang, P.C., Tulsa, Oklahoma

A. A few states still recognize common-law marriage under which the state considers a man and woman who have lived together as husband and wife for a certain amount of time to be married under common law. You can find a list of the states that recognize common law marriage at http://www.unmarried.org/common.html. If your relationship breaks up, you then have to get a divorce to divide assets and determine custody and support.

—Answer by Denice Patrick
The Law Office of Denice L. Patrick, Lynnwood, Washington

Internal Revenue Service generally holds each spouse responsible for the entire tax debt if a couple files jointly. Both spouses are liable for fraudulent statements on a joint tax return. In some limited circumstances, when a spouse who signed a joint tax return can prove that he or she is an **innocent spouse** who did not know and had no reason to know that the tax return understated the true tax, liability may be excused. If you want full protection against possible liability for inaccurate tax returns filed by your spouse, then you can file a "married filing separately" return. The downside of this filing status is that you and your spouse may end up paying more taxes than if you had filed a joint return.

A "marriage penalty" results when a married couple pays more income taxes than they would have if they had remained single. Tax laws passed in 2003 eliminated the marriage penalty for most couples, but those in the highest or lowest income brackets may still be affected. You can find a marriage tax calculator at the Turbotax website, www.turbotax.com/calculators/index.html.

THE WORLD AT YOUR FINGERTIPS

• The American Bar Association's *Complete and Easy Guide to Family Law* (1996) provides more detailed information about marriage and other family law topics.

• The Legal Information Institute provides links to cases, laws, and Internet sources about law and marriage at www.law.cornell.edu/topics/marriage.html.

• Lambda Legal is a national organization committed to achieving full recognition of the civil rights of lesbians, gay men, bisexuals, transgendered people, and people with HIV or AIDS. It engages in litigation, education, and public policy work. The website has many resources, news items, and links to information about marriage at www.lambdalegal.org/cgi-bin/iowa/documents/record?record=1075.

REMEMBER THIS

• Women are equal to men and are held to the same legal standards—especially when it comes to their rights and responsibilities in marriage.

• A woman retains title and full property ownership rights in all the property she owned before she married and in all separate property she acquires after marriage.

- In community property states, all the wages a woman earns during a marriage are community property and are owned by the couple fifty-fifty.

- Premarital agreements most often contemplate the parties' rights upon divorce or death, yet they may also deal with issues of property and support, and include agreements that each will make a will or create a trust to carry out the intent of the premarital agreement.

- You may be responsible for your spouse's debts, but it depends on the nature of the debt and where you live.

CHAPTER 7

Unmarried Couples: Simple Steps You Can Take to Protect Your Rights as a Couple

Anne and Ben lived together as committed partners for ten years. Ben was working his way up the corporate ladder: his pension had vested, he was a junior vice president, and he had purchased a home for him and Anne to share. Anne took time off from her career as an architect to oversee the renovation of their new home, so she was not earning a separate income. They lived like a married couple, sharing everything, and they counted on growing old together. But Ben never got around to making a will.

A month ago, Ben was killed in a car accident. Ben's only living relative is his mother, whom he spoke to once a year and has not seen since he and Anne started living together, because she disapproved of the relationship.

Sad and true: Because Anne and Ben never married, Ben's mother will inherit the house and most likely the pension and all of Ben's other assets as well. In addition, if Ben was killed as a result of the other driver's negligence, Ben's mother—not Anne—will probably be the only person who could file and collect damages in a wrongful death lawsuit.

Not everyone wants, or is able, to marry the person with whom they want to spend their lives. Consider the partnership of Simone de Beauvoir (author of *The Second Sex*) and philosopher Jean-Paul Sartre, who lived together for almost fifty years. Gertrude Stein, author and grande dame of the Paris art scene, lived with Alice B. Toklas for thirty-seven years. Katharine

Hepburn and Spencer Tracy (who was unwilling to divorce his Catholic wife) spent twenty-seven years together.

It is hard to imagine, but just thirty-some years ago, before 1970, it was pretty much illegal in every state for unmarried couples to cohabitate (live together and have sexual relations). Today, a handful of states still have laws prohibiting cohabitation—although they are rarely enforced. But even though cohabitation is widespread and increasingly socially acceptable, unmarried partners who are living together do not generally have the benefits or entitlements that married couples gain at the moment they tie the knot. Laws that define spousal rights relating to property ownership, divorce, and inheritance usually do not apply to unmarried couples. Because of this, it is important to consider the legal consequences of living with another person and take appropriate steps to create private agreements to protect you and your partner. This chapter will consider some of the legal implications of being an unmarried couple—from the perspective of an unmarried woman living with her male or female partner. You may also find the information in this chapter useful if you are single or married, because you can use it to arrange your affairs in the way that you want, rather than relying on legislation that sets up default positions.

THE BASICS

If you live with your partner, there are some simple steps you can take to help you arrange your affairs in the way you want. You may even qualify for some of the same kinds of benefits as married couples.

Powers of Attorney

Powers of attorney are documents that everyone, especially unmarried couples, should consider, because they can be very useful in family matters, property matters, and health matters. A power of attorney is not about giving authority to your lawyer; it is simply a legal document that authorizes your partner, or anyone else you choose, to act on your behalf. For example, a power of attorney can authorize your partner to access your finances and make decisions on your behalf if you are unable to do so. A power of attorney can give your partner the ability to access your bank account and withdraw funds, so only execute one if you really trust your significant other.

Some lawyers will advise you to make a **springing power of attorney,** which only becomes effective if you are certified incompetent. Not all states recognize a springing power of attorney, so check your state law carefully. Other lawyers don't like springing powers of attorney because determining incompetence may be difficult in some cases (e.g., you may be out of the country when you are rendered incompetent, or your incompetence may be intermittent). Talk to your lawyer about your options, and also discuss them with your partner.

Domestic Partnership Registration

In some jurisdictions, an unmarried couple may enter into a **domestic partnership arrangement.** The laws regulating domestic partnerships differ from state to state. In some jurisdictions, only lesbian and gay couples qualify as "domestic partners." You and your partner probably have to live together for a fixed period of time before your partnership will be recognized. Most jurisdictions require that, to register publicly as domestic partners, you and your partner pay a small fee and sign affidavits stating that you meet certain criteria. Domestic-partner status is not simply a personal and private commitment between you and your partner—it can entitle both of you to some of the same benefits as married couples. For example, employers or insurance companies often rely on the registry's information to decide if you are eligible for domestic partner health benefits, different insurance rates, and so on. You may want to consult a lawyer before registering as domestic partners, to ensure that your domestic partnership will not create an implied contract for any

↻ ASK A LAWYER

Q. *A couple can become legally married in some states simply by living together, right? If they move to another state, are they still married?*

A. Yes. A marriage in one state must be given "full faith and credit" in another state, unless honoring the marrigage would be against the public policy of that other state. This means, for example, that partners who are married by common law in one state will be considered married when they move to another state, even if that state does not recognize common-law marriages for its own citizens. You must be a resident of the state in which you have a common-law marriage for the marriage to transfer to another state when you move.

—Answer by Marilyn Ireland
Professor, California Western School of Law,
San Diego, California

Q. *I'm not married to my partner, but I like his surname much better than I like my own. Can I change my name and use his last name even if we're not married?*

A. In most states, the answer is yes. In general, you can use any name you like as your legal name, so long as you do so consistently. But the changeover can be a bureaucratic nightmare, and many people, like clerks at the Department of Motor Vehicles, can be hard to convince. You can go to court in a very simple proceeding and legally change your name to whatever you like, so long as it is not for the purpose of committing a fraud. A well-known performer even legally changed his name to an unpronounceable symbol. Under the law, your name is yours. Taking or keeping a family name is just a custom, not a law.

Be aware if you live in a state that recognizes common-law marriages. Taking your partner's surname could be considered holding yourself out as married, resulting in a common-law marriage.

—Answer by Marilyn Ireland
Professor, California Western School of Law,
San Diego, California

Q. What's the difference between civil unions and marriage per se? And how do "domestic partnerships" fit in? Why are we getting all these alternatives now?

A. There are hundreds of ways in which married couples are legally treated differently from unmarried couples, and many more ways that private people and companies treat them differently. Same-gender couples have been asking for equal treatment for some years, and the courts are beginning to agree that they have been discriminated against by a system that excludes them and their needs. The earliest calls for reform arose because some hospitals refused to allow a gay partner even to visit a dying loved one.

Because many people object, often for religious reasons, to allowing gay marriage, a number of states decided to give gay couples some or all of the benefits of marriage, such as the ability to get insurance for each other. Civil unions and domestic partnership are just two terms that were made up to avoid using the word "marriage" to refer to relationships that are not comprised of a man and a woman.

—Answer by Marilyn Ireland
Professor, California Western School of Law,
San Diego, California

purposes that you might not have intended—like sharing your income, your home, or support.

If there is not a public domestic partnership registry in your city or state, some companies will still provide benefits to the domestic partners of their employees. Your employer may require you to sign an affidavit of domestic partnership to qualify for benefits. These benefits may include health insurance, pension benefits, family and bereavement leave, education and tuition assistance, credit union membership, relocation and travel expenses, and inclusion of your partner in company events. Some companies may only offer benefits to same-sex domestic partners.

HEALTH AND FAMILY LAW ISSUES

Medical Care

Let's revisit our scenario involving Anne and Ben. Suppose that Ben survived the car accident, but required major medical procedures and was unable to give consent because he was unconscious. Would Anne be able to visit Ben while he was in critical condition? Would she have the legal authority to make critical medical decisions on Ben's behalf? What if she and Ben's mother disagree on what is best for Ben?

Anne is in for some bad news. Because she is not related to or married to Ben, she does not have next-of-kin status. Doctors must follow state law, which generally gives decision-making priority to spouses, adult children, and parents. Even if Anne and Ben were registered as domestic partners, they may not have rights to make health care decisions for one another. Anne will only be able to make decisions on Ben's behalf if she and Ben had the foresight to draft a legal **health care directive** designating her as the decision maker.

Health care directives are also referred to as **advanced health care directives**, **health care proxies**, **medical directives**, **directives to physicians**, and **living wills**. They can involve two documents: one for declaring your health care choices should you become incapacitated (e.g., that you do not want to receive blood transfusions), and another for appointing a specific person to act and make decisions on your behalf if you are incapacitated. In some states, these decisions can be covered in the same document, usually called a **durable power of attorney for health care**. If you want your partner to make medical decisions on your behalf, you should document your intentions in writing and consult the law in your state to make sure your intentions will be followed. Creating a durable power of attorney for health care is a particularly important step to take if you are elderly or have an ongoing health condition. Once your partner has properly created a durable power of attorney for health care, you have the right to visit him or her in the hospital, hire and fire his or her medical care personnel, and gain access to his or her medical records.

The slightly better news for Anne is that she will not be liable for Ben's medical bills, unless they are registered as domestic partners and have agreed to assume liability for each other's debts. If Anne and Ben hold property jointly, however, then the property could be taken to pay the bills—although this will depend on the type of property, how it is held, and the laws of the state in which Anne and Ben live.

Wrongful Death Suits

If you are not married to your partner, then in most states you have no legally recognized relationship with your partner. This means that if your partner is killed or injured, you have no legal standing to recover money or other economic benefits you would have received if your partner hadn't been killed or injured. If Ben is killed in a car crash, Anne will have no standing to bring a wrongful death lawsuit against the driver.

Although two states (New Jersey and Ohio) have granted "bystander" rights to an unmarried partner to recover emotional distress damages for witnessing a loved one be killed or seriously injured, this would not help Anne in the previous scenario, because she did not witness Ben's death.

Children

Unmarried couples wanting to start a family, raise existing children from a prior union, or adopt have myriad issues to consider, ranging from paternity and name selection to custody and inheritance rights of children of unmarried parents. Family laws vary by state, so it is important for you to check your state law and consult a good family law specialist.

In 1968, the U.S. Supreme Court held in *Levy v. Louisiana* that it is illegal for any state to give legitimate children more legal rights than illegitimate children. The Uniform Parentage Act, drafted in 2000, also provides that "the parent and child relationship extends equally to every child and to every parent, regardless of the marital status of the parents." This model law, which has been adopted by fourteen states, declares that for the purposes of receiving Social Security benefits and similar government benefits, it doesn't matter whether a child is "legitimate" (born as part of a legal marriage) or "illegitimate" (born outside of a legal marriage).

Even so, a child of unmarried parents may have problems collecting benefits or insurance policy proceeds through his or her father if the father is not listed on the birth certificate. If a couple is married, then the hospital will automatically fill in the husband's name on the birth certificate. If a couple is unmarried, the mother must take this step.

Listing the father on the birth certificate is an extremely significant step for you and your child. That one signature will establish the father's liability for child support. It will ensure that the child is entitled to benefits through the father, such as health, life, and disability insurance benefits. It will also establish the father's liability to reimburse the state for welfare and other aid payments made to the mother. Incidentally, it also has important implications for the father. If the father's name does not appear on the birth certificate, then he must sign a paternity statement. If a father waits too long after the birth of a child to sign a paternity statement, his parental rights may not be fully recognized. As a mother, you also have the option of putting "Unknown" or "Refuse to State" in place of the father's name on your child's birth certificate.

However, just because the father's name is on the birth certificate, the baby will not necessarily have to take the father's name. In most states, naming a baby is no more complicated than filling out a birth certificate. You can give the child your last name or your partner's last name, whichever you prefer. Be aware that giving a baby the father's last name is not sufficient to establish paternity—you must also list the father's name on the birth certificate, as explained earlier.

If you're not married and you want to adopt a child, you will need to check your state's laws to learn what specific rules apply to you. In many states, it is legal for unmarried couples to adopt jointly. You can also adopt if you're single, if you are found to be a "fit parent." But be aware that adoption agencies, though bound by state antidiscrimination laws, may be biased against your unmarried status or, if you are a lesbian, your sexual orientation, and investigators may make it more difficult for you to adopt. Expect a visit and interview from an agent of a local service agency that will report its findings to the court, which must approve your adoption. Because you are more likely to be discriminated against if you are unmarried, you should consult with a good family law attorney. Chapter 11, "Infertility," contains more information about adoption.

TAXES AND BENEFITS

Tax and Social Security laws have special provisions applying to married couples. But if you are part of an unmarried couple, then you'll generally both be treated as if you are single people.

UNMARRIED COUPLES

According to 2000 Census Bureau statistics, cohabitation is more popular than ever. More than 5.4 million unmarried opposite-sex couples (that is 10.8 million people) live together, a 72 percent increase from the 3.1 million cohabitating heterosexual couples in 1990.

The Census Bureau counts only unmarried heterosexual couples and refers to each person as a "POSSLQ" (person of the opposite sex sharing living quarters). Same-sex spouse responses were flagged as invalid on the 2000 census, because the 1996 federal Defense of Marriage Act instructs all federal agencies only to recognize opposite-sex marriages for the purposes of enacting any agency programs.

Taxes

Federal income tax provisions give special treatment to married persons, treating them differently from single people and unmarried couples. Many state income tax provisions are similar to the federal tax laws. In general, the most favorable tax treatment goes to married couples, especially those with children, if the household is of the "traditional" one-breadwinner-plus-one-unemployed-homemaker variety. The tax benefits of marriage decrease as the incomes of a couple become more equal. In the past, a married couple in which each spouse earned about the same amount of income could actually pay more than if they were single. Recent tax changes have tried to improve the situation by removing the "marriage penalty" for such couples.

Unmarried couples are treated like single taxpayers. They are not able to use the special tax rates for married people that permit a kind of income averaging. So, those couples who are most penalized for not being married are those with the traditional lifestyle in which one works and the other has no substantial income. If the stay-at-home partner has no income, it may be possible for the wage earner to claim a partner as a dependent for tax purposes. But if one has a high income and the other a small income, even this tax benefit is not available.

Social Security

Generally speaking, unmarried couples are at a disadvantage compared to married couples when it comes to claiming public benefits. Unlike married spouses who may qualify for either dependent or survivor benefits based on their spouse's earnings, unmarried cohabiting partners are not eligible for these benefits. An unmarried partner is not a "dependent" for the purposes of Social Security. This can be particularly discriminatory to women whose cohabiting partners work outside the home while they stay at home and care for kids or run the household.

ASK A LAWYER

Q. Is it true that you can lose some government benefits if you marry? We're both senior citizens and would like to get married, but don't want to risk losing what we have.

A. That depends on the type of benefit. If one of you, for example, is receiving pension or other retirement benefits as a result of the death of a former spouse, the particular pension or benefit plan may have a provision that your right to receive these benefits would terminate upon remarriage. You would need to check with the individual plan. If you are drawing Social Security benefits based on a prior marriage, those benefits too could terminate in the event of a remarriage. You should check with the individual institution or governmental agency to determine whether marriage would result in a cessation of benefits.

—Answer by Sharon L. Corbitt
Sneed Lang, P.C., Tulsa, Oklahoma

PROPERTY LAW ISSUES

Property law issues for unmarried couples include
- sharing incomes or bank accounts,
- buying a home together or investing in property together,
- debts, and
- inheritance.

When a couple marries, the law automatically provides some protections in the previously listed areas. If a woman's spouse dies, then legislation ensures that she automatically inherits a portion of the deceased's estate. If a married couple divorces, there are legal protections that ensure that the property is fairly divided. If you're not married and do not register—or qualify— for a domestic partnership, the law does not step uninvited into any of these areas, and you may want to make private agreements that both safeguard your rights and limit your obligations. You can make arrangements with your partner about all of these issues by making a **living-together contract** or **cohabitation agreement**. This type of contract can cover a wide range of topics, from who will pay for what and who will own what, to who will inherit what property. While it may seem unromantic to make contracts that regulate these aspects of your life with your partner, they can provide you with important safeguards. They might ensure that you will not be saddled with your partner's debts and that you are entitled to an equal share in the home you bought together.

Experts say that several specific agreements are better than one big and potentially complicated document. Thus, you could have one agreement for sharing living expenses, another for property that you own jointly, and another for keeping specific property separate. The most important thing to remember about these agreements: don't mention sex. Living-together contracts that even hint at sexual services in exchange for support will not be enforced in any court for fear of legitimizing "meretricious consideration" (i.e., legalizing prostitution). Some lawyers even go so far as to discourage use of the term "lover" in your agreement. Living-together contracts may also contain mutual powers of attorney or **mutual guardianships** that enable partners to act on each other's behalf, but again, keep them simple, separate, and targeted to specific powers (i.e., health directives in one and business or financial authority in another). Specific grants of power (pay the utility bills) are better than unlimited powers (manage my finances)—they are easier to change, easier to enforce, and less likely to be ambiguous.

Sharing Income or Bank Accounts

It may seem like a gesture of trust and commitment to agree to share a bank account, but unless you and your partner have a cohabitation agreement outlining your financial responsibilities and expectations in your relationship, it is risky to commingle your assets. Sharing a bank account could put your money and assets at risk should your relationship end. If you live in one of the few states that recognizes common-law marriages (see chapter 6, "Marriage"), a court could find evidence of a common-law marriage, which would require a formal divorce to dissolve the relationship. Or a court might find an implied contract to support your partner for life (which is what palimony suits are all about—see the "Palimony" sidebar below) or find that you intended to hold all of your property jointly with your partner.

If you do not have a cohabitation agreement, you should also avoid

• contributing money to the purchase of a major asset such as a house or car,

• holding a title in both of your names,

• referring to your partner as your "husband" or otherwise holding yourself out as married,

• adopting the same last name as your partner,

• relying on a partner's promise to take care of you (financially) for the rest of your life, or

• leaving your partner in doubt about your intentions and expectations.

Debts

You are not liable for the debts of your partner unless you specifically agree to pay them. For example, if you cosign a note for your partner or a debt is charged to a joint account that you have with your partner, then you are liable. You may also be liable for

---

► **MAKE YOUR INTENTIONS CLEAR**

There are tax and other implications for transfers of money between partners. If you give your partner money as a gift, make it clear that that is your intent and write "gift" on the check. Likewise, if it is a loan, record it as a loan.

▤ PALIMONY

Palimony is a term coined by journalists—not judges—to describe alimony-like support given by one half of an unmarried couple to the other after they end their relationship. Palimony is neither a legal term nor a legal entitlement, and the term is often misused, because in most cases the plaintiff is seeking a division of the unmarried couple's property—not periodic support payments, which is the more narrow and technically accurate analogy to alimony. Nevertheless, the term "palimony" is often used to refer to both the division of property and support payments after an unmarried couple ends their relationship.

your partner's debts if you and your partner register under a domestic partner law that says that you agree to pay for each other's basic living expenses such as food, shelter, and clothing.

Credit

Your unmarried status should not affect your ability to get credit. In fact, under the Equal Credit Opportunity Act, it is against the law for creditors to discriminate on the basis of marital status. Chapter 17, "Women and Credit," contains more information.

ESTATE PLANNING

In our original scenario, Ben died **intestate** (i.e., without making a will). Unfortunately for Anne, the law does not automatically recognize unmarried partners as legal heirs. There are exceptions in some states where the unmarried partners are registered as domestic partners.

If you are one half of an unmarried couple, it is immensely important for you to make a will or living trust (both are a good idea) and ensure that your partner does too. State intestacy laws presume that your blood relatives will inherit your property after you die, so it's particularly important to draw up a will if you want any of your property to go to your partner.

An additional protection for unmarried partners is a **contract to make a will**. Such a contract prevents your partner from changing arrangements in his or her will without your knowledge and consent. A contract to make a will can supersede any updated will. These contracts can only be changed if both parties agree and are obviously not as flexible as wills. They are usually only prepared in anticipation that some kind of conflict will occur. Such contracts usually contain provisions that dis-

---

ASK A LAWYER

Q. If one of us dies, how much will the other inherit?

A. That depends. If you and your partner hold property together in joint tenancy with a right of survivorship, you would automatically take title to the whole property in the event of his or her death (regardless of what the will says). If there is a valid will, you would take property pursuant to the will. If there is no valid will, then property will be distributed according to state intestacy laws, and you may inherit nothing. Other assets such as automobiles may have documents of title that control who owns them. Title can be held singly or in both names. Finally, with respect to life insurance, whether you inherit will depend on whether you are one of the beneficiaries of the policy. With respect to pensions, 401(k)s, or items of this nature, you could inherit to the extent you were named as beneficiary. Caveat: If your partner is still legally married to someone else, that spouse may have federal rights to a portion of the pension, which will preempt your rights.

—Answer by Sharon L. Corbitt
Sneed Lang, P.C., Tulsa, Oklahoma

solve them when the partners agree in writing that the relationship is over.

Another common alternative to a will is a **trust**. A trust is a very flexible instrument that allows you to do what a will does—leave your property to whomever you choose. The advantage is that property in trust does not have to go through probate. You and your partner might each set up a separate living trust for your individual property and possibly a third one for your shared property. The individual trusts can be used to make gifts to your or your partner's friends or relatives. The shared trust can leave property to your mutual friends as well as to the surviving partner. Chapter 19, "Issues for Senior Women," contains more detailed information on how to set up a trust.

THE WORLD AT YOUR FINGERTIPS

- The Alternatives to Marriage Project is a national organization that offers support to people who choose to be unmarried or are unable to get married at www.unmarried.org.

- The American Association of Single People provides education and advocacy to unmarried adults, and advocates for fairness for unmarried employees, consumers, and taxpayers and more recognition of unmarried voters at www.singlesrights.com.

- *Prenups for Lovers* (2001), by Arlene G. Dubin, discusses the need for cohabitation agreements.

- A search for "cohabitation agreements" on the Internet will find many sources of information. A particularly useful site is the Equality in Marriage Institute's website at www.equalityinmarriage.org.

- Many gay rights groups offer publications and other information about the legal rights and needs of people who are in unmarried, committed relationships. A good place to start is the Lambda Legal Foundation website at www.lambdalegal.org. This information is useful for all unmarried couples, not just same-sex couples.

REMEMBER THIS

- A power of attorney and a power of attorney for health care are two documents that can give your partner rights and authority to make decisions in the event of your illness or incapacity.
- You may be able to qualify for health care benefits or other benefits if your employer offers domestic partnership benefits and your relationship meets your employer's qualifications.
- If you are one half of an unmarried couple, make sure you draft a will and ask your partner to draft one as well. If you die without a will, your partner will probably receive nothing.
- If you are part of an unmarried heterosexual couple and have a child, make sure you add the father's name to the birth certificate if you want to have him in your child's life. This simple step can give you and your child valuable rights.

CHAPTER 8

Divorce and Separation: Breaking Up Property, Debt, and Alimony

After several years of marriage, Billy and Emily have decided to separate, and they plan to divorce in the future. They have two children, as well as a house, a car, and a lot of history.

Billy's wages paid off most of the mortgage on the house, and he thinks he is entitled to keep it. He also wants custody of the children. Emily supported Billy while he was in graduate school and then gave up her career as a nurse to raise the kids. She wants custody and would like to continue to live in the house while the children are in school to provide them with a stable environment. Emily also thinks she is entitled to spousal support, so that she and the children can continue to have the standard of living they enjoyed during her marriage.

S ometimes marriages do not succeed. Despite the efforts of the couple, and perhaps the help of counselors and clergy, there is nothing to do but end the relationship. This often means that a couple has to divide assets and make custody arrangements. Sometimes a couple can work this out between themselves; sometimes, where there are competing interests and people just can't resolve them, the law steps in. If you are facing separation or divorce, you might need to face custody issues, receive or pay alimony, and divide property and debts. Just as the state was involved in creating your marriage, so it becomes involved in dissolving it.

A BRIEF HISTORY OF DIVORCE

Before the twentieth century, divorce was rarely a realistic option for women. Prevalent sexual double standards, inferior custody and support laws, and women's lack of control over marital finances made men the chief beneficiaries of divorce. Women infrequently filed for divorce. When a divorce was granted at a woman's request, it was in cases of adultery, long absence, and cruelty. The husband automatically got custody of the children, unless they were very young.

Changes in divorce laws have benefited women for the most part, and the number of women seeking divorce over the course of the last century has expanded. In fact, today more women file for divorce than men. However, generally men are in a more secure financial position after divorce than women.

For many women, divorce brings freedom and independence; for others, it means new obligations, difficulties, and dependencies. This chapter looks at the differences between separation, divorce, and annulment and the basics of property division and alimony. Child custody and visitation are discussed in chapter 9.

ANNULMENT, SEPARATION, AND DIVORCE

An **annulment** is a court ruling that your marriage was never valid or is **void ab initio** ("void from the start"). The most common grounds for an annulment are fraud and misrepresentation. For example, your spouse may not have told you that he had previously been married and divorced, that he has a criminal record or an infectious disease, or an inability to engage in sex or have children. You may also get an annulment on grounds of bigamy or inability to contract (because a person was underage or mentally incapacitated). Pop starlet Britney Spears ended her famously brief marriage in an annulment. The grounds given to the court were that, on learning of each other's desires (with respect to children, state of residency, and likes and dislikes), Spears and her husband found that they were "so incompatible that there was a want of understanding of each other's actions in entering into the marriage."

A **separation** simply means that you and your spouse are living apart. Of course, you may live separately without a formal separation agreement (this is called **separate maintenance** in some states). However, one or both of you may seek a **legal separation**. This has the added element that your arrangement is court ordered, or you and your spouse consented to it in a written agreement. Whether your separation is legal or not, your marriage is not ended. Separation recognizes the possibility of a reconciliation, and you are not free to remarry while you are legally separated. You and your spouse may modify your separation agreement at any time.

Separation agreements or court orders spell out what support, if any, you or your spouse must pay each other. If you have minor children, the agreement or court order will also cover custody and visitation arrangements. Be careful about agreeing to terms in a separation agreement that you would not agree to in a more long-term agreement. Do not be more generous or more conciliatory in a separation agreement than you would be in a divorce. If you agree to the terms of a separation agreement but you and your spouse cannot agree to the terms of a divorce, a court may order continuation of the terms of the separation agreement in the final judgment of divorce if the court thinks the terms have worked out reasonably well.

Some states require a period of legal separation before a divorce will be granted, but in most states you can proceed straight to a divorce without first seeking a legal separation. Keep in mind that while waiting for a divorce, you and your spouse may live separately, without a formal separation agreement, or you may continue to live together.

Legal separation before divorce can offer you some advantages. For example, legal separation can offer structure for you and your spouse while you are waiting for a divorce (or while you are considering a divorce). If one of you wishes to seek a religious divorce or annulment, a legal separation may provide a useful transition while waiting for action by the religious tribunal. In addition, most medical plans permit a legally separated spouse to continue to be covered in a family plan without additional cost. And though legally separated, you and your spouse may elect to file joint or separate tax returns.

A **divorce** or **dissolution of marriage** is a decree by a court that your valid marriage no longer exists. It leaves you and your former spouse free to remarry. The court will award custody and divide property and, if necessary, may order spousal and child support. A **fault divorce** is one in which one party blames the other for the failure of the marriage by citing specific wrongdo-

◖◗ ASK A LAWYER

Q. *My husband and I are heading for divorce, but I'm worried that I won't be able to support myself and the kids when he moves out. How can I get support as soon as we are separated? What if he won't agree— can a court order separation?*

A. In most states, you can file a request for temporary orders at the same time the divorce is filed. A hearing will be held a few weeks later. At the hearing, a judge will decide if there is a need for temporary support to be ordered and will set the amount (unless the parties reach an agreement on this). In addition, the temporary orders will set up a temporary visitation schedule for the noncustodial parent. The judge can also order one of the spouses to move out of the marital home until a final decision is made at the final divorce hearing (or by agreement) as to who will be awarded the marital home, or whether it should be sold. The temporary orders may also include provisions prohibiting both parties from wasting marital assets, hiding marital assets, or making other major changes in the marital assets while the divorce is pending. You should talk to a lawyer about the exact procedures to follow in your state to obtain temporary orders and what the additional cost will be to do this.

—Answer by Irene Jackson
Attorney, Mediator, and Arbitrator, Irving, Texas

ing. Fault divorces are most common where abuse is a factor; however, other bases may include abandonment, adultery, desertion, habitual drunkenness, inability to engage in sex, insanity, imprisonment, physical or mental cruelty, and use of addictive drugs. In many states, the waiting period is shorter for a fault divorce. The use of fault grounds may affect other aspects of your divorce, depending on the state in which you live. In a few states, fault may be taken into consideration when the court makes decisions on property division and spousal support—even if the divorce is granted on no-fault grounds. In some states, fault will be considered if it directly causes waste or dissipation of marital assets (e.g., if your cheating spouse spends significant marital assets on his lover). In some states, if you are the spouse who commits adultery, then you may not be able to receive spousal support. In many states, however, fault is not a factor in dividing your property or deciding spousal support. In custody cases, fault is also not supposed to be considered unless that fault had a harmful impact on your child. For example, if you or your spouse had a discreet extramarital affair, this would not normally be a major factor in deciding custody. But if either of you had an affair or a series of affairs that placed your child in stressful situations, this could be a factor in deciding custody.

A **no-fault divorce** is one in which neither you nor your spouse is considered responsible for the breakup of your marriage, and neither of you has to prove that the other did something wrong. Grounds may include irretrievable breakdown, irreconcilable differences, or incompatibility, but you generally do not have to provide proof of these grounds. No-fault divorce is the most common form of divorce. According to the U.S. Census Bureau, in 2000 no-fault divorces accounted for 80 percent of all divorces.

An **uncontested divorce** is one in which the spouse who is sued for divorce does not fight it and instead reaches an agreement with the other spouse about the terms of the divorce during the proceedings. In other words, you both agree about the divorce and its terms. Uncontested divorces are generally more amicable and economical than other types of divorce. Most states do permit do-it-yourself uncontested divorces—sometimes referred to as **summary divorces**. The ease or difficulty of obtaining a do-it-yourself divorce depends on local laws and rules as well as the complexities of the issues in your divorce.

If you or your spouse has a lot of property, if you pay a lot of taxes, or if there are any contested custody or visitation issues, it is advisable for both of you to have separate lawyers, no matter what kind of divorce you're seeking. You might also consider hiring a certified divorce or financial planner to help protect your financial future—especially if you or your spouse earn 75 percent or more of the family's income, one or both of you owns all or part of a business, or you have been married for fifteen or more years.

Although divorces may be emotionally contentious, 95 percent of divorces do not end up in a contested trial. Usually, the parties negotiate and settle property division, spousal support, and child custody between themselves, often with the help of their lawyers. You can even get a divorce if you do not know where your spouse is, but you will need to contact an attorney who can help you follow the correct procedures for this.

Sometimes you can reach an agreement by mediation, with a trained mediator who can help you and your spouse identify and accommodate common interests. You then present your negotiated or mediated agreement to a judge. Approval is virtually automatic if the agreement is fair. If you agree on some issues but are unable to agree about property, support, or child custody, you may ask the court to decide your unresolved issues.

How long does a divorce take? The answer is that it depends entirely on which state you live in. In Oklahoma, a divorce can be final in just ten days if there are no children. Some states, like California, require a minimum of six months before you can legally be an unmarried person. Others, like North Carolina, require a year's separation before a divorce can be granted. If your divorce is contested and you and your husband cannot agree to the terms, it can take years to litigate some issues.

( ) ASK A LAWYER

Q. My husband insists that he and I can divide our property without either of us having a lawyer, but I'm not sure. How can I find out if hiring a lawyer would be worth it to me?

A. At the very least, you should buy an hour of time from a matrimonial specialist (if you can afford one) or from a competent attorney who practices in the area of family law. Even if your case is fairly simple and straightforward, you will feel better having someone who does a lot of divorces give you his or her opinion. After all, this is your only divorce, but a competent matrimonial lawyer has advised in many divorces and can help you make a determination as to what is fair in your particular circumstances.

—Answer by Sharon L. Corbitt
Sneed Lang, P.C., Tulsa, Oklahoma

Q. I was in a committed relationship with my (same-sex) partner for five years, and we drove up from Texas to get married in Canada last year. For various reasons, the marriage has ended, and we'd like to get a divorce . . . but can we get a divorce in Texas if it won't even recognize our marriage?

A. Since June 2003, when a Canadian court ruled that same-sex couples must be granted marriage equality, many same-sex couples from the United States have gone to Canada to get legally married. Many more couples will marry in those states in the United States that recognize same-sex marriages. But couples who leave the country or their state to get married in a jurisdiction that recognizes same-sex marriages may not realize that they may not be able to get divorced in their home state, if it doesn't recognize same-sex marriage. While there is no residency requirement to marry in Canada, for example, one spouse must live in Canada for at least one year before the couple may be granted a divorce.

At least one court in Iowa has granted a divorce to a lesbian couple that was joined in a civil union in Vermont, but it remains to be seen how same-sex marriages and civil unions will be treated by other jurisdictions.

—Answer by Nicole G. Berner
Jenner and Block LLP, Washington, D.C.

Q. *When things were better, my husband gave me a beautiful pair of ruby and diamond earrings. Now he says they should count as marital property when we divide things up, but I say they were a gift to me and are mine. Who's right?*

A. In most states, a gift given by one spouse to the other becomes the separate property of the recipient spouse.

—Answer by Sharon L. Corbitt
Sneed Lang, P.C., Tulsa, Oklahoma

DIVISION OF PROPERTY

Many women face a significant drop in their standard of living after divorce. Precise figures are debated, but there is general agreement that women and their custodial children are worse off after a divorce, while the standard of living for divorced custodial fathers either rises or declines far less severely. This is true even if the property is split fairly (see the discussion of equitable distribution laws later in this chapter), because courts rarely order alimony or spousal support for a woman at home, either full or part time—divorce can mean giving up her entire way of life. If you have not worked outside the home for some time, you are at an even greater disadvantage, particularly if you lack education or training.

Generally, a couple is free to divide their property as they see fit. They may enter into what is referred to as a **marital-settlement agreement**, also called a **property-settlement agreement** in some states, which is a contract between them that divides their property and debts and resolves other issues of their divorce. When you and your spouse agree on a settlement agreement, you can take it to court, where a judge will usually approve it after a short hearing. In some states that offer simplified divorce procedures, you may not even have to attend a hearing if every detail of your divorce is agreed to ahead of time.

The decision of whether to go to trial and have a judge decide your contested issues often involves some cost-benefit analysis on your part. Will you gain more and spend less with a trial, or vice versa? You must look at the facts objectively and consider the time and expenses involved. Lawyers, financial analysts, and expert witnesses are expensive.

Division of marital property, like ownership of property during marriage (discussed in chapter 6), varies with state law. As a starting point, most states allow parties to keep their **nonmarital** or **separate property**. This includes property that you brought into the marriage and kept in your own name, inheritances received and kept separate during the marriage, and gifts received by just one of you during the marriage. The right of a spouse to keep his or her separate property may depend on the degree to which the property was, in fact, kept separate. For example, if, in the hypothetical that opened this chapter, Emily brought a $20,000 inheritance to the marriage, and held it in the same account that her pay was deposited into, a court might hold that the $20,000 had become marital property because it had been mixed up with marital property (her paychecks). If you are bringing anything of value into a marriage that you would like to keep as separate property, you should keep it in your own name in a separate account to ensure that it does not become marital property.

Once separate property is allocated, a court will consider marital or community property. State laws vary in their approaches to distributing marital or community property. A few community property states divide all marital property fifty-fifty, because they view marriage as a joint undertaking in which both spouses are presumed to contribute equally, though often in different ways, to the acquisition and preservation of property. Feminists suggest that this model is the best way to have the contributions of wives toward the accumulation of marital property recognized and put on equal footing with those of their breadwinning husbands. Other community property states may look at the facts of each case and try to be equitable.

Equitable distribution means a court divides marital property as it thinks is valid, just, and equitable—it does not necessarily mean a fifty-fifty split. States applying equitable distribution principles view marriage as a shared enterprise in which both spouses usually contribute significantly to the acquisition and preservation of property. The property could be divided fifty-fifty, sixty-forty, seventy-thirty, or even all for one spouse and nothing for the other (although this would be very unusual). The percentage distributed need not be the same for all property, thus the percentage of entitlement may vary from one asset to another. For example, you may get 100 percent of the value of a particular painting, but only 10 percent of a money market account.

In equitable distribution states, courts consider a variety of factors and need not give even weight to each factor. Judges have considerable discretion to consider the particular facts and financial circumstances of each case, and this makes the resolution of property issues less certain when you let a court divide your property. For example, courts may take into account the length of your marriage, your and your spouse's age and health, your occupations, and possibly your conduct. In addition, services as a homemaker are recognized by courts as work and as a contribution to the other spouse's ability to earn more money, and thus they may factor in favor of the homemaker. Some courts might also take into account the fact that you may have impaired your earning capacity by being the stay-at-home spouse.

Generally, courts award more property and fewer debts to the spouse who has less earning ability, poor health, or custody of minor children. If the parties have more debt than assets, which is a common situation, then the court will divide whatever property they have, and then allocate the responsibility of each party to pay off particular debts.

DIVISION OF DEBT

The divorce settlement may allocate the outstanding debt on the joint Visa card to your former husband. But be warned—just because the divorce decree orders him to pay off a card does not mean that you are released from responsibility for the debt. If your husband fails to pay the debt, creditors can still seek payment from you and start collection proceedings against you. See chapter 17, "Women and Credit," for more information.

The family home and the retirement accounts are often the most valuable assets acquired by a couple during marriage. Assuming that both are marital or community property and subject to distribution upon divorce, the decision of who gets the house and the pension depends on the facts of each case. If minor children are involved, then whichever one of you spends the most time with the kids or provides their primary care will get to remain in the house while the divorce is pending. If you can afford to keep the house after the divorce, then the law usually favors giving the house to the person who will have custody of the children most of the time. If you cannot afford to keep the house, then it may be sold and the proceeds divided. In some cases, if you have primary custody of the children, you will have a right to live in the house for a certain number of years. At the end of that time, you can buy out your spouse's interest or sell the house and divide the proceeds. If the house is to be sold and divided later, specific provisions need to be included in your final settlement agreement regarding who is responsible for regular maintenance costs as well as major repairs.

Retirement accounts, even though they are earned solely by the labor of one spouse, are still marital or community property if they were earned during the marriage and thus are also subject to distribution upon divorce. Many courts prefer to give the full rights to a pension to the party who earned it, as long as the other party will have a sufficient amount of income and property from other sources after retirement. When a pension is divided, a court can award specific percentages to each spouse or it can award a specific dollar figure for one spouse to receive.

Wives were often discriminated against when it came to property division and pensions before a federal law providing for **Qualified Domestic Relations Orders** was enacted. These orders, when properly entered by a court, require a pension plan administrator to send pension checks not only to the worker, but also to the worker's former spouse. The court cannot order a pension check to be written before the worker is entitled to the pension, nor can the court change the total amount of the pension that is due. But a court can direct that when a worker is eligible for a pension, checks must be sent to the worker's former spouse for the ordered amount.

ALIMONY, MAINTENANCE, AND SPOUSAL SUPPORT

States vary in their approaches to alimony (also called spousal support or maintenance). You should check your state's laws to understand your entitlements and obligations when it comes to postdivorce support payments.

When a divorce is granted, the court may order one person to pay a suitable allowance to the other person for support during the life of that other person or for a shorter period as the court finds just considering the circumstances of each person. The court may from time to time modify support-payment orders if either person's circumstances change. There are essentially three types of alimony:

- Permanent alimony
- Restitutional alimony
- Rehabilitative alimony

Permanent alimony or **permanent maintenance** is awarded when one spouse cannot become economically independent or

▶ **PRACTICAL TIPS IF YOU ARE CONSIDERING SEPARATION OR DIVORCE**

If you are considering moving out during your separation, keep in mind that what you do during this transition period may set a precedent for what is later awarded in the divorce. You should think about taking the following precautions:

- Put a freeze on all joint credit accounts. Don't put yourself in a position of financial responsibility for postseparation spending sprees (see chapter 17, "Women and Credit," for more detail).

- If you rent a home, take your name off the lease. Take your name off the utilities, too. This way, if your spouse fails to pay, you will not be responsible.

- Forward your mail to a post office box or to a close friend or relative.

- Make a note of all important addresses, telephone numbers, account numbers, and any other financial information you will need after the separation.

- List and photograph the contents of any safety deposit boxes and apartments or homes that you leave and remove all personal items.

Finally, if you are considering moving out of the county or state, talk to a lawyer first. Every state has a requirement that you reside in a county and state for a period of time before you can file for a divorce there. If you move, then you may delay your ability to file for a divorce.

maintain a lifestyle that the court considers appropriate given the financial resources of the parties. A common reason for ordering permanent alimony is that the recipient, because of advanced age or chronic illness, will never be able to maintain a reasonable standard of living without such support. Some courts will order permanent support to be paid to a working spouse if the working spouse will never have earning power at a level near the earning power of the more prosperous spouse. When deciding permanent support amounts, the courts often use the same criteria they do for dividing property.

If you want to request permanent alimony, you must establish both that you have a need and that your spouse has sufficient means and abilities to provide for part or all of that need. Although this type of alimony is called "permanent," the amount and duration of the support can lessen or increase or even end if the ability of the payer or the needs of the recipient change significantly. Support generally ends if the recipient remarries, and in some cases it may end if the recipient lives with someone else.

Restitutional or **reimbursement alimony** and **rehabilitative alimony** are, by contrast, only for specified periods of time. **Restitutional alimony** is sometimes awarded to pay back a debt. **Rehabilitative alimony** (called **transitional alimony** in some states) is awarded to provide education or job training to a spouse who was financially dependent or disadvantaged during the marriage so he or she can become self-supporting. Rehabilitative alimony is often awarded to help make up for opportuni-

---

 ### KEEP GOOD RECORDS!

It is not uncommon after a divorce for you to dispute, or the Internal Revenue Service to challenge, the amounts of support that were actually paid or received. Without adequate documentation, you may be required to pay back support if your former spouse makes a claim against you.

It is a good idea to guard against this by keeping careful, accurate records of the payments you give or receive. You can simply start a notebook to keep track of payments, noting the date the payments were made or received, the amounts, the check numbers, and the account names and numbers. For extra protection, you should keep photocopies or carbon copies of the checks and copies of any signed receipts you give (or receive) for cash payments.

---

ties lost by a spouse who left a job or career path to support the other spouse's career or to care for the family. It may also be awarded to a spouse who worked outside the home during the marriage, but sacrificed her career because of family priorities. In setting the amount and duration of rehabilitative alimony, a court will consider the following factors:

• any educational or employment opportunities the person sacrificed during the marriage,
• the length of the person's absence from the job market,
• the person's health, and
• the skills and time necessary for the person to become self-supporting.

An alternative to monthly alimony payments is **lump-sum alimony** or **alimony in gross**. This is a fixed payment that is paid in a lump sum regardless of circumstances and terminates all other spousal support entitlements. For example, lump-sum alimony would be paid even if the recipient remarried or died. Lump-sum alimony can also be awarded instead of a property settlement or as a type of restitutional alimony to ensure that one spouse is paid back for certain expenditures. To date, about fifteen states have laws that expressly allow for lump-sum support payments.

Gender is no longer a factor that courts consider when ordering alimony of any type. In the 1979 case of *Orr v. Orr*, the U.S. Supreme Court struck down as unconstitutional an Alabama statute that could require husbands—but not wives—to pay alimony upon divorce. Justice William Brennan, writing for a six-member majority, said "the old notion that generally it is the man's primary responsibility to provide a home and its essentials, can no longer justify a statute that discriminates on the basis of gender." Before the decision, many state support laws were not gender neutral, and husbands were charged with the primary obligation to support their wives. Alimony was viewed as a penalty imposed on a guilty husband for violating his marriage vows and obligations. The obligation to pay alimony was in direct proportion to the husband's station and position in life. A wife's misconduct (e.g., adultery) was not only grounds for divorce, it also provided a defense to an award of alimony.

After the decision in *Orr v. Orr*, states had to change their alimony laws to be gender neutral. This change, together with equitable property distribution schemes and the influx of women into the labor force, has contributed to a decline in alimony awards. The fault of either party is a factor the courts may consider in awarding support of any kind. Additional factors courts look to in awarding all types of alimony and support include:

- The length of the marriage
- The parties' financial conditions after property division
- The parties' respective ages, health, and physical conditions
- The parties' stations in life or social standing
- The number of minor children at home
- Any premarital agreements

(i) FINANCIAL ASPECTS OF ALIMONY

For tax purposes, alimony is usually treated as income to the recipient and a deduction from income to the person paying alimony. This can result in a major tax benefit to the spouse with the most income, who is presumably paying the alimony. At the same time, it adds to the taxes of the recipient, but usually she pays taxes at a lower rate. Because you have to pay taxes on alimony, it is usually better to get a larger property settlement than to seek a large alimony award.

If you are awarded alimony, then your former husband will have to pay it through thick and thin. In the past, many women found themselves out of luck collecting property settlements and support payments if their former husbands declared bankruptcy. A federal law passed in 1974 states that a bankruptcy court cannot discharge past-due payments for alimony, maintenance, or child support. This means that even if your former husband declares bankruptcy, he will still have to pay you alimony he already owes you and has a legal duty to continue paying alimony.

THE WORLD AT YOUR FINGERTIPS

• The website of the American Academy of Matrimonial Attorneys offers a variety of materials on divorce law and policy at www.aaml.org.

• Some commercial websites have lots of basic information and checklists about divorce law and references to other sources: check out www.divorcelawinfo.com, www.womansdivorce.com, and www.divorcemagazine.com.

REMEMBER THIS

• A divorce is a decree by a court that a valid marriage no longer exists. If you get divorced, you may have to make arrangements about custody and visitation of children and division of property and debts.

• If you are contemplating marrying your same-sex partner, be aware that you may not have the same access to the divorce court as heterosexual couples do in your home state.

• Most divorcing couples are able to settle property division without going to court. However, even if a divorce is uncontested, you may still want to consult a lawyer to safeguard your rights.

CHAPTER 9

Child Custody and Visitation: How the Law Divides Families When a Relationship Ends

When Sarah and Hank split up, she took the car, he took the motorboat, and she stayed in their house. But the two of them have had much more difficulty trying to agree on custody arrangements for their four-year-old daughter. Hank wants joint legal and physical custody; Sarah wants sole custody, but is happy to grant visitation rights. Both Hank and Sarah are sure they know what's best for their little girl. Sarah also wants to leave her hometown, Boston, and move to California, where she has a job offer and can make a new start. Hank is horrified at the possibility—he'd only be able to see his daughter once every few months.

Whether you were married or not, if you are ending your relationship with the other parent of your child, you'll probably find custody arrangements difficult to agree on. Nonetheless, more than 95 percent of people splitting up somehow work it out, and fewer than 5 percent of contested custody cases ever go to trial and require a judge to decide custody. This chapter will first discuss ways to settle custody disputes, such as parenting agreements and mediation. It will then briefly outline the factors that a judge will consider in the unlikely event that a custody case goes to court.

A BRIEF HISTORY OF CHILD CUSTODY LAWS

The law of child custody has swung like a pendulum. Two hundred years ago, fathers were almost always awarded custody in divorce because children were viewed as the property of their father, who had a legal obligation to protect, support, and educate them. This presumption favoring fathers lasted until the late 1800s, when society's increased focus on children's welfare began to weaken it. Mothers became favored for custody under the "tender years" doctrine, according to which mothers were awarded temporary custody arrangements of infants during their "tender years," until they were old enough to be returned to their fathers. By the 1920s, mothers were more likely to be awarded custody in England and the United States, regardless of the child's age. And at one point in time, a preference for awarding custody to mothers was part of the law in all states and frequently reflected in judicial opinions. One often-quoted decision made in 1924 offered this justification: "[I]t is well known by all men that no other love is quite so tender, no other solicitude quite so deep, no other devotion quite so enduring as that of a mother."

The presumption in favor of maternal custody remained firm for many decades and was challenged only after the divorce rate began to rise dramatically in the 1960s. As Dr. Joan Kelly explains, "[s]purred on by fathers' claims of sex discrimination in custody decisions, constitutional concerns for equal protection, the feminist movement, and the entry of large numbers of women into the workforce, most states had substituted the standard of the 'best interests of the child' for the tender years presumption by the mid 1970s. For the first time in history, custody decision-making was to be rooted in a consideration of the child's needs and interests, rather than based simply on the gender of the parent."

This swing in focus to the child's best interest led in part to the next trend: joint custody after divorce. Joint custody was intended to preserve the parental role and status of both parents by continuing the involvement of both parents after divorce. California enacted the first joint custody statute in 1979, and was followed by Kansas and other states. Today, most states have shared-parenting statutes, although judges continue to award sole custody (custody to just one parent) when it is in the best interests of the child.

CHILD CUSTODY DEFINITIONS

Child custody is the right and duty to care for a minor child on a day-to-day basis and to make major decisions about the child. In **sole custody** arrangements, one parent takes care of the child most of the time and makes major decisions about the child. This parent is usually called the **custodial parent**, and the other parent is usually referred to as the **noncustodial parent**. Even when sole custody is awarded to one parent, the other parent almost always has a right of **visitation**, which is a right to be with the child, including for overnight visits and vacation periods.

Joint custody—sometimes referred to as **shared custody** or **shared parenting**—has two parts: joint legal custody and joint physical custody. **Joint legal custody** is when both parents share in making major decisions on issues such as school, health care, and religious training. Other issues on which the parents may make joint decisions include extracurricular activities, summer camp, dating, driving, and discipline. **Joint physical custody** refers to the time the child spends with each parent. The time is flexible, so it does not have to be fifty-fifty. However, parents who opt for equal time have come up with alternatives, such as alternate two-day periods, equal division of the week, alternate weeks, alternate months, alternate four-month periods, and alternate six-month periods. If the child is in school and spends substantial amounts of time with both parents, it is usually best for the child if the parents live relatively close to each other.

Joint custody may be joint legal custody or joint physical custody or both. It is common for couples who share physical custody also to share legal custody, but not necessarily the other way around. Usually, when parents share joint custody, they work out joint physical custody according to their schedules and housing arrangements. **Bird's-nest custody** is a type of joint custody where the child remains in the family home and the parents take turns moving in and out.

⟲ ASK A LAWYER

Q. How does the law handle custody disputes between lesbian couples?

A. An increasing number of lesbian couples are choosing to raise children jointly. Some couples adopt, others choose to have one or both of the partners become pregnant. In many states, the nonbiological or nonadoptive mother can legally adopt her partner's child. These adoptions—called second-parent adoptions—place both parties on an equal legal footing with respect to the child.

   If a same-sex couple separates after a second-parent adoption, it will face the same types of custody issues faced by an opposite-sex couple that separates after having children. The couple will have to reach agreement on custody, visitation, and child support issues, or go to a court to seek orders. If the nonbiological or nonadoptive mother never adopted the child, however, she may have no legal right to custody, or even visitation, in the event the couple separates. For this reason, it is very important for couples in jurisdictions where second-parent adoption is an available option to take advantage of it. Where second-parent adoption is not available, couples should be sure to document clearly their intention to parent their child together and their plans in the event of a breakup.

—Answer by Nicole G. Berner
Jenner and Block LLP, Washington, D.C.

Q. My husband and I have just separated. We're starting to talk about how to share custody of the children. He wants to keep things loose and have a pretty unspecific parenting agreement. I'm afraid that will lead to endless wrangles. I want us to be specific up front. Who's right? Is a compromise possible?

A. A very informal agreement works for many couples and certainly gives them flexibility. However, you are right that if persons do get into a dispute, a less specific agreement can be problematic. My preference is to define minimum periods of visitation for the noncustodial

parent, but then provide in writing that the parties may vary this
arrangement by mutual agreement.

—Answer by Sharon L. Corbitt
Sneed Lang, P.C., Tulsa, Oklahoma

There are several advantages to joint physical custody,
including the fact that it can protect and improve a child's relationship with both parents and can ensure that a child will not
"lose" a parent because of the divorce, and the fact that the
arrangement gives parents the right to spend equal time with the
child. Of course, there are also some disadvantages: Joint physical custody is generally more expensive than other options
because it requires both parents to keep a home for the child.
And it is not for every family—joint custody may be bad for children who are tense and become easily upset by changes in routine, and the potential for conflict means that this option should
only be considered when the parents have an amicable, respect-
ful relationship.

PARENTING AGREEMENTS

A **parenting agreement** is a detailed document that can cover
everything from your financial responsibility for your child's
health insurance, to which kind of summer camp your child will
attend. A well-thought-out parenting agreement can help you
minimize the trauma your child will face during a breakup. You
can avoid many power struggles and headaches in the future by
working out how the details of your child's life are to be handled,
and, if you are getting divorced, including a parenting plan with
your divorce papers. Reaching an agreement with your spouse
before the final divorce decree will also keep your custody decisions out of the court, saving time, money, and public airing of
your differences. Of course, you and your partner can try to

work out a parenting agreement even if you're not married. A parenting agreement allows both of you to feel secure about how your child will be raised.

Parenting agreements might include provisions on

• access to medical records, school records, teachers, and school activities,

• authority to make emergency medical decisions,

• a child's recreational activities,

• financial responsibility for a child's expenses and insurance,

• custody or visitation schedules, including details of where and when a child is to be picked up and dropped off,

• school vacation, holiday, and birthday celebration schedules, and

• long-distance travel for visits to one parent or for vacations.

Drafting a parenting agreement usually requires some negotiation between you and your child's other parent. You may negotiate directly, but more likely you will negotiate in the presence of both your lawyers. When you attend this negotiation session, you should bring all the documents that might be relevant, including

• any divorce-related court documents you have filed or received,

• any correspondence from attorneys, counselors, mediators, or court officials regarding your separation, divorce, paternity, child support, custody, or visitation,

• court orders regarding a legal separation, divorce, paternity declaration, or award of custody,

• any previous parenting agreements between you and the other parent, and

• reports or evaluations from school officials, counselors, therapists, or others who have an insight into your children.

When you and the other parent of your child have reached agreement on these issues, your lawyers can draft a parenting agreement containing the substance of what you decided. The agreement can then be registered in the family court or magistrate's court and enforced as if it was a court order.

MEDIATION

If you and the other parent of your child cannot agree on parenting arrangements, mediation may be a useful way to resolve your custody and visitation disputes. **Mediation** is a nonadversarial process in which the parties to a divorce (or some other dispute) meet with a neutral person (a **mediator**) to help them settle their dispute. Mediation takes place outside of a court. A mediator cannot force the parties to settle, but can assist them in reaching an agreement of their own. In a handful of states— Alaska, California, Delaware, Michigan, New Mexico, and South Dakota—a court may ask a mediator to recommend a solution if the parties cannot agree.

Mediation can be mandatory in some courts for contested custody and visitation disputes. Many courts require both parents to meet with a court-appointed mediator to try to resolve their dispute before they can have their case heard before a judge. Only if they cannot agree will the judge hear the case. Mediation is often cheaper and quicker than taking a case before a judge, and the fact that the process is nonadversarial may increase parental harmony in the long run. However, mediation is not a panacea for all of your custody and visitation disputes. Mediation may be difficult if one or both parents are withholding information, or if one parent is somewhat passive and is likely to be bulldozed by the other. Mediation does not redress power imbalances between parents in the way that the formal processes of a court can. Some women fare even worse in mediation than they would before a judge. Mediation may also be inappropriate if domestic violence (including physical, mental, or emotional abuse) is an issue in the case.

A court will often order mediation. However, even if mediation isn't ordered, you may still agree to mediate. Most mediators are either lawyers or mental health professionals, and although generally they are not licensed or regulated by the state, the American Bar Association has adopted standards and many states require or provide certification for court-mandated

( ) ASK A LAWYER

Q. What if one parent is religious and the other is not? Can the religious parent insist that the child be brought up in his or her faith?

A. Religion can be an important area of dispute between parents who are splitting up. If the children already have an established religious practice, a court probably will not order that it be changed to suit the desires of one parent. But be aware that some judges will favor the wishes of a parent to raise a child in an established religion over those of a parent with no established religious practice. There is no right to have your child raised in a particular religion, unless of course there was some prior agreement or understanding about this.

The question of a child's right to control his or her own religious practices when he or she becomes more mature is debatable, but a strong case can be made for letting an older child make this determination where the parents disagree.

There are special problems when the religion chosen by one parent condemns the other parent, for example, because of a homosexual lifestyle. Sometimes this can even be a basis for changing custody, since courts don't approve of anything that undermines the parent-child relationship.

—Answer by Marilyn Ireland
Professor, California Western School of Law,
San Diego, California

A. This really is a question that should be discussed with your lawyer, since case law varies greatly from state to state. As a general rule, the parent who is the primary physical custodian will have the right to determine the religious upbringing of the child. However, if the other parent is of another faith, it is likely that he or she will have time carved out during his or her religious holidays and may also be allowed to have the child participate in some of his or her religious activities.

—Answer by Sharon L. Corbitt
Sneed Lang, P.C., Tulsa, Oklahoma

mediators. It is not uncommon today for many lawyers specializing in family law to offer mediation services for child custody and other divorce-related disputes, though there are also many nonlawyer mediator groups.

COURTS AND CUSTODY DECISIONS

If you and the other parent of your child are part of the small minority of people who cannot agree on custody and visitation arrangements on your own, with the help of your attorneys, or through mediation, then a judge will have to decide these issues for you. Courts make decisions on custody according to the best interests of the child, and this standard takes priority over all other factors. A court may consider the following factors when deciding what the best interests of a child are in any given case:

• the child's age, gender, and mental and physical health,
• the mental and physical health of both parents,
• parenting skills and each parent's willingness to care for the child,
• emotional ties between child and parent,
• each parent's willingness to facilitate visitation by the other parent,
• each parent's moral fitness, including whether the child will be exposed to alcohol use or secondhand smoke,
• whether there has been any history of child or spousal abuse,
• each parent's ability to provide food, shelter, clothing, and medical care,
• the child's established living pattern, including school, home, community, and religious institutions, and
• the child's preference, if the child is above a certain age (which is usually twelve).

If none of these factors clearly favors one parent over the other, then most courts will look at which parent will more likely provide a stable environment for the child. For younger children, this may be the primary caregiver, because this will give the child consistency and less disruption in daily routines. For older children, this may mean awarding custody to the parent who is best able to foster continuity in schooling, community life, religious practices, and peer relationships. If either parent has a major problem with alcoholism or mental illness, or has abused the child or committed domestic violence, that alone could be the deciding factor.

Courts are generally not allowed to consider the race, gender, sexual orientation, or nonmarital sexual relationships of parents when making custody decisions. For example, in the Florida case of *Palmore v. Sidoti*, a white couple had divorced and the mother was awarded custody. The father petitioned the court for a change in custody after his former wife married an African-American man and moved the family to a predominantly African-American neighborhood. The state court granted the change, but the U.S. Supreme Court reversed in 1984, ruling that social stigma, especially a racial one, is an impermissible basis for a custody decision.

Courts in some states seem willing to assume that a parent's homosexual relationship will have a more harmful effect on a child than a heterosexual relationship. But in a few states— Alaska, California, New Mexico, Pennsylvania, and the District of Columbia—a parent's sexual orientation cannot be considered or cannot in and of itself prevent a parent from getting custody or visitation.

The laws of most states provide that mothers and fathers have an equal right to custody. No state requires that custody be awarded to the mother without regard to the fitness of both parents. Also, courts are not supposed to assume that a child is automatically better off with his or her mother or father. Of course, judges, like the rest of us, are products of their backgrounds and personal experiences. Some judges may have deep-seated beliefs that mothers can take care of children better than fathers and that fathers have less experience in day-to-day parenting.

THE UNIFORM CHILD CUSTODY
JURISDICTION AND ENFORCEMENT ACT

The Uniform Child Custody Jurisdiction and Enforcement Act
(UCCJEA) is legislation providing that only a child's home state
may make a child custody order. The **home state** is the state in
which a child lived with a parent for at least six months immediately before the child custody proceeding started. The state that
makes the original child custody order is given **continuing jurisdiction**, which means that it is the only state that can modify the
custody order. This provision ensures that a parent cannot just
relocate a child to another state in the hope of getting a more
favorable custody decision. Courts in other states have a duty to
enforce the original custody order and have some enforcement
powers. For example, if a court is concerned that a parent with
custody will flee or harm the child, it can issue a warrant to take
possession of the child.

The UCCJEA replaced and updated an earlier act, the Uniform Child Custody Jurisdiction Act, which was not always clear
as to which state had jurisdiction to modify a custody order and
did not provide for enforcement of custody orders. The newer
act has been enacted in thirty-four states and the District of
Columbia (and introduced in another eight states); in the
remaining states, the old act remains the law. Commentators
have described the current situation as a "statutory crazy-quilt,"
but anticipate that all states will adopt the newer act within the
next few years. Having the same law in all states will make consistency in the treatment of custody awards possible and will
help resolve custody disputes and kidnapping allegations
between parents living in different states.

RELOCATION AND TRAVELING

State laws vary widely when it comes to parental ability to relocate. Some states routinely allow a custodial parent to move out

( ) ASK A LAWYER

Q. *My ex-husband took our eight-year-old son out of state for a week's vacation with my permission. Guess what? They dropped out of sight and didn't come back for six weeks. What can I do to see that this never happens again?*

A. You can go to court to modify visitation to require that it be supervised in the future. The disappearance is useful evidence to support such a modification.

—Answer by Marilyn Ireland
Professor, California Western School of Law,
San Diego, California

of state with a child if there is a good-faith reason for the move (such as significantly better employment opportunities, following a new spouse to a new job in another state, or a desire to live near family members). Many states examine requests to move on a case-by-case basis and decide the issue after considering several factors. Some states also impose notice requirements that require the moving parent to notify the other parent of the move at least thirty, sixty, or ninety days before moving, so the other parent has a chance to challenge the move. Usually, the applicable law will be that of the state where the divorce was granted. If the parents were never married, the law of the state where the child is living or where a custody determination was made will likely apply (under the UCCJEA).

Out-of-state vacations are a different story. Unless a custody or visitation agreement provides otherwise, a parent is pretty much free to take a child where the parent wants, so long as the child is not harmed. Of course, it may not be in a child's best interests to be away from the other parent for a very long time or to be unable to communicate with that parent. Planning ahead is the key, so you should ask the other parent of your child about plans for scheduled vacations. If you do not get an answer, you can always request the information in a certified letter addressed to the father's lawyer. Make a copy of this letter so it can be shown to a court at a later date. You can also consider filing a "show cause" motion and ask the court to have the other parent of your child come to court and explain why you are not being told about his vacation plans.

It is important to note that the UCCJEA cannot help you if your child is taken to another country. If your spouse has family or business ties in another country, you might want to consider putting a provision in the custody award forbidding him from taking the child out of the country. Sadly, some foreign countries, even those with treaties governing such matters, are reluctant to return a child to a custodial parent in the United States. It may be important in such cases not to agree to joint custody and to closely monitor visitation periods.

VISITATION

Even when sole custody is awarded to one parent, the other parent almost always has a right of **visitation**, which is a right to be with the child, including for overnight visits and vacation periods. You might be able to work out the details of visitation (times, places, and so on) in a parenting agreement. If a court has to decide visitation, it will often order visitation at reasonable times and places and leave it to the parents to work out the precise schedule. This is called **reasonable visitation**, and for it to work, both parents need to cooperate and communicate with each other frequently. In reality, however, under reasonable visitation the custodial parent has control over dates, times, and duration and is not legally obligated to agree to any particular arrangement.

If your situation is not amenable to reasonable visitation, then a **fixed-visitation schedule** can save you time, angst, and costs associated with going to court to get other arrangements

◯ ASK A LAWYER

Q. My former husband has primary custody of our children while I'm finishing my education. I still have two years to go, but now he wants to move clear across the country to take another job. I say, no way. What can I do to prevent this?

A. Most states have what are called relocation statutes, which set forth how much notice the moving parent must give to the other parent. The statutes generally also set forth what the parent who objects to the move must do to bring the matter before a court. Some states require mediation in advance of court proceedings. Even in states that have no specific statutes, our mobile society has caused a fairly significant number of cases in this area in the past several years. You should check with your attorney in this regard. At one time, relocation of children was generally disfavored. But in most jurisdictions, the pendulum has swung significantly over the past several years. Now, more courts are looking to the best interests of the children, and the person who has been the primary caregiver often is deemed to be the parent with whom the children should live, even if this means a move.

—Answer by Sharon L. Corbitt
Sneed Lang, P.C., Tulsa, Oklahoma

Q. Do grandparents have visitation rights?

A. This varies from state to state. Most states do have statutes that define the parameters of grandparent visitation and when and under what circumstances those rights may be given. However, as a general rule, the rights of grandparents have been somewhat diluted by the U.S. Supreme Court case *Troxel v. Granville*, in which the Court found that fit parents should be given more deference on decisions regarding with whom the child will associate than was provided by state law. The Court left open the possibility that some grandparents could obtain court-ordered visitation if, for example, the grandparents could show that they had a particularly strong relationship with their grandchildren, it would harm the child not to continue the relationship, and it was in the child's best interest to continue. The burden of proof is on the grandparents.

—Answer by Sharon L. Corbitt
Sneed Lang P.C., Tulsa, Oklahoma

enforced. A court will order a fixed-visitation schedule when there is hostility between the parents and/or where contact between them may be detrimental to the child. However, a court will not deny visitation because a parent is behind in child support payments or there is a history of violent or destructive behavior. Instead, the court may limit visitation and require that it be supervised and occur at a public facility. When supervised visitation is ordered, the supervisor must be approved by the court, and it cannot be the custodial parent. A court will usually deny visitation only if parental rights have been terminated.

THE WORLD AT YOUR FINGERTIPS

• Dr. Joan Kelly's online article, "The Determination of Child Custody in the USA," outlines the fascinating history of child custody laws in this country at www.islandnet.com/~wwlia/us-cus.htm.

• The Woman's Divorce website contains information about the issues women face during divorce and separation. The site also includes more detailed information on the kind of material you should cover in your parenting agreement at www.womans-divorce.com/parenting-plan.html.

• The American Bar Association can help you locate mediation resources in your area at www.abanet.org/dispute.

• You can find some more information—and some case law—on custody issues faced by gay and lesbian parents at http://www.lambdalegal.org/cgi-bin/iowa/issues/record?record=5 and at www.nclrights.org/publications/custody.htm.

REMEMBER THIS

- A well-thought-out parenting agreement can help both parents work out what they want and prevent subsequent wrangling over the details of custody and visitation.

- If you and the other parent of your child cannot compromise on custody and visitation arrangements on your own or with the help of your lawyers, mediation may be the best option for reaching a workable solution.

- Courts decide custody according to the best interests of the child, and this standard takes priority over all other factors. The laws of most states provide that mothers and fathers have an equal right to custody. No state requires that custody be awarded to the mother without regard to the fitness of both parents.

- Even when sole custody is awarded to one parent, the other parent almost always has a right of visitation, which is a right to be with the child, including for overnight visits and vacation periods.

CHAPTER 10

Child Support: Your Guide to Getting It and Keeping It

Lorraine divorced Tony when their twin daughters were six years old. It was a fairly amicable divorce, but Tony's new wife took a dislike to the twins, and the relationship between Tony, Lorraine, and their daughters deteriorated.

Tony stopped visiting the twins five years after the divorce. A year after that, at the urging of his new wife, he stopped paying child support. He insisted to Lorraine, who was struggling to make ends meet, that he had no money. His house was in his new wife's name, he was spending a fortune on a new baby, and he quit his job. Lorraine is furious and upset. What can she do?

After the dust of the breakup or divorce has settled, you'll still have children to raise and bills to pay. Of course, you hope support from the other parent will keep flowing in. Unfortunately, a great many women do not receive all the child support to which they're entitled. This chapter explains the laws affecting child support, your rights to receive it, and your obligations to pay it.

CHILD SUPPORT GUIDELINES

Child support is payment one parent makes to another for financial support of children after a divorce, separation, or paternity proceeding. A **child support order** is a document from a court that sets out how often and how much a parent is to pay in child support. Under the federal Child Support Enforcement Act, each state is required to have its own **guidelines** for determining child support. These guidelines generally consider such factors as

- the needs of the child or children (including health care and insurance, education, day care, and special needs),
- the income and needs of each parent,
- the number of children who need support, and
- the child or children's standard of living before divorce or separation.

The guidelines vary considerably from state to state; however, they have the common goal of providing the children who receive support with the same standard of living they had before the divorce or separation. However, maintaining two households on the income that formerly supported just one is often difficult, if not impossible, so this goal is rarely realized.

For women, who most often have custody and who are more likely to be the beneficiaries of a child support order, the guidelines have brought some good news. Since the federal law was enacted in the late 1980s, child support payments have increased by approximately 50 percent. In addition, child support payments within each state have become more uniform.

However, the guidelines do vary considerably from state to state. Some state guidelines give judges a good deal of leeway in setting actual amounts, as long as the general state guidelines are followed. Other states are very strict and allow little judicial discretion. Thus, child support ordered in one state may be far more or far less than that ordered in another state.

Generally, there are two types of child support guidelines. One type is based on the income of the person who is supposed to pay child support and the number of children. The other type of guideline is based on the income of *both* parents and the number of children. This second type of guideline is often referred to as the **income shares model**.

A court will assume that the custodial parent spends the child support money on the child, but there are no hard and fast rules or regulations limiting the way the money is spent. If you are concerned that your child support payments are not being spent on your child, then you might set up a separate checking account for the child's expenses and agree on the type of expenses that can be paid from the account.

( )   ASK A LAWYER

Q. *I was never married to the father of my little boy. We're apart now. Can I collect child support from him?*

A. Even if you were never married to the father of your child, he is obliged to provide for the support of a child. You can bring a paternity action in your state court to establish paternity, set visitation, and deal with incidental of child support such as base support, day care expenses, health insurance premiums, and so on. Alternatively, you can check with your state child support collection and enforcement office, which can bring an action to set child support and collect it for you.

—Answer by Sharon L. Corbitt
Sneed Lang, P.C., Tulsa, Oklahoma

A. Child support is for the child and has nothing to do with marriage or lack of it. The important thing is to be able to prove that the father is really daddy. It is usually enough if he has acknowledged the child as his. If he won't acknowledge the child, then DNA testing is available to determine the paternity of a child born to a woman who is not married to the father. You can't get alimony for yourself, but once paternity is established in court, you are entitled to child support the same as if you had been married and gotten a divorce.

—Answer by Marilyn Ireland
Professor, California Western School of Law,
San Diego, California

DETERMINING A PARENT'S INCOME

When applying child support guidelines, most state legislation requires judges to look to the parent's net income (gross income minus federal and state income taxes, Social Security tax, Medicare tax, and deductions for health insurance), although some states use the parent's gross income. Courts will consider income from all sources (including any assistance programs) and generally do not deduct payments to credit unions or banks or wage attachments. In addition, under most state guidelines a judge can look at the parent's ability to earn an income, along with what the parent is actually earning, and order a higher child support payment if there is a discrepancy.

Some states allow deductions for the paying parent's reasonable living expenses, but will not include dining out or entertainment expenses. The rationale for disallowing these expenses is that family support should come before all personal expenses. While this approach may seem like common sense, it can have adverse consequences for parents who have child support obligations. For example, if you have an obligation to pay child support, you may be prevented from leaving a current job and going back to school, because education expenses may not be considered when a court looks at your income and ability to pay support. If you have child support obligations, you may also be prevented from taking a job with less pay but good potential for higher pay in the future, or from taking a lower-paying job that provides job satisfaction or requires fewer hours to be worked.

If you must determine the income of the child's other parent, and he or she is self-employed, then you may face particular challenges in finding hidden assets and figuring out what business expenses will be deducted from the parent's income and what expenses will not. In this regard, certain expenses that are deductible for tax purposes may not be deductible from income for the purpose of setting child support.

MODIFYING CHILD SUPPORT ORDERS

The most common circumstances in which a court will consider modification of a child support order is where there is a **substantial change in circumstances**. This usually refers to a change in the income of the parent who is paying support. If the parent who is ordered to pay support suffers a loss of income,

---

ⓘ THE EFFECT OF JOINT CUSTODY ON CHILD SUPPORT

The effect of joint custody on child support will depend on the nature of the joint custody arrangement. If you have joint legal custody (where you and the other parent share making major decisions about the child), that by itself will have little effect on child support obligations. But if you and the other parent have joint physical custody, with the child spending substantial time with both of you, and if you both have approximately equal incomes, it is possible that neither of you will have to pay support to the other. Each of you will pay the child's day-to-day expenses when the child is in your respective homes. You may need to coordinate payments on major expenses such as camp, school, clothing, and insurance.

Women with joint physical custody of their children are most affected when there is a significant difference in incomes, and the other parent's income is significantly higher. In such cases, the parent with the higher income will probably be required to make some payments or to pay more of the child's expenses, but the amount paid probably will be less than the guideline amount because of the joint physical custody arrangement. The unfortunate result of this is that children do not in fact enjoy the same standard of living in both homes.

---

that loss could provide a legitimate basis for reducing support; conversely, if that parent's income increases, that gain could be grounds for increasing support.

Changes in the child's circumstances can also be a reason for modifying support orders—for example, if the child has significant new expenses, such as special classes, health needs not covered by insurance, or needs braces or orthodontic work. Significant changes in the income of the parent seeking support can also be a basis for modifying support. If the custodial parent's income drops (particularly through no fault of the custodial parent), this loss could be a basis for increasing support. Likewise, if the custodial parent's income increases, it might be a reason for reducing support from the noncustodial parent.

In some states, support orders may be reviewed automatically every two years. If the parent who is supposed to pay support has a major drop in income, that parent should promptly go to court to modify the order, because the obligation to pay support at the designated amount continues unless and until a court orders otherwise.

Women who receive or are entitled to receive support payments are at risk if the other parent of the child goes to prison. Several courts have ruled that a parent's imprisonment may entitle the imprisoned parent to reduce or suspend child support payments—particularly if there is no evidence to suggest that the imprisonment resulted from the parent's attempt to avoid paying the support.

Generally, there is no break for child support payments when a child goes on vacation. Courts reason that many major expenses for the benefit of the child—such as rent, mortgage, utilities, clothes, and insurance—have to be paid whether the child is with the custodial parent or not. Of course, the parties themselves or the court may set different payment schedules. A lower amount for vacation periods with the noncustodial parent might reflect savings to the custodial parent for food and expenses or child care (but, of course, that, too, sometimes has to be paid even during school holidays).

A related issue may arise if the noncustodial parent wants to reduce child support payments because he or she has spent money on the child, such as for clothes or extracurricular activities. However, this is almost never a basis for reducing child support payments. If the noncustodial parent wants to pay for clothes or extracurricular activities of the child, this is fine (and nice for the child), but the court will treat such payments as gifts to the child, not as part of the noncustodial parent's support obligation. Court orders or divorce settlements almost always provide that child support is to be paid in specific dollar amounts from one parent to the other. Courts do not want the complications of trying to sort out whether the parties on a particular occasion agreed to an alternative way of making child support payments. Courts also do not want the noncustodial parent changing the method of paying child support and potentially interfering with the budget planning of the custodial parent.

Finally, child support payments may be modified when a child turns eighteen. In most states, a parent is not legally obligated to support a child beyond the age of eighteen or after the child has graduated high school. However, in some states support obligations continue until the child is twenty-one or has graduated from college or trade school.

You are not obliged to seek modification of a child support order when one of your older children turns eighteen. But if the other parent insists, it might be to your benefit. The court will look at a variety of factors, including both parents' incomes and the needs of the remaining children. If your incomes have both remained the same, and the needs of the remaining minor children are the same, then a court may decrease the total amount of support paid. However, if the other parent's income has risen since the last order, a new child support order for the remaining children may actually be more than the original amount.

A reduction in child support after a child turns eighteen can have several negative consequences for women receiving child support. For example, if some of the support has been for housing and has gone toward mortgage payments, a woman may be forced to sell her house when the child support payments end. If the woman has more than one child and the eldest turns eighteen and the child support order is child specific (e.g., "child support shall be $200 per month for each of the three children"), then the monthly support will be reduced accordingly.

ENFORCEMENT

It's one thing to work out how much child support one parent should pay the other. It's another thing entirely to ensure that the money is actually paid. According to the Census Bureau

( ) ASK A LAWYER

Q. My husband's ex-wife claims that now that he and I are married, and have two incomes, their kids should get more child support. That doesn't seem fair. Is it possible that she's right?

A. Child support laws vary from state to state. In most jurisdictions, however, the income of a new spouse would not be considered relevant for purposes of a determination of child support. Your husband should check with an attorney to determine the law in your state.

—Answer by Sharon L. Corbitt
Sneed Lang, P.C., Tulsa, Oklahoma

Q. I'm all for us divorced moms getting all the child support we can, but the standard that only takes into account the noncustodial parent's income seems a leftover from the old days when men worked and women stayed at home. Am I missing something?

A. You are right and in fact most legislatures have agreed with you. Most states do take into consideration the income of *both* parents. Child support guidelines vary greatly from state to state, so you should check the guidelines in your own state in this regard.

—Answer by Sharon L. Corbitt
Sneed Lang, P.C., Tulsa, Oklahoma

(from the 1999 Custodial Mothers and Fathers and Their Child Support Report), only 45 percent of the parents entitled to receive child support receive the full amount that is due. The Census Bureau also reported that eight out of ten fathers with joint custody paid support. But of the fathers with no visitation rights, fewer than half paid support.

It is important to remember that child support and visitation are independent rights and obligations. You cannot withhold one to get the other. If you are not getting your child support payments, you may not withhold visitation or contact with the other parent. The correct remedy is to go to court (or activate a wage withholding order) to collect your past-due child support. Similarly, if you are supposed to get visitation or contact and you are being denied this, you cannot withhold paying your child support obligations. Again, the correct remedy is to go to court and get an order to enforce your visitation rights.

The federal government and the states have a variety of techniques for enforcing payments of child support. State child support programs, which are administered through Child Enforcement Units, help locate noncustodial parents, establish paternity, establish and enforce support orders, and collect child support payments. While programs vary from state to state, their services are available to all parents who need them. Any parent or person with custody of a child who needs help to establish a child support or medical support order or to collect support payments can apply for child support enforcement services. Depending on the state, there may be some costs, but they are usually low. These can include the cost of legal work done by agency attorneys and costs for locating a noncustodial parent.

If you want to apply to your state child support program for help in locating the father of your child and enforcing a child support order against him, you should bring the following information and documents to the first meeting:
- the name, address, and Social Security number of the father,
- the name and address of the father's current or recent employer,
- the names of friends and relatives,
- the names of organizations to which he might belong,
- any information you have about his income and assets—pay stubs, tax returns, bank accounts, investments, or property holdings,
- a physical description or photographs,
- your children's birth certificates,

- if paternity is an issue, written statements (letters or notes) in which the alleged father has said or implied that the child is his,
  - your child support order,
  - your divorce decree or separation agreement,
  - records of any child support received in the past, and
  - information about your income and assets.

Some parents have complained of delays in states' handling of support claims. If you can afford it, a private attorney may be able to help you collect child support more quickly. The attorney's regular rates will usually apply, although some attorneys may be willing to handle the case for a contingency fee. A contingency fee means the lawyer will take a portion of whatever is collected, but the client will not have to pay the attorney's fees if nothing is collected. Attorney fees can also be assessed against the party who was supposed to pay support but did not. In that case, the parent who was supposed to pay support will pay for the attorney of the other parent in addition to his or her own attorney fees.

Another way of collecting past-due child support is to use a private collection agency. Some collection agencies will handle collection of child support just as they handle collection of business debts or credit card debts. Collection agencies usually charge a contingency fee.

You can enforce an order for child support even if the other parent of your child lives in another state. State and federal statutes facilitate enforcement of support orders when parents live in different states. In addition, under the federal Child Support Recovery Act of 1992, it is a federal crime to willfully fail to pay child support to a child who resides in another state if the past-due amount has been unpaid for over one year or exceeds $5,000. Punishments under that law can include fines and imprisonment. States also have criminal penalties for failure to pay child support. State and federal prosecutors can help with interstate collections.

Finally, don't lose heart if the other parent of your child declares bankruptcy. Past-due child support is not dischargeable

(i) COLLEGE EXPENSES

In most states, there is no obligation under law for parents to continue to provide support after a child reaches the age of majority (eighteen in most states) or graduates from high school. Thus, parents are generally not under an obligation to pay for college. A few states have legislation specifying that parents should pay so-called **postminority support** in certain circumstances, for example, if the parents can afford it and the child is a good enough student to benefit from college. Other states will consider the circumstances and make a decision on whether a parent should pay for college on a case-by-case basis.

If you plan to send your kids to college, and you want the other parent of your child to share the cost, then you should consider making this obligation a part of your agreement on child support or a part of your divorce settlement if you were married. A court will generally enforce these kinds of private arrangements about college expenses. You should also let your children know that they are expected to help pay for their college expenses by working at summer jobs and using their own savings.

(forgiven) in bankruptcy. A bankruptcy court can discharge many debts, but the court cannot discharge a child support debt.

COLLECTING PAST-DUE CHILD SUPPORT

The following are some of the other ways in which you can collect past-due child support:

Wage Withholding Orders

These are court orders that are served on the employer of the parent who owes support. The employer sends payments to the state government, which then sends support payments to you.

Tax Refund Intercepts

The state government sends a notice to the Internal Revenue Service or the appropriate state department of revenue, directing that the tax refund of the recalcitrant parent be sent to the government for payment of support.

Liens on Property

A lien can be placed on the real estate, automobile, or other property belonging to the parent who owes support. If the support is not paid, the property can be confiscated and sold to pay the past-due amount.

 **ASK A LAWYER**

Q. *My ex is way behind on his support payments. He owns a house (or at least I think he does). A friend told me I could have a lien put on it— but what does that mean, how does it help me get my money, and how do I do it?*

A. You can check out the title to the home at the county recorder of deeds. All you need to know is precisely where the house is. If you think you can't do the research yourself, you can hire a title search company to do it for you. Once you find that he owns a house, you can file a lien on it for back child support. A lien is a legal claim against another person's property. If he doesn't pay after you place a lien, the court can order the property to be sold and a portion or all of the sale price paid to you to cover money past due to you. To file a lien, you should have a lawyer to help you file the correct court papers.

—Answer by Marilyn Ireland
Professor, California Western School of Law,
San Diego, California

Contempt of Court

You can ask a court to hold the other parent of your child in contempt of court for willful failure to pay support. If found guilty, he can be jailed, fined, or both.

Revocation of Licenses

About twenty states will revoke the driver's license or professional licenses of people who have not paid child support.

THE WORLD AT YOUR FINGERTIPS

- You can find information about child support, including links to the support guidelines of each state, at www.support-guidelines.com.
- The official website for the Federal Office of Child Support Enforcement provides a wealth of information and links for parents who have questions about child support or need any information about enforcing child support orders at www.acf.dhhs.gov/programs/cse.
- Every state has child enforcement units that help custodial parents establish and enforce child support orders and locate absent parents through child support programs. These offices are sometimes called IV-D Offices because they are required by Chapter IV-D of the Social Security Act. You can find your local office online at www.acf.dhhs.gov/programs/cse/extinf.htm or by looking under county or state government listings in your local telephone directory.

REMEMBER THIS

- Child support is payment from one parent to another for financial support of children after a divorce or separation or paternity proceeding. A child support order is a document from a

court that sets out how often and how much a parent is to pay
for child support.

• You can ask a court to modify a child support order if there is
a substantial change in the child's circumstances. The parent
paying support might request modification if his or her circumstances change.

• Just because you have an order for child support doesn't
mean that the parent who owes money will actually pay it. Visit
your state child enforcement unit or speak to your attorney
about ways in which you can get money owed to you for your
child.

PART FOUR

Health

CHAPTER 11

Infertility: Where Technology, the Law, and Parenthood Intersect

Deirdre is a successful attorney, is happily married, and has just turned thirty-seven. But her plans for children were derailed last year when she was diagnosed with cervical cancer and underwent a series of operations that left her unable to bear children to term. She and her husband have been looking into a number of different fertility treatments in an attempt to find one that will work for them.

Deirdre, as an attorney, is concerned about the legal implications of various infertility procedures. How does surrogacy work? Who owns the extra eggs or embryos produced through in vitro fertilization procedures? What are the implications of using donor eggs or sperm?

Reproduction used to involve some nontechnical procedures—would-be mothers and fathers having intercourse. Now, women (or couples) who have a medical condition that impairs their ability to have a baby can use assisted reproductive technologies to conceive and give birth to children. When medical professionals and third parties are involved in this process, the law becomes relevant to this sensitive and emotional process of conceiving a child. It's a good idea to understand the basics of how the law applies before you begin treatment.

THE SCIENCE OF CONCEPTION

Let's revisit your sixth grade human sexuality class and take a look at how a child is conceived: A man must produce healthy sperm, the woman's ovaries must produce mature eggs, sperm must swim toward the womb and fertilize the egg in the fallopian tube, and the fertilized egg (now called an embryo) must move from the fallopian tube to the uterine lining and implant in the uterine wall. The embryo must have a complete set of twenty-three chromosomes and divide normally to support its continued growth and development. At any stage of this delicate and complex process, something can go wrong that prevents a woman from conceiving or from carrying a child to term. For example, some men have abnormal sperm—sperm that can't swim well, that have misshapen heads, or that do not carry the requisite twenty-three chromosomes. Or an egg might be successfully fertilized but implant in the fallopian tube, causing an ectopic pregnancy, which can be life threatening if the tube ruptures. Or some women are simply unable to produce healthy eggs.

About 20 percent of all couples who wish to conceive do so within a month. During each subsequent month, about 20 percent of the remaining couples conceive, so that there is about an 85 percent chance of a couple conceiving within six months. However, not all pregnancies are carried to term—there is a high natural miscarriage rate even in fertile couples. Infertility is a term used to describe the inability to conceive or to carry a pregnancy to a live birth after a year or more of regular sexual relations without the use of contraception.

OWNERSHIP AND CONTROL OF SPERM, EGGS, AND EMBRYOS

When would-be parents use their own **gametes** (eggs or sperm) with assisted reproductive technology, the process is relatively clear of legal worries on the issue of the identity of the parents of the baby. However, whether you succeed in having all the babies you desire or decide to stop fertility treatments, there will sometimes be embryos or sperm left over (there may be eggs, too, though it is still experimental and not reliable to freeze eggs). You and your partner will need to make decisions about the creation, storage, use, and disposition of your genetic material.

📋 INFERTILITY TREATMENTS

In vitro fertilization (IVF): The woman is usually given medication to make her body produce more eggs during ovulation. A woman's eggs are removed from her body (usually by using an ultrasound probe and needle while the woman is under anesthesia) and placed into a dish with culture medium and sperm from her partner or a donor. If the sperm fertilizes the egg, an embryo is created. An embryo or several embryos are then placed into the woman's uterus or frozen for later use. If the embryo attaches to the woman's uterus, pregnancy results. Transferring more than one embryo can result in multiple births, generally twins or triplets.

Artificial insemination (often referred to as intrauterine insemination, or IUI, in the medical lexicon): Using a very thin catheter, sperm is placed in the woman's vagina or uterine cavity at the time mature eggs are released. The hope is that the sperm will fertilize at least one of the woman's eggs. Artificial insemination is a technology that is decades old and is still used today.

Gamete intrafallopian transfer (GIFT): This is a slightly more complex procedure than artificial insemination and slightly less complex than IVF. Eggs removed from the woman's ovaries are combined with sperm from her partner or a donor in the laboratory and, using a catheter, the mixture is then placed in one of her fallopian tubes, where fertilization can occur. Then the embryo follows through the fallopian tube to the uterus, where implantation may occur. Some people consider GIFT to be "more natural" than IVF.

You can keep your genetic material frozen for possible future use by you, donate it to another person or couple for their use in creating a child, donate it for research, or have it destroyed. Regardless of your decision, you should inform the infertility clinic—before you start treatment—what you want done with your genetic material. This is an important step. Unless you

168   HEALTH

decide what you want done with it, and inform the clinic and
storage facilities of your wishes, the clinic will decide how it will
treat and use your genetic material. Several states require parties
to create a **directive**, a document in which you formally declare
your intentions for your gametes or embryos, and have it signed,
witnessed, and notarized according to testamentary requirements. Even if your state law does not require it, you should set
out your wishes in writing. You should not just rely on the clinic's
informed-consent documents regarding how you want your tis-
sue treated. You and your partner should create a separate document.

In Virginia, a couple asked their fertility clinic to give them
their frozen embryos so that they could try a different doctor and
clinic. The clinic refused. The couple sued the clinic and won.
The court found the couple did have a kind of property interest
in their embryos. Not all courts are comfortable with declaring
embryos to be "property," and a court in another state might
reach a different decision. Nevertheless, you have a good chance
of controlling your embryos if third parties try to interfere.
Courts tend to provide parents with some form of quasi-property
rights to their embryos, such as the rights to possess, use, or
donate them.

Things become much more difficult when the fight is
between you and your spouse—for example, if you divorce and
cannot agree on what to do with the remaining embryos. This
kind of dispute raises complex emotional, legal, and ethical
issues. If there is no agreement, the court will have to balance
the interests of the people fighting for control. A New York couple had five frozen embryos remaining when they divorced. The
wife asked for sole control of the embryos. The husband wanted
to donate the embryos to the clinic for research. When they
began their fertility treatments, the couple had signed an agreement stating that they would donate the embryos to the clinic.
The court ruled in 1998 that the agreement was valid and the
embryos were to be donated.

However, there are some limits on what couples can agree to.
Even when a husband and wife sign a clear agreement giving one

( ) ASK A LAWYER

Q. My husband died last year, but left some frozen semen. I'm thinking of having a child using his semen, and I wonder if a child will be able to collect Social Security survivor's benefits based on the Social Security he earned.

A. In 2003, several states enacted statutes that prohibit the use of a dead person's gametes, unless that person prepared a written directive giving permission to create a child after his or her death. So you may not be able to use your husband's sperm. If you do have a child, there is differing case law as to whether he or she will be recognized as "a child of the marriage" for the purposes of Social Security.

—Answer by Ami Jaeger
BioLawGroup LLC, Santa Fe, New Mexico

A. Social security rules and regulations state that if you are the natural child of an insured, deceased person and were dependent on him, then you are entitled to Social Security survivor benefits. Normally, just being the natural child of the deceased means you are dependent on him or her. So, technically, under Social Security rules, your child should be entitled to collect Social Security survivor's benefits. Clearly though, the Social Security Administration has not kept up with modern science. In the future, the administration may change its rules so the child would not be able to collect survivor benefits.

—Answer by Denice Patrick
The Law Office of Denice L. Patrick, Lynnwood, Washington

Q. My husband donated sperm several times to get a few extra bucks while we were starting our own family. Our kids are starting to date now, and we have a (possibly unreasonable) fear that one of them might unwittingly get involved with a half brother or sister. Is there any way we can find out how many people used my husband's donated sperm to have children, and the identity of those children?

A. If your husband worked with a reputable sperm bank, you should not have to worry. There are national policies and procedures allowing sperm banks to use each donor only ten times. There are also regional restrictions on the use of a donor.

—Answer by Ami Jaeger
BioLawGroup LLC, Santa Fe, New Mexico

partner control of the embryos, courts are reluctant to enforce such an agreement if it forces one person to become a legal parent against his or her will. For example, if you divorce your husband and, in accordance with the terms of the agreement, he has sole control over the embryos and wants to use them to have a child with his new wife, a court would probably prevent him from doing so without your consent. By the same token, if your former husband objects, a court might prevent you from using these embryos, even if the original agreement says they are yours.

DONOR SPERM, EGGS, AND EMBRYOS

The legal and ethical issues raised by infertility procedures become even more complex when a couple uses donor sperm, eggs, or embryos to conceive a child.

Many women use donated sperm to conceive children—for example, because their male partners have problems with their sperm, because they are in lesbian relationships, or because they want to be single parents. Under the Uniform Sperm Donor Act adopted in many states, if a donor provides semen to a licensed physician for use in artificial insemination, then he is treated by the law as if he were not the father of the child. In states that have adopted this act, a sperm donor has no paternity rights and cannot be liable for child support, as long as he provided the sperm to a doctor. If a doctor is involved, it doesn't matter whether the donor is known or anonymous. A doctor might simply receive the sperm, screen it for sexually transmitted diseases, and give it to a woman for her to inseminate. Or a doctor might actually be involved in the insemination. In the past, many physicians refused to inseminate lesbians or single women. Today, more physicians are willing to provide donor insemination and avoid making judgments about their patients' parental suitability. If a woman is married, in most states her husband is automatically considered the legal father of her child. He may even be liable to pay child support, as long as he consented to the procedure in writing.

On the other hand, if no doctor is involved, a sperm donor may be granted paternity rights. In California, for example, a known donor donated his sperm to a lesbian couple. One of the women was inseminated with the man's sperm at home. There was no assistance from medical professionals and the man was not present when the woman was inseminated. Later, the man decided he wanted paternity rights, including visitation. Because the sperm was not provided to a licensed physician and because the donor was known, the sperm donor was granted paternity rights.

In states that have not passed the Sperm Donor Act, it is a good idea to involve a doctor and to ask a known sperm donor to

FINDING YOUR ANONYMOUS MOM OR DAD

In 2004, a voluntary register of anonymous sperm and egg donors was established in the United Kingdom as part of a pilot scheme to allow people to discover the identities of their genetic parents. The service permits people who donated anonymously to come forward and supply DNA samples. DNA tests will attempt to match offspring with donors and other half siblings who are also on the register. No such register exists in the United States, but some websites provide an opportunity for egg and sperm donors and children of donors to put their details online in the hope of connecting with the person who supplied or received some of their genetic material. Some gamete banks in the United States have a policy of open donation, which means the donors have agreed to be contacted by their offspring.

waive his paternity rights in a written agreement before the insemination takes place. Although such contracts are generally not legally binding in most jurisdictions, they can be used as persuasive evidence of the parties' intent.

If you are infertile because you are unable to produce healthy eggs due to aging, premature ovarian failure, anatomically inaccessible ovaries, or lack of ovarian function due to radiation, chemotherapy, or surgery, then egg donation may enable you to bear a child who is genetically related to your male partner.

A handful of states sanction egg donation and generally treat it the same as sperm donation—that is, if eggs are provided to a doctor, then the donor does not have any rights or obligations with respect to the child. Eggs are less likely to be truly anonymously donated than sperm, and so for the most part the same considerations apply to egg donation as apply to sperm donation from a known donor. Currently, in states without an egg donation statute that have a sperm donation statute, experts suggest that egg donation should be treated in the same way as sperm donation—that is, an egg donor who provides eggs to a doctor should be treated as if she has given up all parental rights and obligations, and the intended parents should be given all parental rights and obligations. This argument is supported by the equal protection clause of the U.S. Constitution. One court upheld the sperm donor analogy in a 1998 California case in which it stated, "We are hard-pressed to think of any reason a woman in an analogous situation [to a sperm donor] should be treated differently" (*Jaycee B. v. Superior Court*). If your state does not have an egg donation statute, and you wish to use a known donor, you are well advised to enter into an egg donation agreement with the donor before treatment begins.

If you and your partner both have infertility issues, you may need to seek a donated embryo. Embryo donation involves the same kinds of issues as egg or sperm donation, although it is slightly more complex because an embryo contains the genetic material of two people: a man and a woman, both of whom must sign an embryo donation agreement. Again, a few states sanction embryo donation and treat it in more or less the same way as sperm donation.

In addition to legal issues, both donors and recipients need to deal with important psychological and emotional issues. Many professionals recommend that donors, recipients, and their families attend counseling sessions both before and after infertility procedures. Independent psychological interventions are also highly recommended in the case of same-family donors and recipients.

Agreements for Donor Sperm, Eggs, and Embryos

Many states have statutes that allow the transfer of parental rights to the intended parents in the case of sperm donation, and a few states have statutes regulating egg donation and embryo donation. If you live in a state that regulates donation, then you will need to draft an agreement with the donor (if you know his or her identity) and state the identity of the intended parents. If you comply with the legislation, the intended parents will be granted parental rights, and the donor will not have any parental rights or obligations.

If you live in one of the states that does not have laws regulating gamete or embryo donation, then it is even more essential that you enter into an agreement. Some states' courts will honor such agreements; in other states, an agreement will provide valuable proof of your intentions, but it will not be conclusive in and of itself. Rudimentary gamete and embryo donation contracts abound on the Internet, but you are well advised to contact a lawyer to draft this important document for you. An agreement for sperm, egg, or embryo donation might cover the following issues:

Legal Parents: Maternity and Paternity

The law presumes that the woman who gives birth is the legal mother of the child, and her husband, if any, is the legal father of the child. Sometimes, this presumption of parentage fits with the intentions of the parties in assisted conception. For example, if a woman who intends to be the mother uses a donated embryo and gestates and gives birth to the baby, she and her husband are presumed to be the legal parents.

However, there is another legal presumption, which is that the person with the genetic connection to the child is the legal parent. If this is not the case (e.g., because you're using a donor egg, donor sperm, or donor embryo), then you must rebut this presumption in an agreement. This means that gamete donation agreements must clarify that the donor is relinquishing his or her parental rights and promises not to establish a parent-child relationship with the child. The same is true with embryo donation agreements: The genetic parents must agree to relinquish their parental rights when they make the donation. The agreement must be drafted to ensure that all parties understand and agree that any child born pursuant to the agreement is, in all respects, considered the child of the intended parents. Generally, this means that the donors will not be able to bring an action to claim their parental rights on the basis of their genetic connection to the child. If donors do bring a lawsuit, then an agreement will provide valuable evidence that the intention of all the parties was that the intended parents would have exclusive parental rights.

Establish Procedures to be Undertaken

The contract should cover the kinds of screening and diagnostic tests (such as tests for HIV/AIDS and ultrasound examinations) that will be performed and any other donor medical information that may be exchanged before the gametes are harvested. Counseling procedures for donors and recipients should also be specified. If there are medical procedures to be followed (including injections and surgery for egg donors), the agreement should make clear what the regimen is. Compensation for the risks and inconvenience should be specified as well as the costs of the drugs, medical procedures, and physician charges.

Confidentiality and Disclosure

If there is a known donor, the agreement should clarify who has the right to tell the child about the involvement of a donor. Also, the agreement should spell out whether or not the child and the donor may have contact in the future and under what circumstances. Finally, the donor should make it clear whether he or she grants permission for the child to have later access to additional health information and under what terms and conditions. These are highly charged emotional issues, and the parties should seek competent professional counseling.

Genetic Disclosure

Certain diseases or conditions may be known to exist in the donor's family or may be found within certain populations or ethnic groupings. These conditions should be disclosed, if known by the donor. The recipient couple can then decide whether to request genetic testing of the donor (which the donor has the right to refuse) or select another donor. The medical and genetic history of the donor and donor's relatives should be provided by all donors.

Disposal and Ownership of Eggs and Embryos

Generally, once the sperm or eggs are donated, the donors relinquish control over their disposal or other use. However, embryos are slightly different because they are not created for the sole purpose of donation (most donated embryos are the "extra" embryos created by a couple undergoing fertility treatment). The donors of embryos can make quite specific requests about how any extra embryos can be used.

SURROGACY

Surrogacy involves many of the same issues raised by gamete or embryo donation, with the added complication that the intended mother (i.e., the woman who intends to be the legal mother and raise the child) is not the woman who actually gestates and gives birth to the child. Again, this situation makes an agreement identifying the intended parents essential. Both legislatures and courts are suspicious of any contract that involves the payment of fees in exchange for a baby. In some states, any kind of surrogacy arrangement involving compensation for a surrogate's services is illegal; in other states, surrogacy is legal and intended parents can pay surrogates. However, in most states parents can only pay surrogates a sum that covers the costs of reasonable living and the medical, legal, and psychological needs of the surrogate mother directly related to the pregnancy. As in egg and sperm donation, this agreement will not be decisive in all states, but at the very least it will provide good evidence of the parties' intentions. The assistance of professionals can help provide a positive, supportive experience for all involved, but state laws regulating the involvement of such professionals are also very different. For example, Arizona prohibits the involvement of any third party to arrange a surrogacy, which has the detrimental effect of subjecting the inexperienced parties to a host of predictable legal, emotional, and psychological risks.

In **traditional surrogacy**, a woman (the surrogate) undergoes intrauterine insemination with sperm from the man who wants to be the legal father. The man providing the sperm is not married to the surrogate, nor does he intend to relinquish his

---

(i) CARRIER AGREEMENTS

Surrogacy agreements usually contain the same kinds of clauses as contracts for egg or embryo donation outlined earlier. In addition, they might include specific clauses setting out

- that the intended parents want to be included in prenatal doctor visits,
- that the intended parents will be present in the delivery room, and
- that the carrier will refrain from behaviors that are harmful to the fetus.

parental rights and be treated as a sperm donor. The baby has genetic material from the intended father and the surrogate. The surrogate voluntarily relinquishes custody of the child to the intended parents at the time of birth. In most states without a statutory definition to the contrary, the surrogate mother's biological and genetic connection to the child defines her as the legal mother, and most hospital administrators will automatically place her name on the original birth certificate. To prevent this, the intended parents should seek a judgment of paternity from a court before the birth, declaring that they are the biological and legal parents of the child. This document allows the hospital to place the names of the intended parents on the original birth certificate.

If a court order is not obtained prebirth, then after the birth, the intended mother must complete a stepparent adoption. First, a social worker from the local department of children's services is assigned to review the file and approve the stepparent adoption. During this process, the surrogate mother signs a final consent decree to formally terminate her parental relationship to the child. At the final stepparent adoption hearing, the judge issues an order that the birth certificate be amended to properly reflect the intended mother's name as the natural and legal mother. The original birth certificate is sealed and a new one is issued with the names of both of the intended parents. This process can be completed within three to six months of the birth of the baby.

Agreements giving parental rights to the intended parents have been upheld in the case of traditional surrogates. But in some states, the fact that a traditional surrogate is genetically related to the child to whom she gives birth has persuaded courts that the traditional surrogate should be recognized as the birth mother and given time to consider whether to relinquish her maternal rights. Entering into an agreement for traditional surrogacy in these states has risks for the intended parents.

In a **gestational-carrier surrogacy**, embryos are transferred to the gestational carrier, who agrees to gestate the baby on behalf of the intended parents. The baby is not genetically

( ) ASK A LAWYER

Q. *I am infertile, but my husband is not. We want to have a baby by using a surrogate impregnated with his semen. Will I have to adopt the baby once it is born? If so, is this difficult or time consuming? Is there a simpler way of doing it?*

A. It is unfair for a couple facing infertility and choosing to undergo treatment to have a child (i.e., specifically rejecting the option of adoption) to undergo the expense, personal invasion, and anxiety of an adoption or stepparent adoption. It is particularly unfair for people with the disability of infertility to be subject to state scrutiny of their parental fitness, which is part of the adoption process. Instead, consider involving a gestational carrier, entering into a contract with her, and obtaining a prebirth order finding you to be the legal parents of the child. It is important that you obtain an experienced lawyer to assist you.

—Answer by Ami Jaeger
BioLawGroup LLC, Santa Fe, New Mexico

Q. *My husband and I are unable to have a baby. We'd like to find a surrogate to carry the baby for me, but how do we do so? What precautions should we take? How can we know that we're not making a mistake?*

A. There are many agencies that provide matches for surrogates and intended parents. Contact fertility support groups and ask your fertility clinic. You may want to find your own surrogate through the Internet or with a newspaper ad. Experienced agencies and clinics have established criteria to select appropriate surrogates and may also be able to help.

Make sure you really understand the legal issues before you consider working with a surrogate and ensure that all parties receive psychological support. You may want to consider using a gestational carrier instead of a surrogate to ease the legal conundrums.

—Answer by Ami Jaeger
BioLawGroup LLC, Santa Fe, New Mexico

Q. *My husband and I are trying to conceive, without luck. I know fertility clinics have worked for some people, but I also know that there are lots of risks. Does the law regulate these clinics? What should we look for? How can we minimize the risks?*

A. After living through the frustrating and emotionally draining experiences of failed pregnancy and perhaps miscarriages, it makes good sense to seek medical information and advice from a fertility clinic. Many times, your general practitioner or gynecologist does not have the expertise to provide you with the best information; seek the advice of a board-certified reproductive endocrinologist. The fertility clinic will help you to evaluate your fertility as a couple before recommending treatment options. Remember, you don't have to undergo all the high-tech interventions, but the information is medically risk-free.

    Physicians at fertility clinics are licensed by the state in which they practice. The laboratory directors at these clinics are not licensed, but the best directors obtain certification from national laboratory groups as a result of rigorous testing. Look for the certification of the lab directors. Both the Centers for Disease Control and Prevention (CDC) and the Society of Assisted Reproductive Technology, which is a division of the American Society of Reproductive Medicine, have a voluntary database of clinics; the clinics provide information about their procedures and pregnancy rates. Remember, this information is provided on a voluntary basis by the clinics—it is not reviewed by the CDC, but it does provide some general information.

    You should look for a physician who will provide you with all the answers to your questions and a clinic in which you feel comfortable asking questions. The physician or clinic should not be uncomfortable involving a lawyer in the process! Avoid clinics that push the latest and greatest technologies—they should be available, but the choice to use the technologies is yours alone. Likewise, be careful of lawyers who push adoption or use adoption concepts in making recommendations about embryos or parentage. The law is clear that adoption and assisted conception are legally distinct.

—Answer by Ami Jaeger,
BioLawGroup LLC, Santa Fe, New Mexico

related to the woman who carries the child. Here is where it gets confusing: The genetic material can come from either of the intended parents (or both), or from an egg donor or a sperm donor, or both. Again, the carrier should sign an agreement with the intended parents, in which she must acknowledge that she will not be the legal mother of the child she gives birth to and must agree that she will not try to form a parental bond with the child. The contract must establish that the intended parents are going to be financially and legally responsible for the support, custody, and care of the child.

If the intended parents have a genetic connection to the child, then this can be asserted prebirth and an order obtained, placing the names of the intended parents on the birth certificate. If there is not a genetic connection to either intended parent, then the agreement that clarifies the intent of the parents may be persuasive to support a prebirth order finding them to be the legal parents. Courts have consistently held that in gestational-carrier arrangements, the intended parents are the legal parents, even if the intended parents did not provide the genetic material.

INSURANCE COVERAGE

Few insurance plans directly cover treatment for infertility, although some policies are starting to cover the cost of in vitro fertilization as the cost decreases and the success rate increases. Policies may also cover treatment for illnesses (such as endometriosis) that contribute to infertility. Some policies will cover infertility treatment if the couple has been trying to conceive for a year or more. Consumers are fighting to get more coverage for infertility treatment. Some states now mandate that insurance companies include infertility treatment in their plans.

ADOPTION

Infertility treatments can be expensive, invasive, and unsuccessful, and many women (and couples) choose to adopt a child instead. There are two basic types of adoption. In **agency**

THERE'S NO SUCH THING AS A PARENTLESS CHILD

In the most extraordinary surrogacy case to date, a California appellate court was faced with the challenge of balancing the parental rights and interests of six parties to a surrogacy contract. In *Jaycee B. v. Superior Court*, John and Luanne Buzzanca, the intended parents, executed a gestational carrier contract in California with a carrier and the carrier's husband. Both the egg and the sperm were to come from anonymous donors.

Things started to fall apart when John and Luanne separated and John petitioned for divorce one month before the expected birth of the child. The child was born and the hospital released the child to Luanne based on the surrogacy agreement. Luanne then sought child support payments from John.

John convinced the trial court that support payments could not be ordered because he was not genetically related to the child. The court also stated that neither the carrier nor Luanne was the legal mother and that Jaycee was in fact parentless. The appellate court overturned the decision and ruled that John Buzzanca and Luanne Buzzanca were the legal father and mother of Jaycee. The court decided that the genetic makeup of the child does not necessarily dictate whose names appear on the birth certificate. Instead, the "first causes, prime movers, of the procreative relationship" are to be viewed as the legal parents, and John was the child's parent because he entered into the surrogacy agreement. The court explained, "John admits he signed the surrogacy agreement, which for all practical purposes caused Jaycee's conception every bit as much as if he had caused her birth the old fashioned way."

adoption, the parents work though a state-licensed agency. The agency often supervises the care of biological mothers who are willing to have their children adopted by others, and it assists in the placement of children after birth. Some agencies specialize in placing children born in foreign countries. Agencies screen adoptive parents—often extensively—before the adoption proceeds and often have long waiting lists of parents.

Private adoptions bypass the use of agencies and may bypass the long waiting lists as well. The process may begin when people who seek to adopt a child contact a lawyer who specializes in adoptions. The lawyer may work with physicians who are aware of women willing to give up children for adoption. Sometimes would-be parents will place ads in newspapers seeking women who are willing to place their babies for adoption. In most states, adoptive parents are allowed to pay a biological mother's medical expenses and certain other costs during the pregnancy. But adoptive parents are not allowed to pay the biological mother specifically to give up the child. The law treats this as a black-market adoption—the buying and selling of children—and it is a crime in every state. Court approval is needed for both agency and private adoptions. Many states also require that the adoptive parents be studied and approved by a social service agency.

Many states allow single persons to adopt. Some agencies strongly prefer to place a child with a married couple, while other agencies—particularly those dealing with children who might be hard to place—are willing to place a child with a single person. Single-parent adoptions are usually possible in private adoptions. Gay and lesbian couples can adopt a child in some states.

THE WORLD AT YOUR FINGERTIPS

• You can delve more deeply into the ethical and legal debates surrounding infertility treatments in a book edited by Sarah Franklin and Helena Ragone: *Reproducing Reproduction: Kinship, Power, and Technological Innovation* (1997).

• John Robertson, a bioethicist, provides a framework for evaluating sperm donation, surrogacy, and other technological advances in his book *Children of Choice* (1996).

• In *Beyond Second Opinions: Making Choices about Fertility Treatment* (1998), Judith Turiel, a medical writer and infertility patient, provides a valuable guide to the process of seeking infertility treatment and educates the reader in accessing, understanding, and evaluating the relevant medical literature.

• The American Society for Reproductive Medicine website has a section devoted to patients, with FAQs on fertility and reproductive issues, at www.asrm.org.

• The National Infertility Association is dedicated to providing advocacy, information, and support to men and women facing infertility and includes a bulletin board at www.resolve.org.

• You can find links to information on surrogacy laws in the states at www.surrogacy.com/legals/states.html. A map showing the status of surrogacy laws is at www.surrogacy.com/legals/map.html.

REMEMBER THIS

• Before you start any infertility treatment, take time to draw up an agreement stating what you and your partner would like to happen to any extra sperm, eggs, or embryos.

• State laws differ on the rights of sperm donors, egg donors, and embryo donors. Check out the law in your state, and always draft an agreement with the parties. If you are receiving donated gametes or embryos, make sure you are identified as the intended parent and that you will have all parental rights and responsibilities.

• Relationships in collaborative reproduction are complicated—legally, medically, and emotionally. Agreements are important because they help to solidify understanding about the roles and expectations each person has. Work with experienced legal and psychological professionals to craft an agreement that defines and supports the relationships being created.

CHAPTER 12

Contraception: Your Rights to Contraception

Sarah is sixteen and has just started having sex with her boyfriend. She's paid attention in sex-ed class and would like to use the most reliable contraception possible so that she can avoid becoming another teenage pregnancy statistic. She wants to ask her family doctor to prescribe her the contraceptive pill, but she has several concerns. Can she ask the doctor not to tell her mother, who would definitely disapprove? Will insurance pay for the consultation and the pills, and can Sarah ask the insurance company not to send a statement showing the consultation to her home?

Sarah would never guess that her mother, Beth, has her own issues getting affordable contraception. Contraception isn't covered under her health insurance and she pays a small fortune every month for the contraceptive pill.

Sarah is sixteen now, and, like her mother, will probably use some form of contraception for many of the next thirty years. This chapter will take a look at this important area for women and girls, focusing on laws affecting the availability of contraception, its cost, and confidentiality issues.

WHAT IS CONTRACEPTION?

There is evidence that various forms of contraception have been used in many societies, modern and ancient, for thousands of years. Ancient contraceptive methods included herbs taken orally; withdrawal by the male; melting suppositories designed to form an impenetrable coating over the cervix; diaphragms, caps, or other devices inserted into the vagina over the cervix and withdrawn after intercourse; vaginal suppositories; douching after intercourse to kill or drive out the sperm; condoms; and varieties of the rhythm method. Many of these contraceptive methods have been in use in different cultures for thousands of years, although their rates of success in preventing pregnancy have increased over the last century or two as understanding of female biology has improved. The newest additions to this battery of ancient contraceptives are the hormonal contraceptives. This group includes the birth control pill, which was introduced in 1960, and more recent types of contraceptives that control fertility in the same way, but deliver doses of the necessary hormones through patches, injections, or implants beneath the skin.

Over half of all pregnancies in the United States are unintended, and according to a report developed by the Alan Guttmacher Institute in 2003 (www.agi-usa.org/pubs/abslides/abort_slides.pdf), almost half of these pregnancies end in abortion. Access to contraception is critical to preventing unwanted pregnancies and enabling women to control the timing and number of their children. The rate of abortion per one thousand women has decreased over the last twenty years. Statistics show that affordable, readily available contraception reduces the incidence of abortion, improves women's health, saves public health funds, and decreases the incidence of infant mortality.

THE RIGHT TO CONTRACEPTION

On June 7, 1965, in *Griswold v. Connecticut*, the U.S. Supreme Court struck down state laws that had made the use of birth control by married couples illegal. Estelle Griswold was the executive director of the Planned Parenthood League of Connecticut. Both she and the medical director for the league provided information, instruction, and other medical advice to married couples concerning birth control. Griswold and her colleague were convicted under a Connecticut law that made it a crime to provide counseling and other medical treatment to married persons for purposes of preventing conception. The

ⓘ A FAMILY PLANNING PIONEER

Margaret Sanger was born in New York City in 1879. She was the sixth of eleven children and watched her mother die at the age of fifty after eighteen pregnancies.

Margaret and her sister, Ethel Byrne, both nurses, opened the first birth control clinic in the United States in 1916. Dozens of Jewish and Italian immigrant women from Brooklyn lined up when the center opened to receive counseling and birth control information. Nine days later, police closed the clinic and arrested the sisters. Ethel was tried, convicted, and went on a hunger strike. Margaret was convicted and served thirty days in jail. But legal failure brought victory of a kind. The publicity surrounding Margaret Sanger's activities made birth control—which had previously been a private, closeted issue—a matter of public debate. In 1952, Margaret Sanger founded the International Planned Parenthood Federation and served as its first president until 1959. She died in 1965 in Tucson, Arizona, aged eighty-seven years, a few months after the decision in *Griswold v. Connecticut*, which upheld the legality of contraceptive use.

Supreme Court found that although the Constitution does not explicitly protect a general right to privacy, the various guarantees within the Bill of Rights create "zones" of privacy, including a right to privacy in marital relations. The Court also found that the right to bear or conceive a child is a fundamental right that is protected by the U.S. Constitution. The Court found that the Connecticut statute was therefore unconstitutional. The Court's landmark decision—which was handed down five years after oral contraceptives became available to American women— legalized the use of birth control for married couples and paved the way for social acceptance of contraception.

Seven years later, in *Eisenstadt v. Baird*, the Court struck down a law in Massachusetts that permitted married couples to obtain contraceptives to prevent pregnancy but prohibited unmarried women from obtaining contraception. The case recognized that unmarried couples and individuals have a constitutionally protected right of privacy to choose contraception. Thus, reproductive rights and protections were extended equally to married and single people.

The final step in ensuring availability of contraception to all women was taken in 1977, in *Carey v. Population Services International*. The Supreme Court ruled in this case that New York's interest in discouraging teen sex could not justify denying minors and their parents choices that would reduce the chance of unwanted pregnancy. The decision extended to minors the individual's constitutionally protected right to make choices regarding contraception.

HOW DO WOMEN GET CONTRACEPTION?

It's one thing to have a constitutionally protected right to contraception; it's another thing entirely to go out and actually get

---

ASK A LAWYER

Q. *I've been told that the Constitution does not ever, not even once, mention the word "privacy." If this is true, then how do we have a constitutionally provided right to privacy that deals with so many intimate matters?*

A. The Constitution does not say "privacy," but it does say "liberty" in the Fourteenth Amendment. The Supreme Court has concluded that certain basic rights, including the right to privacy, are encompassed in the right to liberty.

—Answer by Marilyn Ireland
Professor, California Western School of Law,
San Diego, California

it. Depending on the kind of contraception you want to use, you may simply need to visit the local drug store, or you may need to get a prescription from a doctor for any of the different types of hormonal contraceptives.

Title X Clinics

Title X clinics are available to you regardless of your economic status, but they are particularly helpful to you if you are a lower-income woman. Title X of the Public Health Service Act was passed in 1970 to provide public family planning services and fulfill Richard M. Nixon's historic 1969 promise that "no American woman should be denied access to family planning assistance because of her economic condition." The Title X program is the only federal program devoted solely to the provision of family planning and reproductive health care, and through a network of clinics across the country it provides services to approximately 4.5 million people each year. Services are delivered through a network of community-based clinics that include state and local health departments, hospitals, university health centers, Planned Parenthood affiliates, independent clinics, and public and nonprofit agencies.

Title X also established a set of principles that guide the ethical delivery of contraceptive services, which require that services be voluntary, confidential, and affordable. These principles mean that a Title X clinic must offer you a broad range of contraceptive methods and cannot pressure you to accept a particular method; it must guarantee your confidentiality, even if you are a teenager; and it must offer services free of charge to you if you have a low income. All women are entitled to use Title X clinics, although if you have a higher income you will be required to pay for services. Fees are charged on a sliding scale based on income.

If you need access to contraception or family planning advice and you are uninsured or can't afford to pay a doctor, you can find your local Title X clinic in the phone book under "Family Planning Services" or by entering "Title X" and your city or state into your favorite search engine on the Internet.

States also pay for family planning services through Medicaid. See chapter 18, "Welfare, Poverty, and Government Benefits," to find out whether you could be eligible.

Insurance

If you have health insurance, you would probably visit your doctor if you needed a prescription for contraception. But wait a minute—are you sure your insurance will pay for contraception? Despite several false starts, there is no generally applicable federal law mandating insurance coverage of contraceptives. The proposed federal Equity in Prescription Insurance and Contraceptive Coverage Act, which would prohibit insurance companies that cover prescription drugs from excluding contraceptives, has not been passed. The current law governing insurance for contraception is a patchwork quilt across the states, and existing federal law does not apply to all employers.

Here is a brief rundown of how the law might affect you:

• Good news if you are an employee of the federal government. There is legislation that requires all health insurance plans available to federal employees to include coverage of prescription contraceptives if other prescription drugs are covered.

• Good news, too, if you are employed by an employer with fifteen or more employees. In December 2000, the Equal Employment Opportunity Commission (EEOC) ruled that an employer's exclusion of contraceptives from a health insurance plan that covers prescription drugs constituted impermissible sex discrimination under Title VII and the Pregnancy Discrimination Act (discussed in chapter 3). In a case the following year, a district court in Washington similarly held that an employer's failure to cover prescription contraceptives in its otherwise comprehensive prescription drug plan constituted sex discrimination under Title VII. The court stated that "[t]he special or increased healthcare needs associated with a woman's unique sex-based characteristics must be met to the same extent, and on the same terms, as other healthcare needs." The court found that the employer discriminated against its female employees "by providing less complete coverage than that offered to male employees." If you think your employer is covered by Title VII, but your health plan does not cover contraception, you can—and should—complain. Start with a complaint to your employer, and follow that up with a complaint to the EEOC. Chapter 3 provides more detailed information about filing a complaint or a lawsuit based on sex discrimination. But be aware that complaints and lawsuits can take years to resolve.

• As for state laws, it depends on where you live. Twenty-odd states have enacted legislation that specifically requires private insurance coverage of contraceptives when other prescription drugs are covered. In addition, many states have their own laws against sex discrimination in employment, which should be interpreted in exactly the same way as Title VII: if a health plan covers prescription drugs, then the failure to cover prescription contraceptives is sex discrimination. If your plan does not comply, you can tell your employer about the applicable state laws and pursue your state's remedies.

Another contraceptive option for some women is a permanent sterilization procedure called a tubal ligation, in which the fallopian tubes are cut, tied, or blocked, preventing eggs from getting to the uterus. This is a surgical procedure and is generally covered or partly covered by health insurance—read your policy or call your insurance company to find out whether you'll need to pay anything. And of course, women can ask their partners to use condoms, which, like other nonprescription drugs and devices, are typically not covered by health insurance.

ISSUES FOR YOUNG WOMEN

If you are a young woman and are becoming sexually active for the first time—and current statistics show that more than half of young women in the United States have sex before their seventeenth birthdays—you are probably most in need of reliable information about and access to contraception. There are several

○) ASK A LAWYER

Q. I'm the mother of a teenage girl, and frankly I would find it sickening if I was not told about matters that are basic to her health. Is that the law, and if so, under what convoluted reasoning did it get that way?

A. Unfortunately, some parents are abusive to sexually active girls. While most parents are good parents, a law that forces doctors to tell parents in all cases can actually be life threatening. How to solve this problem is complicated, so state laws vary. If a minor is sexually active, it is better for her to use contraception than to get pregnant, and telling parents can hinder this objective.

—Answer by Marilyn Ireland
Professor, California Western School of Law,
San Diego, California

A. A health care professional is permitted to tell a parent any medical information that a teenager gives permission to disclose. The teenager can also tell the parent directly. But in many states, a health care professional must treat a teenager's medical information as confidentially as she would an adult's medical information, even if the teenager's health care or health insurance is paid by the parent.

There is considerable variation from state to state as to (a) the age at which teenagers' medical information must not be disclosed directly to parents, (b) whether health care professionals must, by law, encourage teenagers to disclose their information to parents, and (c) what information the law covers. Studies indicate that adolescents are reluctant to receive medical care if they believe health care providers will disclose their secrets to parents.

—Answer by Bethany Spielman
Associate Professor of Medical Humanities and Law Director,
Medical Ethics Program, Southern Illinois University School
of Medicine

ways to obtain a prescription for contraception. Title X clinics provide confidential services for minors, with no need to show parental consent (although Title X guidelines require clinics to encourage parental involvement). Services are also confidential for minors under Medicaid programs. Several states have tried to place conditions on the provision of contraception and other reproductive services to minors through these services, but courts have not allowed such conditions on the basis that they are inconsistent with the federal requirements for Title X clinics.

If you are a minor and you visit your family doctor to seek a prescription for contraception, you will not necessarily be guaranteed the same confidentiality; the law differs from state to state. The rules often hinge on what the state defines as the **age of majority** (i.e., the age at which you become legally recognized as an adult) for health care purposes—in a few states, it's fourteen; in others, it's eighteen. In Montana, for example, your parents retain the right to access your medical records if you are under eighteen because they are considered to have the right to protect you from decisions you make as a minor. In Pennsylvania, on the other hand, you can receive contraception in confidence on the basis that when you have the right to consent to treatment or testing, you also have a right to confidentiality. Some states resolve the issue by letting the doctor decide whether it would be in your best interest to let your parents see the information.

If you're a young woman, you should also be aware that even if you are able to receive contraception from your doctor confidentially, notices sent to the person named on the insurance policy (usually the employee) may inadvertently disclose confidential information to your parents. If you are particularly concerned about confidentiality, you could ask your doctor not to bill the insurance company, but you would then have to bear the cost of the consultation and the prescription yourself. You should also remember that several kinds of contraception are available over the counter without a prescription, including condoms and spermicide.

(i) EMERGENCY CONTRACEPTION

Emergency contraception, sometimes called the "morning-after pill," is an option for women who have had unprotected sex or whose contraception has failed during sex, exposing them to the risk of pregnancy. The morning-after pill prevents pregnancy from occurring in several different ways: depending on the point at which it is taken in the cycle, it can prevent ovulation or prevent a fertilized egg from implanting in the uterus. These are the same ways in which regular contraceptive pills work. Emergency contraception is not the same thing as the abortion pill, which disrupts an established pregnancy after the fertilized egg has implanted in the womb. Emergency contraception is available by prescription from your doctor. In some states, pharmacists can dispense emergency contraception without a prescription.

Emergency contraception is not always available to women who need it because some state and federal legislation contains refusal clauses or "conscience clauses" that permit doctors and pharmacists to refuse to dispense medication that conflicts with their religious or moral beliefs. Advocates are seeking to reduce the scope of existing conscience clauses and prevent them from being added to new legislation. Catholic health care providers and hospitals may not provide emergency contraception in their hospitals. In some states, legislation requires hospitals to offer the pill to survivors of rape. Visit www.backupyourbirthcontrol.org or call 1-888-NOT-2-LATE for more information. Health professionals recommend that you learn about how and where to obtain emergency contraception in your area before an emergency arises.

THE WORLD AT YOUR FINGERTIPS

• The Office of Family Planning website at http://opa.osophs. dhhs.gov/titlex/ofp.html provides information on federal funding for family planning, including Title X. The National Family and Reproductive Health Association website includes a useful tool that allows you to find family planning clinics and Title X clinics in your city by entering your zip code at www.nfprha.org/clinics/.

• Many states mandate coverage of contraception in insurance plans that cover other prescription drugs. Find out about the law in your state by reading the National Women's Law Center (NWLC) report "Contraceptive Equity Laws in Your State" at www.nwlc.org/pdf/ConCovStateGuide2003.pdf. This guide gives you detailed information about how to file a complaint about your insurance company in states where contraception coverage is mandatory. The website also provides a guide for employees seeking to get prescription contraceptives covered under their employer health plan at www.nwlc.org/pill4us/index.cfm.

• The website of the Center for Reproductive Rights contains a web page showing in which states emergency contraception is available over the counter from a pharmacist, without a prescription, at www.reproductiverights.org/st_laws_ec.html.

• The Planned Parenthood Association of America has up-to-date information on the latest court cases and news related to contraception at www.ppfa.org. It includes links to Planned Parenthood Centers in your area, some of which allow you to get a prescription for emergency contraception online or over the phone.

• The Alan Guttmacher Institute at www.agi-usa.org contains a wealth of information about contraception and other reproductive health issues.

• The National Campaign to Prevent Teen Pregnancy contains valuable resources and research, for teenagers and for parents, at www.teenpregnancy.org. Another site, www.teenwire.com, includes practical information on how to use birth control effectively.

REMEMBER THIS

• Women can seek low-cost reproductive health services, including contraception, from Title X clinics across the United States. Medicaid also covers contraception.

• Not all insurance plans pay for contraception. Check the law in your state. If you think your insurance plan should, by law, cover contraception, take the initiative and make a complaint.

• Young women can seek contraception on a confidential basis from Title X clinics. Depending on state law, their confidentiality may not be protected if they seek a prescription from their family doctor.

CHAPTER 13

Pregnancy and Childbirth: The Facts of Life and the Law

Emma is five months pregnant and is enjoying pregnancy by eating (a lot!) of healthy food, going to yoga classes, and listening to music. She always planned on giving birth at home with the assistance of a midwife, as her mother did in the 1960s, surrounded by her friends and family. But the father of the child, Stephen, has other ideas. He worries about Emma's high blood pressure and thinks that she should give birth in a hospital, where doctors can step in if anything goes wrong. Stephen is also worried that Emma has occasionally drunk alcohol during her pregnancy and wants to know if there's anything he can do to stop her. Emma figures it's her baby, it's her body, and she can do whatever she wants when it comes to her pregnancy and giving birth.

Making the decision to have a child is one of the most important and personal decisions you can make. But the state, as well as your doctor, has a powerful interest in protecting you and your fetus from harm and may place limits on some of the choices you can make. This chapter will look at some of the ways in which the law might affect you during pregnancy, childbirth, and immediately after you've given birth.

PREGNANCY AND THE LAW

Drug and Alcohol Abuse During Pregnancy

If a woman can decide whether or not to use contraception or have an abortion, then she can decide what she wants to do with her body while she is pregnant, right? To a certain extent, this is true. For example, according to the National Center For Chronic Disease Prevention and Health Promotion, surveys show that up to 22 percent of all pregnant women smoke tobacco during pregnancy, despite the fact that smoking has been shown to cause low birth weights and other problems in newborn children. A woman can even continue to smoke despite the recommendations of her doctor and the wishes of the father of the child. But when it comes to drugs and alcohol, a pregnant woman does not always have the same freedom of choice.

No state has enacted laws specifically criminalizing a woman's behavior during pregnancy that poses a risk of harm to the fetus, but that hasn't stopped prosecutors in many states from filing criminal charges against women. Traditionally, a pregnant woman was exempt from criminal liability for conduct that harmed the fetus. Even in states in which abortion was a crime, only the doctor could be charged; the woman was considered a victim. Recently, though, prosecutors in many states have tried to prosecute women under existing criminal laws for behavior that endangers their fetuses. For example, prosecutors have argued that pregnant women delivered drugs to minor children—fetuses—through the umbilical cord, and a new mother's positive drug test has led to charges of assault with a deadly weapon (cocaine). The Center for Reproductive Rights estimates that over two hundred women have been prosecuted in more than thirty states for alleged drug use while pregnant. Many of them have pleaded guilty or accepted plea bargains.

In cases where women have gone to court to dispute the charges, they've won almost every time. Some courts have interpreted criminal legislation narrowly so that legislation referring to a "child" does not include a fetus; others have recognized that such prosecutions violate women's rights to due process and privacy.

The exception is the South Carolina Supreme Court, which in 1997 upheld the prosecution of a woman who smoked crack cocaine during her pregnancy and whose baby was born with cocaine in its system. The woman was subsequently imprisoned for eight years. In *Whitner v. South Carolina*, the court held that a viable fetus was a "child" under the state's criminal child endangerment statute. The U.S. Supreme Court would not hear Cornelia Whitner's appeal, so the South Carolina decision still stands. In a later South Carolina case, Regina McKnight, another crack cocaine addict, was convicted of murder and jailed after her daughter was stillborn. The U.S. Supreme Court also declined to hear her appeal.

Can a hospital test you for drug use without your consent? The answer is no, but do be careful of what you sign. One hospital in South Carolina developed a policy of administering drug tests to pregnant women and cooperating with the city in prosecuting women whose infants tested positive for drugs. Some obstetrical patients arrested after testing positive for cocaine filed a suit challenging the policy, on the theory that drug tests conducted as part of a criminal investigation were unconstitutional searches unless there was a search warrant or unless the person being tested consented. The U.S. Supreme Court ruled in 2001 that the drug tests were indeed unconstitutional.

If you are pregnant and addicted to drugs or have a problem with alcohol, doctors recommend that you continue to seek prenatal care and get treatment for your addiction from a professional. If you are charged under state laws with endangering your fetus, seek advice from a lawyer about whether to challenge the charges in court. Courts have found in favor of the woman in every state except South Carolina.

Discrimination Laws

In 1998, television soap star Hunter Tylo was awarded $5 million in damages in a pregnancy discrimination lawsuit. After Tylo revealed that she was pregnant, Aaron Spelling fired the actress from a new role in the show *Melrose Place* before filming began.

Many women want to work when they are planning to have a child or during their pregnancy. As long as you can perform the major functions of your job, your employer cannot fire you, change your responsibilities, or refuse to hire you because you are pregnant. You may also be entitled to pregnancy leave or leave to give birth if your employer gives sick leave to other employees. Chapters 4 and 5 contain more information on the Pregnancy Discrimination Act.

(i) FETAL HOMICIDE LAWS

Laci Peterson was in her eighth month of pregnancy when she disappeared. Her husband, Scott, was charged with her murder and the murder of her fetus under fetal homicide laws. Fetal homicide laws have been passed in some states to enable the conviction of people who cause the death of fetuses. All of these laws have an exception for abortion. Under California law, murder charges can result if the fetus is older than seven weeks. To convict Peterson of murdering his unborn son, prosecutors must prove that he intended to kill the fetus or knew that it would die as a result of his wife's death. Not all fetal homicide laws require prosecutors to show that a person intended to kill a fetus. Opponents of fetal homicide laws have expressed concern that these laws could be used to convict pregnant women whose abuse of drugs or alcohol harms their fetuses. Such laws could also be used to prosecute women whose fetuses are harmed during pregnancy as a result of their failing to adhere strictly to medical advice, for example, bed rest orders.

The federal Unborn Victims of Violence Act, also known as Laci and Conner's Law, was passed on April 1, 2004. The act has been criticized as an attempt to undermine a woman's right to have an abortion by granting separate legal personhood to a fetus. It has been suggested that crimes of this nature are more appropriately addressed by enhancing penalties for injury to a pregnant woman, rather than creating crimes for injury to a fetus.

CHILDBIRTH CHOICES

Childbirth certainly hasn't changed much in millennia, but the choices women make when it comes to giving birth drift in and out of vogue. A century ago, American women usually gave birth at home, attended by a female midwife if they could afford it, in varying levels of cleanliness and safety, and usually in a great deal of pain. Some women gave birth in hospitals, but infections were so rampant that even that was unsafe. By 1960, most women were giving birth in hospitals. Often, their husbands were not allowed to be present at the birth, and women were given medication for pain without being asked for their consent.

Today, women have some choices about the way they want to give birth. A number of communities offer women the option of giving birth in a hospital, at home, or at a birthing center. The majority of births still take place in the hospital, but that experience has changed as well. Today, women may accept or reject medication for pain and other procedures. The woman's family and friends are allowed to remain with her throughout the labor and delivery. Some hospitals even allow couples to videotape the birth; other hospitals do not permit this for fear of malpractice suits. The new mother decides whether to keep the baby with her in her room or allow the baby to be cared for in the nursery. These changes were not, in large part, brought about by changes in the law. Rather, hospitals changed their policies as a result of societal changes, such as women becoming stronger advocates for their health care. Also, as health care has become more competitive, hospitals have had to become more attuned to the needs and wants of pregnant women and change their policies accordingly.

Not that parents haven't tried to use the legal system to change the status quo. Several couples who had taken Lamaze classes sued a hospital because the hospital prohibited fathers from being in the delivery room. The couples argued that they had a constitutional right to choose whether or not the fathers should be present at the birth. The court ruled that there is no constitutional right to choosing birthing methods, and the couples lost their case.

Home Births

Many parents look to home births because they want to deliver their babies in a familiar setting where they can be more in charge. Some literature concludes that for low-risk women, a planned home birth is as safe as a planned hospital birth.

(i) INFORMED CONSENT

In order to perform surgery or administer drugs, a doctor must have your informed consent. This applies during childbirth—a doctor must tell you what a procedure involves in a way that you understand and secure your consent before he or she can give you drugs or commence a surgical procedure. Informed consent gives you more power in decisions about your medical care, but it also gives you more responsibility. And there are limits: You cannot force your doctor to step outside the bounds of good medical judgment, to violate medical ethics, or to perform alternative treatment he or she considers too risky. You can also withdraw your consent to a procedure. Obviously, it is best to change your mind *before* the doctor begins a surgical procedure.

For example, in Wisconsin a woman went into labor and was admitted to the hospital. She had planned on, and was prepared for, a vaginal delivery. During delivery she changed her mind and three times asked her doctor to perform a cesarean. The doctor continued to prepare for a vaginal delivery. When complications arose during delivery, the doctor delivered the baby by cesarean. The baby was paralyzed from the neck down.

The woman sued the doctor because he did not acknowledge that she withdrew her consent to a vaginal delivery. The doctor argued that once the vaginal delivery began, the patient could not withdraw her consent. The woman won the case. Because a cesarean delivery was a viable medical alternative to a vaginal delivery, the woman had the right to withdraw her consent to a vaginal delivery. When she withdrew her consent, the doctor was obligated to discuss with her the consequences of her withdrawal and her options at that point.

Although the woman won in Wisconsin, the law varies from state to state. In every state, though, you have the right to withdraw your consent. Your doctor should discuss with you the effects this will have on your treatment, but the ultimate decision is generally up to you.

It is legal in all states for doctors to attend home births. However, the majority of doctors refuse to do home births because of the fear of malpractice lawsuits or because their insurance does not cover home births. Nevertheless, some doctors are in favor of home births, believing them to be the better choice for expectant mothers at low risk for a difficult childbirth.

↻ ASK A LAWYER

Q. *I am thirty-four years old and am pregnant for the first time. My doctor would like me to have an amniocentesis so that he can examine the baby's cells in the amniotic fluid. I am more worried about the risks associated with amniocentesis—including miscarriage. Is there any way my doctor can force me to take a test that I don't want to take?*

A. Unless you live in California, where by law pregnant women must undergo prenatal testing for neural tube defects (brain defects caused by incomplete development of the brain, spinal cord, and their protective coverings), a physician cannot compel you to undergo prenatal testing. However, a physician may refuse to treat you if you refuse to undergo testing. Usually, the physician is more concerned about his or her malpractice liability if you refuse a test than about your health. In making a decision about whether to have a prenatal test, it is important to really consider what you will do with the test results. Will you take action? Will it answer questions about your baby? Will it provide you with emotional relief? Too often, women undergo testing because their doctor recommends it, but they don't think about what they will do with the information once they get it. If the test results aren't going to change your feelings or actions, why bother with an expensive and risky procedure? Stick to your guns and resist the doctor's pressure; you know what is best for your body and your pregnancy.

—Answer by Ami Jaeger
BioLawGroup LLC, Santa Fe, New Mexico

One doctor in Chicago claims his group of physicians has delivered fourteen thousand babies in home births in the last twenty-five years.

Midwives

Midwifery is a body of knowledge regarding normal maternity care. This was originally the province of midwives and women, but was slowly taken over by obstetricians, who were known as man-midwives. If you do decide to deliver at home, then being attended by a midwife becomes an option. In some states, midwives can also have a role in hospital births. The following is a guide to the choices you may have in your state:

Certified nurse-midwives are registered nurses trained in obstetrics and often work in conjunction with a doctor. How closely they are regulated varies from state to state. Some hospitals ban certified nurse-midwives from attending births in the hospital, preferring that only the hospital's doctors be present. On the other hand, some states allow certified nurse-midwives to obtain hospital privileges, prescribe medications to women, and attend births in homes, hospitals, or birth centers. They can provide family planning and women's health care, as well as prenatal and birthing care, and are trained through programs approved by the American College of Nurse Midwives. An estimated four thousand nurse-midwives are presently certified throughout the country. Certified nurse-midwives often staff midwifery centers. These are good places to go because they always have hospital backup, emergency transfer arrangements in place, and an agreement with an obstetrician-gynecologist. They often have as good or better outcome rates than hospital maternity rates. Nowadays, many hospitals own midwifery centers.

Licensed or **certified midwives** (sometimes also called **direct-entry midwives**) are not required to be nurses, although nurses are not excluded from being licensed or certified. These midwives are trained through a combination of apprenticeships, correspondence courses, self-study, and formal schooling. These midwives must meet or exceed the state's requirements for midwifery by documenting their experience and passing both skills and academic exams. Direct-entry midwifery is legally recognized in some way in more than half the states. A handful of these states allow Medicaid reimbursement for licensed midwives, as do many insurance companies. Licensed midwives can sign birth certificates and are generally required to have doctor backup and emergency procedures lined up in case something goes wrong during delivery.

Traditional or **lay midwives** are not licensed by a state and are not required to be trained as nurses. States differ widely as to how they regulate lay midwifery. This means that the quantity and quality of available midwives varies greatly from one state to the next. Some states make traditional midwifery illegal, no matter what. Other states have laws regarding certified nurse-midwives, but do not mention traditional midwives at all. In those states, lay midwives are generally considered acceptable as long as they do not engage in the unlicensed practice of medicine. In some states, this may mean that midwives are banned from asking for payment for their services. Some midwives are part of a religious group and practice only within that specific community. There are currently an estimated two to three thousand traditional midwives practicing in the United States.

Lay midwifery is considered in some states to be the **unlicensed practice of medicine**, which is illegal. Midwifery is considered practicing medicine because courts have held that pregnancy is a physical condition that requires medical attention, the use of medical instruments, and possibly drugs. These are the essential factors in practicing medicine, which only licensed doctors are allowed to do.

Midwives are rarely brought up on charges of practicing without a license, although it occasionally does happen. In California, several women who acted as traditional (unlicensed) midwives for women in childbirth were arrested and charged under a California law. The women argued that the law deprived pregnant women of their right to privacy. The court said that the law against attending and assisting a pregnant woman in childbirth did not violate the expectant mother's right to privacy. It also said that the state has an interest in the life and well-being of the unborn child. Thus, the state could require midwives to be licensed, even though that would significantly reduce the number of midwives available to expectant mothers.

For the most part, traditional midwives regulate themselves within their states. Opinion is sharply divided over whether that self-regulation is enough to guarantee quality. Some observers point out that qualified midwives perform good work and provide an alternative for parents who may not be able to afford a physician-assisted hospital birth or may not choose to seek such assistance. But unqualified, unlicensed midwives can (and unfortunately sometimes do) cause real harm.

Some self-regulation programs appear to have real merit. In Oregon, the Oregon Midwifery Council puts forth its own certification standards for traditional midwives and requires intense training for its midwives. It offers advanced certification for midwives who wish to specialize in higher-risk births such as breech or multiple births. Some of the Oregon Midwifery Council's regulations were later enacted by the state legislature to license traditional midwives and allow them to be reimbursed under the state Medicaid program.

If you want to give birth at home with the assistance of a midwife, you should ask about her education, credentials, and experience attending home births. Ask whether she has been sued. Find out whether she has admitting privileges at the hospital (meaning whether she can continue to care for you if you're transferred there) or whether she can at least accompany you and stay with you if you're transferred there. You'll also want to ask her whether she has a consulting physician at the hospital and whether the physician is willing to take home-birth transfers.

MINIMUM HOSPITAL STAYS AFTER BIRTH

If you choose to give birth in a hospital, the law steps in to regulate the length of time that your insurance company must pay

---

(i) BREASTFEEDING

Health professionals agree that breastfeeding provides benefits to babies, and more than half the states have enacted laws relating to breastfeeding. Nineteen states allow mothers to breastfeed in any public or private location, and thirteen states exempt breastfeeding from public indecency laws. Ten states have laws related to breastfeeding in the workplace. Five states exempt breastfeeding mothers from jury duty. Four states have implemented or encouraged the development of a breastfeeding awareness education campaign. There are no laws that prohibit breastfeeding in a public place. You can find more information on the laws relating to breastfeeding in your state at www.ncsl.org/pro-grams/health/breast50.htm.

---

for you and your baby to stay in the hospital after you give birth. The federal Newborns' and Mothers' Health Protection Act does not require health plans to include coverage for hospital stays after childbirth. But if your plan does include this kind of coverage, then insurers and health plans may not restrict benefits to less than forty-eight hours following a vaginal delivery or ninety-six hours following a delivery by caesarean section. If you have your baby in the hospital, the time period begins at the time of delivery. If you deliver outside the hospital and are later admitted to the hospital in connection with childbirth, the period begins at the time of the admission. This does not mean that it is compulsory for a new mother to stay in the hospital for the entire period—she can leave if she wishes and if her doctor or other health provider agrees. But a mother cannot be encouraged to accept less than the minimum protections available to her under the act.

The federal act might not apply to you depending on whether your plan is insured or self-insured. There are confusing distinctions here, and it's probably best for you to contact

(i) WRONGFUL PREGNANCY AND WRONGFUL BIRTH

If you or your husband has been sterilized and you subsequently become pregnant, you may be able to sue the doctor who performed the faulty sterilization procedure for wrongful pregnancy or wrongful birth. You might be able to recover money damages for pre- and postnatal delivery expenses, pain and suffering incidental to pregnancy and delivery, loss of income, and loss of consortium (sexual relations). A few states let parents sue doctors for all of the expenses involved in raising the child.

You might also be able to bring a wrongful birth claim if you were not informed during pregnancy that your child has birth defects and were therefore deprived of the choice of whether to continue the pregnancy.

your plan administrator to find out if the federal act applies. Remember, federal law does not require plans to provide any hospital coverage for childbirth. And the federal act does not prevent a health plan from imposing deductibles or copayments relating to hospital stays for childbirth.

THE WORLD AT YOUR FINGERTIPS

• The website for the Center for Reproductive Rights contains the paper "Punishing Women for their Behavior during Pregnancy," which discusses the kinds of actions that have been brought against pregnant women whose actions endanger their fetuses. You can find it at www.reproductiverights.org/pub_bp_punwom.html. The center also provides links to some of the reproductive laws in each state at www.reproductiverights.org/st_laws.html.

• You can find a chart showing fetal homicide laws state by state at the Alan Guttmacher Institute at www.agi-usa.org/media/pdf/fa_chart042403.pdf. The American Civil Liberties

Union website contains some information on the perceived problems of fetal rights legislation; search "fetal rights" on the website at www.aclu.org.

• The American College of Nurse Midwives in Washington, D.C., can direct you to home-birth resources, including a list of certified nurse-midwives in your area. You can visit its website at www.midwife.org.

• The Midwives Alliance of North America contains more information about midwives, including a link to the laws on direct-entry midwives in each state, at www.mana.org.

• Tracie Hotchner's *Pregnancy and Childbirth* (1997) includes an extensive section on home birth, from how to choose a home-birthing midwife to what to do in various emergencies.

• You can find more information about the Newborns' and Mothers' Health Protection Act at www.cms.hhs.gov/hipaa/hipaa1/content/nmhpa.asp.

• Contact your local state department of insurance to find out whether your state has laws that may take precedence over the federal Newborns' and Mothers' Health Protection Act. You can find your state office's website at the National Association of Insurance Commissioners website at www.naic.org/state_contacts/sid_websites.htm.

REMEMBER THIS

• So-called fetal rights get a lot of press, but only South Carolina's courts have upheld convictions against women for their actions during pregnancy that have harmed their fetuses. Many states do have specific laws criminalizing fetal homicide by persons other than the mother, and a federal law protecting fetal rights was passed in 2004.

• Doctors must ask for your consent to surgical procedures like a cesarean and before they administer drugs, if it is practicable to do so.

• State law regulates midwives. If you want a midwife to assist in your home birth, you should ensure that she is experienced.

Regardless, you should still have a backup plan for getting to the hospital if something goes wrong.

• Federal and state laws regulate the amount of time that your health insurance must pay for you to stay in the hospital after you've given birth.

CHAPTER 14

Abortion: A Deeply Felt and Controversial Issue

Caroline is twenty-one years old and is six weeks pregnant by her former boyfriend, Mike. Caroline just finished school, doesn't have a job yet, and can't expect any support from her family if she has a child out of wedlock. Uncertain about what to do, she is thinking about her options. Mike wants Caroline to have the baby. He says he will provide support and help look after the child, although Caroline doubts that he will be willing—or able—to fulfill these commitments indefinitely.

Every year, millions of American women find themselves having to make the very personal and emotional decision that Caroline faces. The U.S. Supreme Court's decision in *Roe v. Wade*, and the fact that Caroline is over eighteen, means that it is a choice that only she can make. But if Caroline decides she wants to have an abortion, state laws may require her to go through a waiting period after she has seen her doctor and made an appointment. If Caroline has a low income she may not be able to afford an abortion since it is not federally funded through Title X clinics or Medicaid, except when necessary to save the life of the woman, or in cases of rape or incest.

This chapter will take a look at the history of abortion and then explore the law—and some of the controversies—relating to abortion today.

THE HISTORY OF ABORTION

You might think of abortion as a practice made possible by relatively recent advances in medicine, but in fact abortion was induced surgically and by herbs in ancient Greece, Rome, and Egypt. In the thousands of years that followed, abortion continued to be a legal and socially accepted, if private, practice. Fetuses were generally aborted before "quickening," that is, before the woman felt the fetus move, which generally happened in the fourth or fifth month. But in the nineteenth century, the law and public opinion started to change. The first English act outlawing abortion was passed in 1803. A similar act was passed in Connecticut in 1821, and by 1860 abortion was prohibited in most states.

Abortion became more difficult for women to procure after these laws were passed, particularly as midwives were replaced by doctors and the practice of abortion moved from the home to clinics and hospitals. As abortion became more public and more visible, it became correspondingly more vulnerable to medical and legal sanction. By the 1940s, the practice was often an illegal back-alley procedure. Having an abortion became a dangerous business for a woman, who faced the possibility of a botched operation by an untrained and inexperienced person, resulting in infection, injury, excessive bleeding, or death. Whiskey was sometimes used as an anesthetic.

In the 1960s and early 1970s, the Supreme Court handed down a series of rulings that recognized a zone of personal privacy in reproductive matters. These rulings limited the authority of states to interfere with private reproductive decisions. In 1973, in the landmark case *Roe v. Wade*, the Court decided that women have a fundamental right to have an abortion. In *Roe*, a single pregnant woman (who appeared under the pseudonym Jane Roe) brought a lawsuit against the state of Texas. Texas law made abortion illegal except in situations where the mother's life was at stake. The Court held that women have a constitutional right of privacy that is "fundamental" and "broad enough to encompass a woman's decision . . . to terminate her pregnancy." Because the right is fundamental, the state must demonstrate a "compelling state interest" in order to restrict it and the state is unable to demonstrate such an interest before the fetus becomes viable. So only a woman can make a decision whether to have an abortion in the first trimester of pregnancy. Once the fetus becomes viable, meaning it can live outside the womb, the government can regulate—and even outlaw—abortion unless the woman's health or life is endangered. There is no definite point, however, at which a fetus becomes viable, and this determination is left up to the judgment of the woman's physician.

In 1992, the Supreme Court heard the case of *Planned Parenthood v. Casey*. The Court in *Casey* affirmed the core holding of *Roe*: that states cannot outlaw abortion before the fetus becomes viable. However, the Court added that states can regulate abortions before viability, so long as any restriction does not impose an "undue burden" on the pregnant woman's right to have an abortion. An undue burden is a "substantial obstacle in the path of a woman seeking an abortion before the fetus attains viability." In this case, the Court held that a law's requirement that a woman notify her spouse before having an abortion was an undue burden. However, a requirement that a woman wait twenty-four hours before having an abortion was not an undue burden; neither was the law's requirement that a minor notify one parent or appear before a judge before having an abortion.

The decision in *Roe* recognized the right of women to have an abortion, but there is still no absolute right to have an abortion at any time or under any circumstance. The state cannot completely override a woman's right to terminate a pregnancy, but it does have an interest in protecting the health of pregnant women and the potentiality of human life and can place some limits on abortions as long as it does not cross certain boundaries. Abortion remains a highly contentious topic, caught between the competing worlds of law, religion, and privacy. In the words of the majority of the Supreme Court in *Sternberg v. Carhart*, decided in 2000, "Millions of Americans believe that life begins at conception and consequently that an abortion is akin to causing the death of an innocent child; they recoil at the thought of a law that would permit it. Other millions fear that a law that forbids abortion could condemn many American women to lives that lack dignity, depriving them of equal liberty and leading those with least resources to undergo illegal abortions with the attendant risks of death and suffering. [These are] virtually irreconcilable points of view."

(i) HUSBANDS AND ABORTIONS

In a perfect world, a husband and wife would agree on whether or not the wife should have an abortion. In the present world, if a husband and wife do not agree, then the wife's decision is final. Husbands or biological fathers do not have the right to have input into the decision of a woman on whether to have an abortion. This is not because their opinions do not matter. It is because the woman's right to control her body is paramount over any right of her husband or boyfriend.

WAITING PERIODS

The Supreme Court upheld laws mandating waiting periods in the 1992 case of *Planned Parenthood v. Casey*. Several states currently require a waiting period, usually twenty-four hours, before a woman can have an abortion. If there is a waiting period in your state, then you will need to make two visits to the clinic where the abortion will be performed. At the first visit, you will need to talk to the doctor or other medical professional about your choice to terminate the pregnancy. State law may require the doctor to give you specific information about fetal development to assist you in making a final decision about what to do about your pregnancy. You'll then have to wait at least twenty-four hours to think about whether or not to terminate your pregnancy and return to the clinic for the procedure. Some view this requirement as a burden to discourage you from having an abortion and argue that a woman already has time to think over her decision between the time she finds out she's pregnant and the time she schedules an abortion. Others think that twenty-four hours is a small inconvenience in light of the significance of the decision you will be making about your pregnancy. There are exceptions to the waiting-period requirement where your health or life may be endangered by the delay.

⚠ REFUSAL CLAUSES

Many states' abortion laws contain "refusal clauses" that give doctors the right to refuse to perform abortions on moral and religious grounds. Hospitals and clinics that are owned by churches may also refuse to perform abortions. In some states, doctors can even refuse to perform sterilization procedures, like tubal ligations. You should check with your doctor and hospital to find out whether these medical services will be provided when necessary if you want them.

BANS ON PARTIAL-BIRTH ABORTIONS

The most controversial debate today is over so-called partial-birth abortions. Although this is not a recognized medical term, state laws have usually defined a partial-birth abortion as any abortion in which a doctor "partially vaginally delivers a living fetus before killing the fetus and completing the delivery." These bans generally apply to nonviable as well as viable fetuses. This definition is broad enough to include several kinds of abortions, including some abortions commonly conducted in the second trimester of pregnancy.

Several states have passed laws prohibiting partial-birth abortions. In almost every state that has passed such laws, courts have found them to be unconstitutional. These laws often impose an undue burden on a woman's right to terminate a pregnancy (by outlawing safe and commonly used methods of second-trimester abortion) and fail to include adequate exceptions for abortions in situations where the woman's life or health is endangered.

Bills have been repeatedly introduced in Congress to make partial-birth abortions illegal on a national level. On November 5, 2003, President George W. Bush signed the first federal ban on partial-birth abortion into law. The law is similar to laws that the Supreme Court has previously determined to be unconstitutional, in that it includes an exception where the abortion is necessary for the life of the mother, but does not include an exception to protect the health of the mother. It imposes a two-year prison sentence on doctors who perform this type of abortion. In the days after the law was enacted, several federal judges temporarily blocked enforcement of the law, stating that it is unconstitutional because it does not contain an exception to protect a woman's health. These rulings prevent the law being enforced against the majority of abortion providers across the country until hearings on the constitutionality of the law. The case, *Carhart v. Ashcroft*, was heard in Nebraska federal courts in 2004. The issue may well go to the Supreme Court again.

PARENTAL CONSENT LAWS

The right of parents to raise their children as they see fit collides with a woman's right to privacy when she is under the age of eighteen. When it comes to women under eighteen years of age seeking abortions, state laws fall into three groups:
- Young women do not have to get permission or notify their parents of the abortion.
- Young women do not have to get their parents' permission, but they do have to notify their parents that they are planning on having an abortion.
- Young women have to get their parents' permission to have an abortion.

All parental consent laws are required to be very limited in their range, and they must include what is called a **judicial bypass option**. A judicial bypass option allows you to go to court for a judicial hearing if you are under eighteen, if you do not want to tell your parents about your pregnancy, or if your parents refuse to consent to an abortion. Judges are likely to grant your request for an abortion if you can show that you are mature enough to make this decision on your own. If the judge finds that you are not mature enough, then he or she will consider whether it would be in your best interest to have an abortion

(i) ABORTION PROTESTERS

Several nationwide antiabortion groups have organized protests against doctors who perform abortions or against clinics where abortions are performed. Such protests have occasionally included serious violence against clinics performing abortions, including murder, bombing, arson, invasion, and vandalism. In 1993, antiabortionist Michael Griffin shot and killed Dr. David Gunn, a doctor who had performed abortions. One year later, President Bill Clinton signed the Freedom of Access to Clinic Entrances (FACE) Act. FACE makes it illegal to use force or "physical obstruction" against a person who is engaged in "obtaining or providing reproductive health services."

Several states have also passed legislation designed to protect clinic staff and women seeking an abortion. Some states have passed "buffer-zone" legislation that requires antiabortion protesters to keep a minimum distance away from patients seeking reproductive services at a clinic. There have been several First Amendment challenges to these state laws by activists who claim that in picketing clinics they are simply exercising their right to free speech. The Supreme Court has upheld aspects of some buffer-zone laws and struck down others, balancing the right to free speech against the government's interest in ensuring public safety and order. The Supreme Court has upheld a law that prohibits demonstrators from approaching within eight feet of anyone coming to or leaving from medical clinics. It has rejected a law that prohibits displaying images, approaching patients within three hundred feet of a clinic, and peacefully picketing within three hundred feet of an employee's residence. The First Amendment Center provides a good summary at www. firstamendmentcenter.org/assembly/topic.aspx?topic=buffer_zones.

(taking into account, for example, your home life, your education, and whether you have the support of your family).

This can be a traumatic experience if you are a young woman. Courtrooms are intimidating, hearings are scheduled during school hours, and you must discuss your most personal concerns with the judge, a total stranger. If you would like an advocate to assist you, a free lawyer must generally be appointed to help you.

Those in favor of parental consent laws say young women need the support of their families when making such significant decisions about whether or not to have an abortion. Many believe that parental consent laws promote abstinence, arguing that if girls knew they couldn't have abortions without telling their parents, then they would not be so willing to have sex and risk pregnancy. Those against parental consent laws point out that such laws may exacerbate already-difficult situations in certain families and may even increase instances of abuse against the girls involved. A 1992 study by the American Medical Association showed that parental consent and notification laws "increase the gestational age at which the induced pregnancy termination occurs, thereby also increasing the risk associated with the procedure." A first- or second-trimester abortion is considered medically safer than childbirth. For each week that goes by after the first eight weeks, the risk of death or major complications significantly increases. When Massachusetts passed its parental consent law, one study found that one-third of the minors who had abortions traveled out of state to do so. Those minors tended to be affluent teenagers with access to the cash and transportation required to cross state lines.

PAYING FOR AN ABORTION

Insurance

There are several states that prohibit coverage of abortion by private insurance plans unless a woman pays an extra premium, but for the most part it is a matter for the individual insurance provider, and you can choose a provider that includes abortion coverage if you wish to do so. The Pregnancy Discrimination Act does not require plans to provide coverage for abortions.

( ) ASK A LAWYER

Q. If a "viable" fetus is a fetus that can live outside the womb, won't the meaning of this standard change as medical technologies enable premature babies to be born earlier? Is it possible that in the foreseeable future abortions over, say, four months could be illegal?

A. The viability standard is, indeed, dependent on medical technology. It is not a clear and unchangeable legal standard and could lead, over time, to a reduction in the length of time a woman has to decide on an abortion.

—Answer by Marilyn Ireland
Professor, California Western School of Law,
San Diego, California

A. A fetus is viable at approximately twenty-six weeks, but this is a moving target as neonatal care and technology interventions increase.

—Answer by Ami Jaeger
BioLawGroup LLC, Santa Fe, New Mexico

Q. How can a young woman convince a judge that an abortion is in her "best interests"? Doesn't it basically come down to the judge's personal beliefs on abortion?

A. A judge's personal belief should not, but sometimes does, interfere with a fair determination. If you think that the judge was biased, a rapid appeal may be your answer. It is rarely true that a minor who is too immature to make a decision to have an abortion would be better off having a child she does not want.

—Answer by Marilyn Ireland
Professor, California Western School of Law,
San Diego, California

(i) THE ABORTION PILL

The Food and Drug Administration (FDA) approved mifepristone—commonly referred to as the abortion pill or RU 486—in September 2000, after the pill had been available in Europe for more than a decade. The pill offers women an effective medical alternative to surgical abortion. Under the current FDA-approved regimen, it can be administered by your doctor and requires several visits to a clinic or doctor's office. The abortion pill is not to be confused with the "morning-after pill," discussed in chapter 12, which can be taken within seventy-two hours of unprotected sex to prevent pregnancy.

Medicaid Coverage for Abortions

In 1976, Congress passed a law called the Hyde Amendment that prohibits federal Medicaid funds being used to fund abortions. There are some exceptions under this law, including in cases of rape or incest, or where a pregnant woman's life is endangered by a physical illness, disorder, or injury.

This federal law does not prevent states from using state funding to pay for the abortions of low-income women. However, fewer than half of the states provide public funding for abortions. In some of these states, courts have ordered that abortion must be publicly funded on the same terms as other pregnancy-related and general health services, in accordance with state constitutions.

THE WORLD AT YOUR FINGERTIPS

• The Alan Guttmacher Institute provides overviews of abortion laws in the states. You can find a map of the states at www.agi-usa.org/pubs/sfaa.html—simply click on your state to access a fact sheet about abortion, which includes statistical and demographic information on who receives abortions.

• The Kaiser Family Foundation provides research, analysis, and fact sheets on women's health issues, including abortion, at www.kff.org/womenshealth/repro.cfm.

• You can visit the American Civil Liberties Union website to find out whether your state funds abortion for low-income women at http://archive.aclu.org/issues/reproduct/funding_abortion.pdf.

• *Abortion* (1998), by Rita James Simon, compares American abortion laws with those in other countries. In addition, she discusses how a nation's policies on population control affect its laws on abortion.

• *The Politics of Abortion and Motherhood* (1985), by Kristen Luker, charts the history of attitudes toward abortion and examines the issues, people, and beliefs on both sides of the abortion conflict.

REMEMBER THIS

• States cannot make abortion a crime before the fetus is viable. However, states can restrict access to abortion prior to viability, as long as the restrictions do not place an "undue burden" on a woman's right to have an abortion. For example, states can require a woman to go through a waiting period to have an abortion.

• Laws regulating abortion must contain an exception, allowing abortion if a woman's life or health is at stake.

• The federal law prohibiting so-called partial-birth abortion has been challenged. Stay tuned to see if it is found constitutional.

• Some states require minors to get parental consent before seeking an abortion. The laws are constitutional, but only if they give minors the option of seeking a judicial bypass.

PART FIVE

Violence Against Women

CHAPTER 15

Sexual Assault:
Sexual Assault and the
Legal Process

Adrienne was in her first year of college when she started dating Dean. After they'd been out a few times, he started pressuring her to have sex with him. Adrienne didn't feel ready and fended off his advances. He said he was okay with her decision, but a few weeks later he took Adrienne to a party and forced her to have sex with him afterward, despite the fact that she said no.

Adrienne feels like it's her fault she was assaulted and does not know what to do. Dean will just tell everyone that she consented, so how can she prove otherwise?

Violence against women and girls takes many forms, including physical, psychological, and economic abuse. It may manifest itself in violent crimes including murder, rape, and sexual assault. Unfortunately, in many cultures violence against women is legitimized and perpetuated by long-standing beliefs, norms, and social institutions. Violent acts often go unchallenged when men direct them at women—especially within the home and family. In the United States, the two most common forms of violence against women are sexual assault and domestic violence. According to the U.S. Department of Justice, over 2 million women are actually victims of violence—from strangers, acquaintances, and family members—across the United States every year. Many women do not report their abuse to authorities, so they are not represented in official crime statistics.

This chapter will take a close look at some of the law relating to sexual assault and will provide you with some useful and prac-

ⓘ I'M A SURVIVOR

We use the term "victim" in this section to describe women who have suffered sexual assault. Some people suggest that using this word reinforces the notion of women as weak and passive, and instead urge that the term "survivor" should be used, to emphasize the strength of women who persevere after the trauma of sexual assault. Our intent is to empower you with information. The law speaks in terms of victims of crime and we use the same word here—not to insult or belittle but to be precise and consistent.

tical information on what do and what to expect if you are a victim of sexual assault.

SEXUAL ASSAULT

Sexual assault can occur in your childhood, adolescence, or adulthood. The offender can be your friend, your employer, your relative, your husband or partner, or a stranger. It can happen to you regardless of your age, race, physical ability, sexual orientation, economic status, or religious heritage.

You may have noticed that crimes that once were called "rapes" are now reported in the news media by other names, such as "criminal sexual conduct." **Rape**, as used in the Department of Justice's annual National Crime Victimization Survey, is forced sexual intercourse, whether the force is psychological or physical. The force can take the form of threats, bribes, manipulation, or violence. Sexual intercourse means vaginal, anal, or oral penetration by one or more offenders. Penetration by a foreign object (such as a bottle) is included. The definition includes attempted rapes, male and female victims, and heterosexual and homosexual rape. **Sexual assault** is the umbrella term we use in this chapter to cover all illegal unwanted sexual conduct—of which rape is a subcategory. It covers all types of rape, as well as child molestation, incest, sexual harassment, and indecent exposure.

Sexual assault laws are gender neutral. This means that women can sexually assault men, women can sexually assault other women, and men can sexually assault other men. State laws generally categorize different types of illegal conduct (i.e., penetration or unwanted touching or fondling) by degree. You

---

(i) FEDERAL LAWS HELP ABUSED WOMEN

Congress has passed several laws that seek to prevent or reduce violence against women. For example, the **Victims of Trafficking and Violence Protection Act** includes provisions to strengthen law enforcement and services to victims of violent crimes and limit the effects of violence against children. The **Jacob Wetterling Act** requires released sexual offenders to report to or register with local law enforcement authorities. The most significant federal law that seeks to prevent and punish violence against women is the **Violence Against Women Act of 1994 (VAWA)**. The law was enacted in response to the inadequacies of state courts in dealing with violent crimes against women. It created the federal Office of Violence Against Women, which provides federal funds to states for criminal law enforcement against perpetrators of violence against women. It also provides for other kinds of assistance to women, taking into account the particular needs of women of color and immigrant women.

The law is broad and bold. It

- creates tough penalties for sex offenders,

- requires sexual offenders to pay restitution to their victims,

- requires states to pay for rape examinations, and

- extends rape shield laws to protect crime victims from abusive inquiries into their private conduct.

can check your state's law to learn how sexual assault crimes are defined and punished.

STEPS TO TAKE IF YOU ARE SEXUALLY ASSAULTED

If you are sexually assaulted, you can take some steps immediately to ensure your safety and health. These steps are basic common sense, but are worth repeating: get to a safe place, call the police or a friend, and get medical attention. Even if you do not think that you have physical injuries that require immediate medical care, seek medical attention right away because of possible internal injuries, pregnancy, AIDS, or other sexually transmitted diseases.

A **rape kit** includes the materials and instructions for a health care professional to collect the evidence necessary to establish that a crime occurred and, if possible, establish who committed the crime. A victim must consent before a health care professional will be able to collect and preserve evidence. Most rape kits instruct health care professionals to perform an internal examination and take swabs of any secretions left by the perpetrator. In addition, a doctor or nurse will comb through the victim's pubic hair to recover any foreign hair and pluck samples of the victim's hair and pubic hair. The hospital will also hold the clothes the victim was wearing as evidence (so it's a good idea to bring a spare set of clothes to the hospital). A doctor or nurse will also take photographs, including anywhere there are bruises, scrapes, or cuts. This can be an invasive process for a woman, but the evidence (of DNA, blood type, and other factors) can be sufficient to convict an assailant.

Finally, in the aftermath of an assault it's important for you to find someone you can trust and talk to that person about what happened. All community rape crisis centers will provide support, information, and referrals to victims of sexual assault, even if the victim chooses not to go to police. **Victim advocates** from such local organizations can be assigned to victims of sexual assault to

⟲ ASK A LAWYER

Q. If there is substantial physical evidence that a victim was raped by the defendant—for example, semen samples, pubic hairs, and evidence of force—does a victim really have to give evidence that the defendant raped her? Wouldn't a prosecutor have enough evidence without her cooperation?

A. Theoretically, you can sometimes prove rape without the victim's testimony. But any prosecutor will tell you that it is very difficult and often impossible to prove a case without eyewitness testimony. Since most rapists do not commit their crimes in public, the only witness is often the victim. Remember that consensual sex is not a crime. Often, only the victim's word is available as evidence of lack of consent. Without it there is usually no chance of a conviction.

—Answer by Marilyn Ireland
Professor, California Western School of Law,
San Diego, California

make sure that assault victims are treated in a consistent, responsible, and sensitive manner by all service personnel—in the hospital, the police department, and the court system. You should also write down all the details you can remember about the assault—this kind of written record can provide valuable, accurate evidence to a court. Remember that a sexual assault is not your fault. Many counseling services may be able to help you, including the National Sexual Assault Hotline (1-800-656-4673).

SEXUAL ASSAULT CASES AND THE CRIMINAL LEGAL PROCESS

Let's be honest, the court system can be daunting. If you decide to press charges against the person who assaulted you, you may face what seems to be a long, drawn-out process as the case is prepared for trial and goes to court. But for many women, the psychological benefits will outweigh the burdens. Taking charge and confronting an assailant is an empowering step in giving crime victims back their lives. Punishing the assailant is not only good for society (it punishes a criminal and may deter that criminal and others from further abusing women), it also may help restore some sense of order to the victim. The legal process for dealing with sexual assault cases is similar in all the states. Knowing ahead of time what the process is like will help you cope with that journey.

The first step to take if you have been assaulted is to file a report with the police. Filing a report does not mean that you have to pursue formal sexual assault charges, nor does it guarantee that the state will prosecute the case. Most local authorities provide counselors who can meet you at the hospital and provide you with information that you will need to get through the process. "Jane Doe" reports are an option in places that allow victims to report incidents without giving their names or other personal information. You get to protect your anonymity and the authorities or institution get the information for prevention and statistical purposes.

If you do want to press charges after you have made a report, then police will conduct an investigation and will take the evidence to the local prosecuting attorney, who will decide if there is enough evidence to bring a case. If the prosecuting attorney decides to prosecute, the next step depends on the state in which you live. In some states, the case will go before a **grand jury**, which involves a jury hearing the prosecutor's evidence in secret and then deciding whether there is enough evidence to pursue charges. In other states, a prosecutor will bring evidence of charges in open court before a judge. This is called a **preliminary hearing**, and the alleged offender has a right to challenge the evidence. More rape cases get dismissed when there is a preliminary hearing than when there is a grand jury, because at a preliminary hearing the defendant has a right to confront the accuser to some extent and challenge the accusations and evidence. In addition, rape shield laws (see page 231) do not always apply in preliminary hearings or at a pretrial conference.

You can expect to be asked to cooperate with police and prosecuting attorneys and their investigations. This could include giving a statement and testifying at a preliminary hearing and again at trial. You may also be asked to sit with the prosecutor during the trial, but this is not obligatory. It's not like television—you do not always need to be present for the duration of the trial and may be spared sitting through all that goes on. In addition, some states have rules or guidelines that apply in sexual assault cases. These require the police to inform you of all criminal proceedings where the defendant has a right to be present and allow you to refuse to give a deposition with the defendant present. A deposition is a procedure in which a witness is questioned under oath outside court—this testimony can then be used later at a trial.

The legal process culminates in the **trial**, during which each side presents evidence. In a criminal trial, a defendant has a Fifth Amendment constitutional right against self-incrimination and the right to remain silent. This means that the prosecutor cannot make the defendant give evidence in court. The victim, on the other hand, must nearly always give evidence in court. The burden is on the prosecutor to prove beyond a reasonable doubt that the defendant committed the crime, and the prosecutor needs the victim's evidence to convince the jury that the defendant is guilty. Often, an entire case rests on the word of the victim.

If you testify for the prosecution, then you can be cross-examined by the defense, because criminal defendants have a constitutional right to confront their accusers. During cross-examination, the attorney for the defense can ask you questions about your evidence and will try to identify inconsistencies or weaknesses in your side of the story. Rape shield laws can prevent the defense from introducing evidence about your past sexual history, but that won't keep the defendant from presenting other evidence to cast doubt on your credibility.

If you bring charges against your assailant, you may have to recount intimate details of the crime more than once to a courtroom full of strangers. But keep in mind the defendant is the one on trial. It is not a crime to be a victim of crime, to say no, or to dress in any particular manner. Focus on what the defendant did wrong and what you are doing right. Remember, only if women agree to testify will assailants be punished and deterred.

Proving that illegal contact or, if required, penetration took place often requires a medical professional's testimony, and this may require an expert to give some personal, private, and sensitive information about a victim. This testimony may address intimate details about the state and nature of a victim's sexual organs, whether there were any tears, bruises, signs of forced intercourse, or the presence of semen or pubic hairs. In addition, to demonstrate this evidence to a jury, a victim's torn clothing or underwear may be displayed and offered into evidence.

Sexual assault cases present unique problems in court. Often, the assault occurs in a private place and there are no witnesses. If a victim of sexual assault does not go straight to a hospital for a medical examination, physical evidence (e.g., semen) may not be preserved, and it may be difficult to prove lack of consent. Sexual assault cases that have been successfully prosecuted have generally had corroborating evidence, including police evidence, a medical report, and witnesses. Witnesses are not necessarily witnesses to the crime, but people such as medical examiners and others who the victim talked to about the crime after it occurred. The value of corroborating evidence highlights the importance of going straight to the hospital after an assault.

Many women are justifiably concerned about privacy and confidentiality if they go to trial. However, the law does provide some protections. In many state and federal courts, your identity and address is considered confidential if you are a victim of a sexual assault. In some courts, you may be referred to in all public court records by your initials only; in others, you may be referred to by a pseudonym if the court requests this. States may try to restrict the release of your name and identifying information by court personnel, law enforcement, and medical and social services, and preliminary trial proceedings may be closed to the public. Most states' paroling boards keep victim-impact statements confidential from inmates and their attorneys.

However, your right to privacy may conflict with two of our fundamental constitutional guarantees. First, criminal defendants have the right to confront their accusers. Thus, the perpetrator will be allowed to know who you are. Second, the media has the First Amendment right to freedom of speech. Some states have laws that prohibit the media from publishing or broadcasting your name, photo, address, or other identifying information. However, in the 1989 case of *The Florida Star v. B.J.F.*, the Supreme Court held that it was unconstitutional to impose damages on a newspaper that had violated state law by publishing the name of a young woman who was a victim of sexual assault. Most media nevertheless follow self-imposed policies and refrain from publishing the names of sexual assault victims who have been identified in open court at trial. A judge can also issue a gag order, which prohibits the parties and their lawyers from discussing the case.

In states that have confidentiality laws, there may be exceptions for victims' services agencies to get certain information to help them provide services to a victim or her family. And some states allow researchers access to some confidential informa-

---

(i) **VICTIMS' RIGHTS**

If the defendant is convicted of assault, some states allow victims to contribute to a presentencing report that will be read by the judge before sentencing. Victims can explain the extent of the physical and psychological damage suffered and can even make a recommendation for sentencing. In addition, some states also allow victims to be present and speak when the rapist is up for parole or other postconviction release.

tion as long as they agree to delete victims' identifying information.

RAPE SHIELD LAWS

Rape shield laws prevent the defense from inquiring into a victim's prior sexual history when the victim gives evidence in a sexual assault case. Rape shield laws were enacted by forty-nine states (Arizona is the only state without a rape shield law) and by the federal government in the 1970s in response to pressure from feminist activists, lawyers, and legislators who urged the need to ease the emotional burden of rape victims who must testify in court.

Proponents of rape shield laws contend that if evidence of a woman's prior sexual history is admitted at trial, it diverts the jury's attention from the issue of the perpetrator's guilt by putting her, her clothing, her attitude, and her past sexual behavior on trial. Asking questions about a woman's prior sexual history can bias the jury against her and be humiliating. Not surprisingly, such fears can discourage women from reporting and pursuing charges for sexual assault. Those opposed to rape shield laws contend that they prevent a defendant from receiving a fair trial and that they are discriminatory against men.

There are several specific exceptions to rape shield law protection where

• there is an issue of consent and the victim had prior consensual sexual relations with the defendant,

• the issue is the source of the victim's sexual contact, and the defendant is alleging that it is not his semen or that he did not cause the victim's venereal disease, or

• the defendant is attacking the credibility of the victim's testimony on what the victim says is her past sexual history. This means that if the victim has introduced an issue about her sexual history into the lawsuit by her own statements (e.g., a statement that she had not had sex before), the defendant can cross-examine her on that statement.

( ) ASK A LAWYER

Q. *There seem to be several mechanisms designed to protect the identity of a rape victim. But a person accused of rape can suffer just as much harm from having his identity made public as a victim. What happened to innocent until proven guilty? Why aren't there laws to keep the identity of a defendant secret?*

A. In some countries, accused criminals' names are protected and cannot be published by the press. But in the United States, the First Amendment prevents the law from censoring the names of criminal defendants or criminal victims. A criminal defendant, unlike a victim, is a party to the lawsuit, so it is very hard for the law to keep his name private.

Defendants have a number of rights that victims don't have, because the defendant is a party to a case. Defendants have a right to remain silent. They have a right to have a lawyer who can question witnesses. The victim has no such rights since she is, legally, only a witness. So, while it is easier to keep the name of the victim private, she does not have any of the legal rights of the defendant.

—Answer by Marilyn Ireland
Professor, California Western School of Law,
San Diego, California

Q. *Rape shield laws sounded like a powerful tool . . . until I read about the exceptions to them. A victim's credibility is an issue in almost every rape trial, isn't it? Does this mean that the defendant can almost always ask questions about a victim's sexual history?*

A. It used to be that women who testified against their attackers were faced with questions about their "wanton" promiscuity, and evidence of promiscuity was accepted as evidence that a woman was not honest, the assumption being that a woman who was not chaste was a liar. Most states, either by statute or court decision, have changed this unfair assumption. Sexual history may be used to show credibility today only if there is a specific fact situation that puts the victim's credibility about sexual matters in question. The exceptions do exist, but they are much narrower than they used to be.

—Answer by Marilyn Ireland
Professor, California Western School of Law,
San Diego, California

If the victim's past sexual history is going to be inquired into, most courts require that she be given prior notice (usually at least ten days), so she has an opportunity to have the judge rule on any objections she has and set limits on what may be asked. The defendant cannot inquire about the victim's sexual history without first showing the judge that there is a good reason for doing so—for example, evidence of two semen sources, one of which is not the defendant's. These issues are almost always handled before trial and outside the presence of the jury. Victims should not be ambushed or surprised at trial by questions about their sexual histories. In addition, defendants will not be allowed to go on "fishing expeditions"—asking questions about a victim's sexual history in the hope that they will find something useful.

CIVIL REMEDIES FOR SURVIVORS OF SEXUAL ASSAULT

You can file a civil lawsuit against a perpetrator of sexual assault and recover money damages. You can do this in addition to or instead of pressing criminal charges against the perpetrator. If you reported the assault to the police and the perpetrator has been found guilty in a criminal trial, then it will be easier for you to pursue your civil suit. It may not even hurt your civil case if your offender was found not guilty in the criminal trial. In a criminal trial, you must prove that the crime was committed beyond a reasonable doubt. In a civil trial, there is a lesser burden of proof—you must only prove the crime "by a preponder-

(i) NO RIGHT TO SUE IN FEDERAL COURT

VAWA, as originally enacted, included a civil rights provision (Title III) that gave women unprecedented access to federal courts, by making violence against women a violation of women's rights guaranteed by the U.S. Constitution. This provision meant that women could sue sexual assault offenders in federal court instead of state court and be guaranteed uniform application of laws and processes no matter which state they hailed from. Title III was intended to give women a federal remedy similar to the federal civil rights remedies for injuries motivated by race.

However, Title III's civil rights provisions under VAWA were struck down by the U.S. Supreme Court in 2000 in *United States v. Morrison*. This case involved an eighteen-year-old freshman at Virginia Tech, Christy Brzonkala, who alleged that she was raped twice by two male football players who then boasted about it the next day. Brzonkala did not immediately report the rapes. Two months later, she pursued charges under the school's Sexual Assault Policy. (She did not file criminal charges because she had not preserved any physical evidence of the rapes.) She withdrew from school after she learned that the school took no action against one of the players and gave the other a deferred suspension that permitted him to keep playing varsity football. Brzonkala, who asked that her name be used in articles about the case, then sued the two football players and the school in federal court. Her complaint alleged that the attack violated Title III of VAWA and that Virginia Tech's handling of her complaint violated Title IX of the Education Amendments of 1972. She sought money damages.

This was the first federal case brought under Title III of VAWA, and it garnered much public scrutiny and debate. Chief Justice William H. Rehnquist, writing for a 5-4 majority, held that Congress lacked authority to enact a law that provides a federal civil remedy for victims of gender-motivated violence—under either the federal Constitution's commerce clause or the Fourteenth Amendment.

ance of the evidence," which means you must show that it was more likely than not that the crime happened. If you want to file a civil suit, you will need to hire your own attorney, who may charge you an hourly rate or may work on a contingency fee basis, in which he or she takes a percentage of any money that you win.

It is important to keep in mind that rape shield laws do not necessarily apply in civil lawsuits. Filing a civil lawsuit will also constitute a waiver of your right to the confidentiality of your medical records and other records. Thus, if you are in therapy with a psychologist or psychiatrist, records of your sessions may no longer be confidential. You may also have to produce private journals or other documents in court.

If you are successful, you may win damages to cover the cost of past and future therapy and the long-term emotional damage resulting from the assault. In cases where the assault occurred during your childhood, you may also seek damages for loss of childhood and failure to fulfill potential.

HELP FOR CHILDHOOD VICTIMS

Victims of childhood sexual abuse can file civil lawsuits as a way to seek justice and accountability from their abusers. Such suits are only allowed in states that have extended **statutes of limitation** for victims of childhood sexual abuse. Normally, each state's statute of limitations sets a time limit on cases, and cases filed after a certain period, say two or three years, fall outside the limitation period and will be thrown out of court. Statutes of limitations exist to give law enforcement personnel an incentive to act swiftly and to ensure that cases are conducted while witnesses can remember clearly what happened and can give reliable evidence. However, the majority of states now have some type of **tolling provision** for sexual abuse cases. This is a rule that "stops the clock"—that is, stops the limitation period from running until a certain event takes place.

In states with **minority tolling** provisions, limitation periods do not start to run until victims reach age eighteen. Some states allow for **delayed discovery or realization** for cases in which a person's repressed memory of abuse is later recovered. In such cases, the limitation period does not begin to run until a victim discovers the injury and/or the fact that the injury or illness was caused by the abuse. So if you were victimized as a child, you might be able to have your day in court many years after the abuse occurred. Recovered-memory cases can be difficult to prove, however. In states that have provisions on **incapacity tolling**, limitation periods do not run during a period of mental incapacity or insanity, which in some states may be shown by repressed memory or posttraumatic stress disorder. Keep in mind that the window of legal opportunity is not open forever. When limitation periods do begin to run, you have to act within the limitation period set by state law.

Women who are assaulted as adults do not generally have the benefit of these extended limitation periods, and in some states the limitation period may be as short as one year to file a civil suit—but in most states it is two to three years.

DATE RAPE

Date rape, which is also referred to as "acquaintance rape," occurs when someone you know or are dating forces you to have sex. This may include your boyfriend, a classmate, a neighbor, or a friend. Date rape is a crime, and it is, unfortunately, a common occurrence among teenagers and college students. You may fear rape from a stranger, but in fact most victims are raped by someone they know. It is especially important to remember that if you are raped, even by a friend or a boyfriend, you should not blame yourself or feel that it was your fault. If you said no or were unable to consent (e.g., because you had passed out) or if you were coerced or threatened into consenting, then it's rape. The law applies to date rape in the same way it applies to other forms of sexual assault. Thus, it is important for you to seek medical attention, report the assault right away, and be careful not to do anything that will destroy evidence.

INCREASING THE LEGAL SYSTEM'S SENSITIVITY TO VICTIMS OF SEXUAL ASSAULT

Feminists have criticized the legal system for decades because its adversarial structure and emphasis on hard evidence makes bringing charges for sexual assault a harrowing process for many women. Many states have instituted procedures designed to make the legal system more sensitive to the victim's needs in sexual assault cases.

• In many states, a victim's advocate, often a rape survivor herself, will be assigned to assist you. The advocate may accompany you to the hospital for medical examinations, help you work with police and prosecutors throughout the investigation and trial, and tell you about community resources available to you.

• Many states have also enacted crime restitution and victims' rights laws. Victims' rights statutes, which cover not just rape but other criminal offenses, often require states to keep you informed about the status of your case and the dates of impor-

ⓘ EMERGENCY CONTRACEPTION LAWS

Emergency contraception is used in sexual assault cases to prevent a pregnancy (chapter 12 provides information about the way in which emergency contraception works). Relatively few states have passed laws requiring hospitals to give victims of sexual assault information on and prescriptions for emergency contraception, though bills proposing this have been debated all over the country. However, many clinics and hospitals throughout the country do provide emergency contraception to survivors of sexual assault if they request it.

tant legal proceedings and may allow you to deliver a "victim impact" statement at the defendant's sentencing.

• As a condition of receiving federal funding under VAWA, your state must not require you to pay for your medical exams following a sexual assault.

• Many states have passed legislation requiring convicted child molesters and/or sex offenders such as rapists to register with local law enforcement agencies when they change addresses; law enforcement agencies are then often required to notify citizens living near the sex offender's residence.

THE WORLD AT YOUR FINGERTIPS

• For an overview of reforms in the area of sexual assault, see the American Bar Association's *Facts about Women and the Law* booklet at www.abanet.org/media/factbooks/womenlaw.pdf.

• For general information on sexual assault, see the Information for Health Organization's "Population Reports: Ending Violence against Women" at www.infoforhealth.org and the Center for the Prevention of Sexual and Domestic Violence's abstract "Sexual Violence" at www.cpsdv.org/Sexual-Violence/index.htm.

• For more on VAWA, see Kathryn Kish Sklar and Suzanne Lustig's study, "How Have Recent Social Movements Shaped Civil Rights Legislation for Women? The 1994 Violence Against Women Act," at http://womhist.binghamton.edu/vawa/intro.htm.

• For more on sexual assault trials, see John Hamlin's "Courts and Rape" at www.d.umn.edu/cla/faculty/jhamlin/3925/courts.html.

• The Office on Violence Against Women offers lists of and links to federal laws and regulations relating to violence against women at www.ojp.usdoj.gov/vawo/regulations.htm.

• The Rape, Abuse and Incest National Network can help you find help centers and hotlines in your city at www.rainn.org/counseling.html.

• The website of the National Conference of State Legislatures offers links to various state programs designed to increase

access to emergency contraception at www.ncsl.org/programs/
health/ec.htm.

REMEMBER THIS

• If you are sexually assaulted, it is important to preserve evidence of the assault.

• Sexual assault trials can be harrowing for victims of sexual assault, who may have to give evidence about the assault in court and be cross-examined by the defense. Many women, however, find it empowering to confront their assailants and know that, because they had the courage to testify, the assailants will be punished for their crimes.

• In some states, the criminal law contains rights for victims, including the right to contribute to a presentencing report.

• Rape shield laws may protect the victim's privacy to some extent, but the laws may still permit some tough cross-examination.

• The most significant federal law relating to violence against women is the Violence Against Women Act, although the Supreme Court has ruled that one of its most powerful provisions is unconstitutional.

CHAPTER 16

Domestic Violence: It's a Crime—And the Law Can Offer You Some Protections

James always had a temper and was a bad loser, but Rosie never thought he would turn on her, his wife and loyal supporter for the past seven years. James never actually hit her, but when he drank with his buddies he threatened to harm her and to withhold the household budget.

Simon, on the other hand, physically abused his girlfriend, Stefanie, when they lived together, right up until the day she left him. After she moved out, he began showing up at her workplace. He then started following her on weekends, despite her pleas for him to leave her alone.

Jackie was jealous of every woman who spoke to or looked at her partner, Roberta. She would criticize Roberta's social skills in the hope of keeping her from engaging in activities outside their home. And when Roberta did go out, Jackie would interrogate her upon her return and insult Roberta's friends and associates.

Would it surprise you to learn that all of these women are in abusive relationships? That threats and psychological abuse can be almost as damaging and demeaning as physical violence? That domestic abuse among homosexual couples is as prevalent as domestic abuse among heterosexual couples? That the rate of domestic violence against white women is about the same as the rate against black women, regardless of their socioeconomic status? No matter what kind of abusive relationship you might be in, this chapter can explain some of your legal options.

WHAT IS DOMESTIC VIOLENCE?

Domestic violence does not just occur among married couples. It occurs whenever one person in an intimate relationship gets and keeps control over another person through a variety of tactics. It can include violence and other abusive behavior by your spouse, intimate partner, or family member. States have their own definitions of domestic violence and sexual assault. **Domestic violence** is usually defined as a systematic pattern of abusive behaviors (which may be psychological, sexual, physical, and/or economic) that are used by an individual to establish power and control over his or her partner. The abuser is able to maintain power and control through fear and intimidation. Remember, **sexual assault** is defined as one person forcing another person to have sex or perform sexual acts through coercion, threats, or physical violence. Thus, you may be the victim of one or both of these crimes. For example, if your partner physically abuses you, this is domestic abuse. If your partner sexually abuses you, this is both domestic abuse and sexual assault.

 **SPOUSAL RAPE**

Under English common law, a man could not be charged with rape of his wife, because rape was defined as illegal sexual contact, and sexual contact between husband and wife was lawful. In 1975, South Dakota became the first state to abolish the spousal exception to rape. By 1993, every state and the District of Columbia had also eliminated this exception, making it possible for a woman to press a rape charge against her husband. To sustain a charge of rape against your spouse, however, many jurisdictions require you to show that a significant level of force was used against you or that you had a reasonable fear of immediate harm.

USING THE LAW TO PROTECT YOURSELF FROM ABUSE

If your partner is abusing you, you can take legal steps to protect yourself. All victims of domestic abuse can seek a protective order. These orders are the result of a civil (as opposed to criminal) procedure. However, if your spouse is physically abusing you, then you may also be able to press criminal charges, discussed in the next section.

Protective Orders

Civil protective orders are one of the core legal mechanisms for the prevention of domestic violence. Protective orders evolved as a useful tool for helping domestic violence victims in the 1970s, when domestic violence cases were rarely criminally prosecuted. By making this civil court procedure available to victims of domestic violence, communities gave victims the opportunity to petition state courts for protection on their own behalf, rather than leaving victims with no remedy if local prosecutors failed to go forward with their criminal cases.

A protective order is a legal order you get from a state court that requires a person to stop harming you. You may have heard such orders referred to as **protection orders**, **restraining orders**, **temporary protection orders** (**TPOs**), **temporary restraining orders** (**TROs**), or some other similar name. Such orders typically prohibit your abuser from having any contact with you or from coming within a certain geographical distance (e.g., five hundred feet) of you. In many states, you can also ask for "stay-away" and "no-contact" provisions to prevent your abuser from contacting you in any manner—for example, by telephone, mail, fax, e-mail, or delivery of flowers or gifts. Protective orders can also limit contact with children.

In many states, it is fairly simple to get a protective order. Often, you can begin the process by getting a packet of forms from the clerk of court, who may even assist you in filling them out. In other states, there may be nonlawyers available to help you fill out the forms. Women's advocacy organizations and women's centers often provide assistance with applying for protective orders as well. Some of the forms require your signature, and in many jurisdictions you must sign in the presence of the clerk of court, who will witness the signature and notarize the forms without charge. There are modest fees for filing and service of your forms, but if you do not have the money, you may apply for a waiver of any filing fees on a separate form. If you cannot afford the fee, be prepared to provide the court with financial information about your inability to pay.

When you've completed the forms, in most states you will have to appear in court before a judge to show evidence of your abuse. Hearings on protective orders are usually **ex parte**, which means that only the person seeking the order is present in the court. The other party is not present to give evidence and usually is not even aware that the hearing is happening. In some states, you must appear in court again to prove your allegations after the defendant has been served with the protective order. In other states, you only need to appear before a judge if the defendant challenges the protective order.

Don't be discouraged simply because you have no physical evidence of abuse. Your statements alone may be sufficient in many courts. Ask a victims' advocate or representative from a women's shelter about local practice and experience. Evidence you give of nonphysical violence may be sufficient evidence, depending on the judge and the definition of domestic violence in that jurisdiction. Because domestic violence does not keep regular business hours, judges are often available to issue protection orders outside business hours. If a judge is not available, then you can check with your local police department—in the absence of an available judge, the police are often authorized to issue emergency protective orders, and you can go to court the next business day to get a more permanent protection order.

If your forms are in order and you have showed sufficient evidence of abuse, then a judge will issue a protection order. A judge may also give you temporary provisions for child support,

ASK A LAWYER

Q. How long does a protective order last? Can I get an order to prevent my husband from contacting me indefinitely? Or do I have to keep reapplying for orders?

A. The duration of a protective order is controlled by state law. Temporary orders—the ones obtained ex parte (meaning only the person seeking the order is present in court)—usually last only a short period of time, perhaps thirty days or less. At the hearing on the validity of the temporary order, the court will determine how long the regular protective order will last. Most states limit a regular protective order to a period of one year. In most places, you will need to reapply if you want to extend the protective order beyond that time. Permanent protective orders are more difficult, but not impossible, to obtain.

—Answer by Klaus Sitte
Executive Director, Montana Legal Services Association,
Missoula, Montana

Q. My partner never physically abused me, but the psychological abuse was enough for me to get a protective order after we split up. As a result, he is unable to see our children. Now he's trying to get the order removed. Can he do that?

A. Psychological or mental abuse is certainly sufficient to qualify for protection orders. Some courts are now recognizing that such abuse of the victim also adversely affects the children, and often these "no-contact" orders result in a prohibition on contacting children. Can he get a protective order removed so that he can visit the children anyway? It depends on the severity of the abuse, whether the children have been exposed to it, and the current or potential impact on the children. Certainly he has a right to try, but it will be up to the court to decide whether visiting with him is contrary to the best interests of the children.

—Answer by Klaus Sitte
Executive Director, Montana Legal Services Association,
Missoula, Montana

Q. Can I get a protective order if my abuser is not my spouse?

A. Most states now provide victims of domestic and sexual violence with the right to obtain protective orders, regardless of marital status. In other words, you need not be married to the abuser in order to obtain an order of protection. On the other hand, a distinction is often made for casual relationships. Most frequently, the victim and the abuser must be partners for some period of time, such as a year, or be family members to meet the "domestic" part of the definition.

—Answer by Klaus Sitte
Executive Director, Montana Legal Services Association,
Missoula, Montana

custody, and visitation to reduce your need to negotiate these issues with your abuser. Because these orders are issued in family courts, which are civil, not criminal, your abuser may only be warned or fined for contempt if he breaches the orders. However, some jurisdictions, such as the District of Columbia, treat a violation of a civil protection order as a form of criminal contempt, and your abuser may face jail time for a violation. In other jurisdictions, such as Maryland, a violation of a protection order may be treated like a misdemeanor: if your abuser is found guilty of breaching an order, then he may face a criminal punishment.

It is a good idea to have several copies of your protective order. Keep one at your home, one at your place of employment, one in your purse or on your person, and, if it covers children as well, one at your children's school and/or day care facility. It is also important for you to register it with the police located in the communities where your abuser has been ordered to stay away from you. This might include the police precincts that cover where you live, where you work, where you attend church or school, and where your children go to school. If you are unsure how to register your protection order, simply call your local police station or contact a victim's advocate. And don't worry about crossing state lines—federal legislation requires all states and territories to recognize and enforce protective orders (as well as other domestic-law orders) issued by other jurisdictions.

Studies show that issuing protective orders and arresting persons who commit domestic violence does reduce future incidents of domestic violence. But protective orders are not guarantees. You should always report any violation of a protective order to police. Police can enforce stay-away, no-contact, cease-abuse, and custody orders by restraining or arresting the person to prevent further violation of the order and threat of harm. You should bring serious violations to the court's attention.

If your abuser is determined to harm or harass you, his or her anger or rage may not change just because you got a court order. If you do not believe that a protective order will protect you, then you need to take every step you can to protect yourself. Hide a bag packed with important documents and basic necessities for you and your children should you need to make a safe exit. You might also want to hide some money, hide a spare car key or house key, and memorize the numbers of hotlines such as the National Domestic Violence Hotline at 1-800-799-SAFE (7233) or the Safe Horizon Hotline at 1-800-621-HOPE (4673). And if you are in danger, get to a shelter and consider your options. You can find more advice on safety planning at the website of the American Bar Association's Commission on Domestic Violence at www.abanet.org/tips/dvsafety.html.

Criminal Charges

Domestic abuse is a crime in every state. Specific state laws may cover different kinds of domestic assault, from attempts to kill to minor physical injury. There are other offenses that do not require you to be injured at all if you reasonably feared an immediate assault. If your partner made a fist and threatened to beat you, and you believed you were about to be injured, then he could be charged with battery. Police may also charge domestic abusers with other offenses, including violation of a protective

(i) SELF-DEFENSE

Self-defense is not against the law, and you will not be prosecuted for defending yourself from domestic violence. Self-defense is based on the notion that you should be allowed to protect yourself from physical harm. You do not have to wait until you are actually struck to act in self-defense. If a reasonable person in your position would think that she was about to be physically attacked, then you have the right to strike first and try to prevent the attack. However, you cannot use more force than is reasonable—otherwise you could be charged with assault. Some states use a combined objective/subjective test for self-defense, and you would be justified in using deadly force if you honestly believed it was necessary to prevent death or bodily harm and if the jury finds a reasonable person would believe it necessary to use deadly force to protect herself.

The situation is different if a victim of domestic violence commits a premeditated act of violence against her abuser. For example, in 1977 Francine Hughes, who had suffered abuse at the hands of her husband for years, set fire to his bed while he was sleeping, causing his death. Her action was not self-defense, because she was in no imminent danger of attack. Her lawyer argued that as a result of continual abuse for years, Hughes was temporarily insane when she committed murder and was suffering from "battered women's syndrome." She was acquitted. The term was in vogue for some years and evidence on the syndrome was frequently given in court to help explain the state of mind of a victim of domestic violence. It has since fallen out of favor, and the term has been criticized for its vagueness and its implicit assumption that all women respond in the same way to domestic violence. Contrary to popular perception, evidence of domestic abuse has never been a defense to murder or any other crime. Evidence of domestic violence may help a person prove self-defense or duress, but battered women's syndrome cannot be used to escape conviction for premeditated crimes.

order, harassment, or endangering the welfare of a child. If your abuser unlawfully enters your property, then police could charge him with trespass; if he enters your house intending to commit a crime, he could be charged with burglary.

The federal Violence Against Women Act (VAWA), discussed in chapter 15, has several clauses designed to prevent domestic violence. The act specifically makes it a federal offense:

- To cross state lines to commit an act of domestic violence
- To cause an intimate partner to cross state lines by force, coercion, duress, or fraud, as a result of which there is bodily harm to the victim
- To engage in interstate stalking
- To travel across state lines to violate a protection order
- For an abuser subject to a protection order to possess a firearm
- To transfer a firearm to an abuser who is the subject of a protection order
- For an abuser to possess a firearm after he or she has been convicted of a domestic violence crime

In many jurisdictions, it is common practice for police to report a firearm violation to the federal Bureau of Alcohol, Tobacco, and Firearms or the Federal Bureau of Investigation, both of which will investigate violations.

VAWA has been used in real federal cases. For example, in *United States v. Michael Casciano* the defendant was convicted of crossing state lines to violate a protection order. He had followed his girlfriend from Massachusetts to New York and had continued to stalk and harass her. He was sentenced to thirty-seven months in jail. In *United States v. William Romines*, the defendant was convicted of forcing his wife to cross state lines. He had violated a protective order to see his wife in Tennessee, threatened to kill her, and forced her and their son into a car. After a high-speed chase, he was captured in Virginia and prosecuted. He received a 151-month sentence, which was upheld on appeal. Finally, in *United States v. Christopher Bailey* the defendant was convicted of kidnapping and interstate domestic violence after he severely beat his wife in their home in West Virginia and locked her in the trunk of the car while he drove to Kentucky. Several days later, he took her to a hospital in Kentucky. Because of the delay in treatment, she is now in a permanent vegetative state, and the defendant is serving a life sentence in federal prison.

Other Federal Laws

Federal tax laws are also sensitive to domestic violence issues. You can apply to the Internal Revenue Service (IRS) for **innocent-spouse status,** which relieves you from part or all of your liability for the tax due on a joint return you may have filed with your abusive spouse. You will need Form 8857, Request for Innocent Spouse Relief, and you should write on the top of the form "Potential Domestic Abuse Case." You should also explain why you think you qualify for innocent-spouse status and attach any legal documents (such as a protection order) that may support your claim. The IRS is required to inform your spouse that you are seeking innocent-spouse relief, but it will not release to your spouse any information regarding your new name if you have one, your employer, your phone number, or any other personal information not related to the determination of your innocent spouse status.

For additional information or forms, visit the IRS website at www.irs.gov or go directly to the IRS Innocent Spouse Q&A at www.irs.gov/individuals/innocent/article/0,,id=109283,00.html.

The Social Security Administration also recognizes the difficulties that domestic violence survivors face in reestablishing their lives. They have a program that issues domestic violence survivors new Social Security numbers so that abusive spouses cannot track them down.

DOMESTIC VIOLENCE AND THE CRIMINAL PROCESS

In many states, police can arrest an abuser for the misdemeanor of domestic violence, with no need for a warrant or a formal

↻ ASK A LAWYER

Q. *My spouse physically abuses me, but I don't want to leave the house and go to a shelter because it would be so destabilizing for the kids. Can I get a protective order and prevent my spouse from coming back to the house, even if the house is in his name?*

A. Orders of protection can prevent entry and residence by your spouse into the shared family home and are generally called "vacate orders." For example, to get an order preventing your spouse from entering the home in New York, you have to show that this step is reasonable and furthers the purposes of ending the violence, ending family disruption, and obtaining protection. If your spouse does have sole ownership of the residence, he or she can pursue a case in civil court to evict you, but this could take some time.

—Answer by Christa Stewart
Senior Director, Safe Horizon Anti-trafficking Initiative,
New York, New York

complaint. Most police are instructed to get the abuser out of the house immediately, using their arrest power if necessary.

If the police have made an arrest, you can expect them to do the following:

- Conduct separate interviews with you and your abuser
- Ask you about any history of abuse
- Give you the relevant officer's name, badge number, and phone number
- Give you the number of a domestic violence shelter, a number to call for information about your case, and information about any local victims' advocate programs that are available to help you
- Make a written report of the incident whether or not an arrest is made

The police will also check for any prior domestic violence incidents involving you or the abuser, including phone calls or contacts, even if no arrest was made. The police should treat you with respect and not dismiss your allegations out of hand as a "private matter." If the police don't take any of these steps, you should ask them to do so.

The police may pass the report on to a prosecutor, who will read the police report, consider other available evidence, and decide whether to file charges. The prosecutor will have evidence about the incident of abuse from police and will not necessarily have to talk with you. However, you may need to give the prosecutor copies of any documentation you have from any previous incidents of abuse, as well as a list of names and addresses of any witnesses to the domestic violence against you. You should also keep copies of photographs that you, the police, or the hospital have taken of your injuries and of any property damage that your abuser has caused. If there are people who witnessed the abuse, saw you after an injury, or heard an angry outburst, you should give the names, addresses, and telephone numbers of those people to the police and the prosecutor. Remember as well that there are other types of photographs that evince inappropriate responses to anger, such as photographs of holes in the wall, broken items, and so on.

If your abuser has physically or sexually abused you, then police may request that charges be filed against him or her, even if you do not want charges to be filed.

Just because the prosecutor files charges against your abuser does not mean that the case will go to trial. Most domestic violence cases are resolved before trial through **plea bargaining**, in which the defendant agrees to plead guilty in exchange for a more lenient recommended sentence or a lesser charge. Many plea bargains are subject to the approval of the court, but some may not be. Plea bargaining is essentially a private process, but this is starting to change now that victims' rights groups are becoming recognized. Under many victims' rights statutes, you may have a right to have input into the plea bargaining process.

If the case does go to trial, the process works in more or less the same way as a trial for sexual assault, discussed in the previous chapter. The abuser may have to attend a preliminary hear-

▶ **APPEARING IN COURT**

Domestic violence cases are stressful and involve heightened emotions on both sides, but if you have to go to court it is important to be fully prepared for the experience. A judge's decision on whether to grant a protective order or other relief in a domestic abuse case is a legal decision based on the requirements of your state's law—not on his or her sympathies or prejudices. It is important to make your case as strong as possible, and to do so it helps for your testimony to be clear and confidently given. While everyone recognizes the trauma that you have been through, judges do not generally respond well to tears, jealousy, outrage, or anger (though at the time this is what you may be feeling). You should try to stay calm and state the facts slowly and clearly. If you take time to prepare and practice what you will say before you go to court, you will be that much calmer when you appear in court. It is daunting enough for most people just to set foot inside a courtroom, let alone take the stand and testify. If you are the victim of abuse or violence, you are to be commended for taking this step. The following tips will help you make a good impression:

- Dress smartly, as if you are going to a job interview or to work.

- When the judge or the opposing side is speaking, try to keep your thoughts, opinions, statements, and questions to yourself. Remember that both you and your abuser have the right to speak freely. Self-control is especially tough when your spouse is not telling the truth or is speaking ill of you, but you will get your chance to deny or explain what he has said.

- Keep your composure during the proceedings. Don't make faces, roll your eyes, shake your head in disbelief, or pound the table.

ing, at which a judge or magistrate will decide whether there is enough evidence, or **probable cause**, to believe that the suspect committed the crime with which he or she is charged. More often than not, the defendant waives the preliminary hearing in domestic violence cases, and even if it goes ahead the victim usually will not need to be present. If the court finds that there is probable cause, then the matter will be listed for trial.

A trial can be a long, drawn-out process, and you may need to give evidence about the abuse. The payoff is that a successful trial can help you to feel empowered to break out of a violent relationship, punish or rehabilitate your abuser, and deter him or her from further abuse. You do not need to hire a lawyer for a trial, but it may be helpful to have a victim advocate with you at court. If you are seeking additional court intervention (support, custody, or divorce orders), then you may need to consult with an attorney and make sure you are advised of your legal rights in these matters.

If the defendant is found guilty of a charge related to domestic violence, a jail sentence may be imposed, but probation is more likely. A judge can order an abuser to attend a drug or alcohol program or a batterer's program, usually as a condition of probation. A judge can also order an abuser to pay you restitution for injuries caused to you. Finally, just as for sexual assault, you can bring a civil suit seeking compensation for injuries caused to you by your abuser.

PROGRESS AGAINST DOMESTIC VIOLENCE

In the last few years, state legislatures have been paying increased attention to domestic violence. You may have seen advertising campaigns designed to increase your awareness of domestic violence and to educate you about local resources for help. You may have even noticed that October is now officially designated as "Domestic Violence Awareness Month." There have also been significant changes in local courts. Many jurisdictions, such as the District of Columbia and New York City, have developed specialized courts to handle domestic violence cases. Some courts, like those in Dade County, Florida, give their courts and judges concurrent civil and criminal jurisdic-

◖◗ ASK A LAWYER

Q. My sister suffers abuse at the hands of her husband, but she refuses to report him to police. What kind of evidence, and how much evidence, would police need to prosecute my sister's husband without her cooperation? Is there anything I can do to help?

A. As citizens, we have an obligation to look out for each other and report crimes that affect other people. If someone abused another individual on the street, you would probably not hesitate to call the police. Here, your reluctance is based on your relationship with the victim. What will my sister think if I report her husband as an abuser? What will that do to my relationship with my sister? What will happen to my sister if I report this domestic violence? Or, more importantly, what will happen to my sister if I do *not* report this domestic violence?

The reasons victims remain in violent relationships are complicated. Sometimes, victims lack information about options and what resources are available to them should they decide to leave. Perhaps you could gather that kind of information for your sister. There are many ways she can receive this information. The information does not need to come from you. Even Mary Kay Cosmetics has a substantial national role in the distribution of domestic violence resource information to victims. You may even want to help her develop a safety plan. You can also assure her that there are, in fact, resources to help her. Her situation is not as hopeless as it may appear to her now.

Recall that witness cooperation is not always necessary to prosecute a crime, whether that crime is domestic violence or some other crime. Obviously your sister's statements would be good evidence, if she was willing to make such statements to a prosecutor. If your sister has received medical treatment for her injuries, those injuries may be sufficient for prosecution. Some states require medical personnel to report evidence of domestic violence to law enforcement officials if children are in the home. So getting your sister medical attention, if necessary, may begin the process on its own.

Check with a shelter in your area. Talk to a victims' advocate. Some police departments have set up special units to deal with domestic violence. You could talk to an officer from such a unit, without revealing your sister's identity. At the very least, your sister has your nonjudgmental supportive encouragement, along with accurate local resource information, as a significant asset. Many victims who break the cycle of violence lack even that support.

—Answer by Klaus Sitte
Executive Director, Montana Legal Services Association,
Missoula, Montana

A. Many jurisdictions, including California, will prosecute domestic violence cases even if a victim refuses to testify or recants her testimony. Evidence to prosecute without the victim may include police reports, 911 tapes, photos taken at the scene, and doctors' reports.

—Answer by Lydia Brashear Tiede
Attorney, San Diego, California

A. Some victims of domestic violence may have chosen not to seek assistance from the criminal justice system or the health-care system for fear of reprisal from the abuser. Often, credible evidence of abuse comes from outside sources such as reports and affidavits from clergy, social workers, school officials, and social-service personnel. Other types of credible evidence include corroborating witness statements, counseling or mental health records, or evidence of property damage.

—Answer by Christa Stewart
Senior Director, Safe Horizon Anti-trafficking Initiative,
New York, New York

Q. *My neighbor is battered by her husband, but she's afraid to report him to police because she immigrated to the United States illegally and thinks she could be deported. Are there any protections for her?*

A. VAWA allows women who are illegal immigrants to obtain legal status in the United States if they are married to U.S. citizens or permanent residents who batter them. If an immigrant woman can prove that she was abused by a U.S. citizen or legal permanent resident, then she may be able to petition for legal permanent resident status for herself and her children. Recent changes to VAWA also relaxed the requirements for battered immigrant women and allowed them to get legal status even if divorced, as long as they applied for legal status within two years of divorce.

As to her husband, legal permanent residents who commit certain domestic-violence violations can lose their green cards and be deported for most domestic-violence convictions, as well as for violating protective orders.

—Answer by Lydia Brashear Tiede
Attorney, San Diego, California

tion, so that one judge can handle all of the issues that might arise in your domestic violence case, including protection orders, misdemeanor and felony charges, custody and support issues, and divorce. In such courts, you may be able to get a protective order as well as an order directing your abuser to continue to make mortgage payments on a home owned by both of you. In addition, some courts can also order your abuser to turn over any firearms and ammunition to police, attend a batterers' treatment program, appear for regular drug tests, and stay away from your children's doctors, day care, school, or after-school job.

Local law enforcement authorities have also implemented changes designed to reduce domestic violence. Police in some counties have implemented proarrest policies in domestic violence situations, and they will prosecute your case even without your cooperation if the violence is severe. Police will take this step because they find that many victims become unwilling or unable to continue to hold their abusers accountable for a variety of reasons, including fear, financial need, lack of affordable housing options, and poor self-esteem.

THE WORLD AT YOUR FINGERTIPS

• The ABA's Commission on Domestic Violence provides valuable resources for survivors of domestic violence, including information about how to recognize violence, what to do if you are a victim of violence, and some of the myths and realities about domestic violence, at www.abanet.org/domviol/home. html.

• To learn more about the specific laws in your state, you can contact your local prosecutor, district attorney, or state attorney general's office. There are also many online sources that you can check for individual state and federal laws. For example, the Women's Law Initiative offers comprehensive state-by-state legal information and resources for domestic violence at www. womenslaw.org/more_info.htm. On each state's page, you will find local and statewide programs that provide direct services and information.

• Many communities have temporary homes called battered women's shelters, where you and your children can go until a domestic violence crisis passes or you are able to permanently relocate. The police can help you find a shelter in your community or you can call any number of local or national hotlines for assistance in finding a shelter. The National Coalition Against Domestic Violence provides information and referrals at www.ncadv.org or 1-303-893-1852. Or you can contact the National Domestic Violence Hotline at www.ndvh.org or 1-800-799-SAFE (7233).

• The Leaving Domestic Abuse Safely site acts as a "how-to" guide for women who want to escape from abusive relationships. It includes specific information on safety, divorce, immigration, legal help, obtaining credit, training for the job market, confidential mail forwarding, and more. There is also an active message board where women come together to support each other, ask questions, and vent frustrations. Check it out at www. leavingabuse.com.

• The Family Violence Prevention Fund website contains many resources about escaping and preventing domestic violence at http://endabuse.org.

REMEMBER THIS

• You may think of domestic violence as something that involves a man using his fists against his wife. Domestic violence is bigger and broader than that—it includes physical and non-physical abuse in every type of family, between both married and unmarried couples.

• Civil protective orders are a powerful tool to prevent domestic violence. You can apply for a protective order quickly and cheaply by showing evidence of abuse to a judge.

• If you are physically and sexually abused, then a prosecutor may bring criminal charges against your abuser. In some circumstances, prosecutors will bring charges even if you do not want to cooperate, because violence is a crime, and the state will take action to enforce state laws.

• Most domestic violence cases are resolved through plea bargaining. You may be able to have some input into the plea bargaining process.

• If the case does make it to trial, then you may need to give evidence against your abuser. The prosecutor and a victim's advocate can tell you more about the process.

PART SIX

Money

CHAPTER 17

Women and Credit: Protecting Your Good Credit—Whether You Are Single, Married, or Divorced

Nancy had never had a car loan in her own name. Her father held the loan to her first car in his name, and she paid cash for her next car. When she was in her thirties and doing well professionally, she decided she wanted a better car. She already had a mortgage in her name and excellent credit, so she thought the timing was right.

Nancy went to a local dealer one weekend to sign the papers for a Lexus. Within an hour, her credit was approved with no conditions and she took delivery of her new car.

But about a week later, she got a phone call from the credit manager at the dealership where her loan was approved. The finance company was now insisting that Nancy's husband's name be added to her loan, since she had never before had a car loan in her own name. She reminded the manager of the favorable credit check a week before and that she had a mortgage in her name in addition to her excellent credit. She was told that none of that mattered, because she had never proved herself with a car loan.

Sound like fiction? In fact, this really happened to Nancy King (and the full story appears in her book, cited at the end of this chapter). And Nancy is not alone. Lenders do not have the best track record when it comes to approving loans for women. Indeed, sometimes their discrimination is blatant. It ranges from denying loans even when women are qualified, to requiring cosigners and charging higher interest rates, to asking women all sorts of demeaning questions that would never be asked of male applicants, such as "how many children do you plan to have?" or "how much time off will you take to care for your newborn child?" Such discrimination is often compounded for women of color. Nancy took issue with the car dealer's request in the real-life scenario, and the dealer did not change the terms of Nancy's credit. But that was only because she knew her rights to credit and was willing to stand up for them.

This chapter takes a look at the different types of credit and explains their legal significance to you. It discusses ways in which your credit history might—or might not—be entwined with the credit of your partner, husband, or former husband, and it describes relevant discrimination laws that prevent lenders from discriminating against you just because you are a woman.

BASIC FORMS OF CONSUMER CREDIT

Simply put, your **credit** is your ability to make payments when they are due. "Credit" also refers to the sale of money to you for

---

⚠️ PAYDAY LOANS

You've probably driven by a payday loan office or heard ads on television or radio promising to help you out with cash until payday. To obtain one of these short-term loans from a payday loan office, you write a personal check for the amount you wish to borrow, plus a sizeable fee, postdated to your next payday. The check casher holds the check until the effective date and gives you the principal in cash. So if you want to borrow $100, you might write a check for $120, and receive $100 cash.

Beware the payday loan! Many women—especially single women with children—resort to payday loans to help them with short-term cash needs. But this kind of loan is incredibly expensive—this example uses an annual percentage rate of over 400 percent—and many women fall into the trap of using it on a regular basis. The other disadvantage is that you do not establish a credit history by using payday loans.

---

a certain price. You may use credit to get money to make a purchase, build a home, or go to school. Credit allows you to buy and use goods and services now and pay for them later. For example, credit lets you use a car or a dishwasher before you have fully paid for it. You pay for it as you use it. Of course, you could save now to buy the car in the future, but you may want or need the car now—not three years from now. Similarly, on a small scale, you may buy a pair of shoes or a dinner on your credit card now and pay for them later. A **creditor** is simply the person or company that lends you money. The words "creditor" and "lender" are used interchangeably in this chapter, but don't worry, they mean exactly the same thing. The **debtor** is probably you—the person who owes the money to the creditor.

There are three basic forms of consumer credit:

1. Noninstallment credit (sometimes called thirty-day or charge-account credit)

2. Installment credit (also called closed-end credit)

3. Revolving or open-ended credit

Noninstallment, or **thirty-day or charge-account credit,** requires you to pay the balances you owe in full within thirty days. Travel and entertainment cards, such as American Express and Diners Club, operate this way, as would a charge account you have with a local business, like your dentist, plumber, or other service provider. **Installment** or **closed-end credit** is credit that you schedule to repay in two or more equal installments over a definite period of time. Your car loan or other personal loans are examples of this type of consumer credit. **Revolving** or **open-end credit** is more flexible and allows you to draw (take money out) on a preapproved open-ended credit line from time to time and then decide whether you want to pay off the entire balance, only a specified minimum payment, or something in between. With revolving credit, you may use the credit, make a payment, and use the credit again. Credit cards such as your MasterCard and Visa, as well as your major retailer cards like Sears or Home Depot, are examples of revolving credit.

Of particular relevance and interest to women is the fact that there are different ways to hold credit accounts with another person. The way in which you are named on an account may greatly impact your creditworthiness. You may have credit in an individual account or in a joint account, or you may be an authorized user on another person's account.

Authorized users are able to use another person's credit without being financially responsible for the debt. If you are an authorized user on your husband or partner's account, the creditor must report the credit history on the account in both names (assuming the account was opened after June 1, 1977). This is true for any other authorized user on an account. However, authorized user status is not a great way to establish your own creditworthiness. Being able to charge on another person's account is useful if you do not qualify for credit on your own. But such status also shows that you are relying on that person's income to pay the account, and thus it will be of little value to you should you later want to establish individual credit in your own name. If the person whose name is on the card does not pay, then a creditor might seek to make you, as an authorized user, responsible for payment of debts that you incurred when you used the card. However, courts have held that authorized users are not liable for the credit card holder's debt or even for their own charges on the card, because the credit card agreement makes payment the sole responsibility of the credit card holder.

With an **individual account**, on the other hand, the creditor will assess your income, assets, and credit history. Whether you are married, partnered, or single, if you designate your account as an individual account, you alone have responsibility for payments, and the account will appear on your credit report. The exception is if you live in one of the nine community property states, in which case you and your spouse will both be responsible for debts incurred on your individual accounts during your marriage, and each individual's debts may appear on both of your credit reports (see the "Credit Rules Are Different in Community Property Jurisdictions" sidebar below). If you are married and you do not have a source of income separate from your spouse's income, it may be more difficult for you to get and establish credit in an individual account. If you are able to open an individual account, you will be in a stronger financial position should your marital status change through divorce or the death of your spouse, because these accounts do not link your use of credit or your ability to get credit to your spouse's income or credit history.

With a **joint account**, the creditor looks at the incomes, financial assets, and credit histories of both you and your husband or partner. Both people named on the joint account are financially responsible for paying the debt. Since June 1, 1977, creditors who report credit histories of joint accounts are legally required to report the history in both account holders' names. Joint credit accounts are not just for married couples—any two people can open an account. You can create a joint account with a sibling, with an older parent, or with a person with whom you are in a relationship.

The good thing about joint accounts is that you are more likely to be granted credit when the assets of both you and the other person are considered. The downside is that when you pool your assets for joint credit, you also sign on for joint responsibility for the debt. You are both responsible for the debt, and it will appear on both of your credit records. If your relationship ends, it's a good idea to close the joint account immediately, before one person can indulge in some retail therapy for which you may both be responsible. Even if a divorce decree assigns responsibility to pay off joint debts to your former husband, you are still legally liable for the debt. This means that if he doesn't pay, the creditors can come after your assets.

Of course, there are other circumstances in which you may be liable for another person's debt. If you cosign for any debt, then you are ultimately responsible for the debt if the person doesn't pay. This is the case even if you didn't read the documents, so be very careful what you put your name to. Another common situation arises in the case of gifts. If your boyfriend gave you some jewelry but did not pay off the debt, the store may have a lien over the jewelry and be able to take it back. You are not legally liable for the debt, but if you want to keep the jewelry, you'll have to pay for it.

CREDIT RULES ARE DIFFERENT IN COMMUNITY PROPERTY STATES

Arizona, California, Idaho, Louisiana, Nevada, New Mexico, Texas, Washington, Wisconsin, and the Commonwealth of Puerto Rico are community property states. In all of these places, you and your husband are considered economic partners, and your earnings and assets are considered to be jointly owned **community property** (see chapter 6, "Marriage," for more information about community property jurisdictions).

In a community property state, some individual credit accounts you open are treated like joint accounts and you may both be liable for individual debts. For example, Suzie and Jack are a married couple living in a community property state. Each earns $50,000 a year and each owns separate assets. Suzie applies for a credit card for herself. The application asks for "household" income. She fills in $100,000.

Suzie receives the card and uses it for vacations with a girlfriend and to help her mom out by paying for her mom's phone bill and groceries. Suzie never uses it for household needs. After several years of using the card, Suzie is injured and unable to make monthly payments. The credit card company sues Suzie and discovers that she has no earnings and no longer has assets in her name.

If Suzie lived in a common-law state, then the creditor would have no rights against her husband's earnings or assets. However, in a community property state, creditors might assume that the debt was a community debt because Suzie included Jack's income under "household" income. In order to prevent Jack from being liable, Suzie would have to establish that it was her separate debt, not used for community expenses (like food, clothing, medical costs, and shelter), and that she had the ability to pay from her separate assets at the time the credit was established. If Suzie could show this, then Jack's income and separate assets would not be subject to the debt.

If you apply for credit in your own name in a community property state, the rules are a bit different from those in other states. A creditor is allowed to ask you about your marital status and request information about your husband because your marital status is relevant to the creditor's right to obtain payment. In addition, creditors in community property states may require that your spouse sign the legal document that makes you financially responsible for the debt.

You need to be aware in community property states that you generally do not get the same opportunities to establish and benefit from individual credit accounts as you do in a separate-property state, and you may be less able to separate yourself from your husband's, or former husband's, credit troubles. Contact a credit expert in your state.

DIVORCE, SEPARATION, AND CREDIT

If you are contemplating divorce or separation, then you should pay close attention to the status of your credit accounts. You might want to consider closing any joint accounts or any accounts on which your partner is an authorized user. A joint account can be closed at either your or your partner's request. If the joint account involves a mortgage or home equity loan, your creditor will probably make you refinance before relieving your partner of a financial obligation on the property. If you don't want to close the account, then make sure that regular, timely payments are made on joint accounts with outstanding balances. Remember that you are jointly liable for paying a joint account, regardless of the status of your marriage or relationship.

You can ask your creditor to convert a joint account to an individual account, but your creditor is under no obligation to do so and, in some cases, may require you to reapply for credit on an individual basis and base a decision on your new economic status. For women facing a reduced income after a divorce or separation, this may result in a rejection of credit.

Many women who have had their names on joint accounts with their husbands face difficulties when applying for individual credit after a divorce, even if they faithfully paid the bills. Why? Because creditors only reported account histories in the husbands' names, and the women have no credit history in their own names. Another pitfall awaits women who revert to their maiden names after divorce. Even if you have had several successful credit accounts in your married name, you might be denied if creditors cannot find a credit history under the name you gave on your application form. Generally, credit agencies track you by your Social Security number, but some creditors may not be willing to extend you credit without an established credit history in your current name. Therefore, it is important that you check with the credit bureau after you change your name to make sure that any old account information gets transferred to a file under your new name.

WIDOWS AND CREDIT

Widowhood, whether you have time to plan for it or it comes on you unexpectedly, presents unique financial challenges for women. If you have time to prepare before your husband's death, you may want to take some of the following steps:

- Build a credit history in your name
- Correct any credit problems in your name or your husband's name
- Explain any adverse information in your credit file—especially if it was the result of your husband's and not your mismanagement
- Consult with an experienced financial advisor

It is not out of the realm of possibility for you to continue to use your husband's credit for a short time after his death; however, doing so may jeopardize subsequent attempts to establish credit in your own name. For older women, this may not be much of an issue, but if you are a young woman with decades of financial independence ahead of you, this is something to consider. When you apply for credit, creditors must count all of your income from all sources, including annuities, pensions, and Social Security, and must also consider your husband's credit history if you can show that his history reflects yours. Of course,

( ) ASK A LAWYER

Q. I was an authorized user on my partner's card for years, until we broke up. I have no credit history in my own name, and am having problems getting a credit card, renting an apartment, and connecting utilities without one. What can I do to establish credit?

A. Apply for a secured credit card with a small balance. You will have to give the company $250 to $500 as security for a $250 or $500 line of credit. Once you use the card and make payments on time at least four months in a row, this will be reported on your credit report.

Apply for a loan and see—you may not be turned down. If you are turned down, often you will be approved if you get a cosigner.

—Answer by Denice Patrick
The Law Office of Denice L. Patrick, Lynnwood, Washington

Q. I live in a community property state. Is my husband automatically liable for my debts?

A. In Texas, a community property state, a husband and wife are not automatically liable for each other's debts. It depends on various factors. One factor is whether the wife obtained credit relying only on her own income. In that case, the husband is not responsible for the debt unless it is for food, clothing, or shelter (necessary items). As a practical matter, creditors may not take action to collect a debt against a husband for a debt incurred only by his wife, in his wife's name, and relying on his wife's credit, even in a community property state. You should consult a lawyer in your state if you have a specific issue of concern in this area.

—Answer by Irene Jackson
Attorney, Arbitrator, Mediator, Irving, Texas

a creditor may also consider the continuity and reliability of your income sources. It will be easiest to show your own creditworthiness if you established and maintained credit in your own name in an individual account during your marriage.

Whether or not you will be liable for your husband's debts after his death will depend on a number of things, including

- the type of debt it is (e.g., whether it is in an individual or joint account),
- whether there is enough money in his estate (including insurance proceeds) to pay off the debt,
- whether you live in a community property state, and
- whether any of the debts were secured with his property or property that you owned jointly.

CREDIT DISCRIMINATION LAWS

How many women do you suppose have been asked to supply a spouse's signature or financial information before a lender would take them seriously? How many women do you suppose have been denied credit when men with comparable finances have been granted it or charged less for it? There are a number of state and federal laws that protect you from being discriminated against by creditors just because you are a woman.

Since the late 1960s, dozens of federal statutes have been enacted to protect consumers like you from any number of bad and discriminatory credit practices on the part of creditors. The 1968 Consumer Credit Protection Act compelled creditors to use plain English in their forms and contracts for the first time, so that you and other ordinary consumers could understand exactly the terms of your credit charges, compare costs between lenders, and shop around for the best deal for you. Ironically, this act, which was designed to help you and other ordinary consumers, is one of the most lengthy and complicated federal laws in existence. Federal judge Richard A. Kohn summed it up best shortly after the law was passed, declaring it to contain some of the most "complex statutory and administrative regulations . . . ever."

For women, the most significant and helpful part of the Consumer Credit Protection Act is the Equal Credit Opportunity Act (ECOA). This law is designed to ensure that all credit applicants are considered on the basis of their actual qualifications for credit and are not rejected because of certain personal characteristics. The law protects both men and women from discrimination based on gender and marital status. In general, a credit grantor may not deny you credit or take any adverse action, such as lowering your credit limits or raising your annual percentage rate, just because of your gender or because you are married, single, widowed, divorced, or separated. There are some specific prohibitions:

• A credit grantor usually may not ask your gender when you apply for credit. One exception would be a loan to buy or build a home, or to repair, rehabilitate, or remodel a home, when asking your gender helps the federal government look for housing discrimination by determining whether equally qualified females and males are able to obtain residential mortgage loans. However, you may refuse to answer this question.

• Normally, you do not have to use a title (Mr., Miss, Mrs., or Ms.) when applying for credit. Sometimes credit grantors may ask whether you are married, unmarried, or separated if your marital status relates to their right to obtain repayment. Such a request would most likely be made in a state with community property laws or if the credit will be secured.

• A credit grantor may not ask you if you use birth control, whether you plan to have children, or whether you will take time off of work to care for your children. Neither are they allowed to make any assumptions about your plans.

• You do not have to reveal child support or alimony payments to a credit grantor unless you wish the credit grantor to consider it as income. If you do ask a creditor to include child support payments as part of your income, then creditors can consider whether these have been steady and reliable.

The act also requires lenders to tell you the reasons why you are denied credit and allows you to find out about your credit records and challenge your billing disputes.

You have a right to choose the name that you want to use on your account, which may or may not be your married name. For

⚠️ **FEDERAL LAW NO GUARANTEE OF CREDIT**

Beware: These laws do not guarantee that you will receive credit. You must still meet the creditor's standards and qualify for credit based on relevant factors, such as your income and credit history.

example, your married name may be "Mary Kate Smith" and your maiden name "Mary Kate Jones." You may use your married name, your maiden name, or a combination ("Mary Kate Jones-Smith"). Unfortunately, many married and widowed women have suffered severe financial hardships when they are cut off from credit when they divorce or lose a spouse. Unless there is clear evidence that your creditworthiness has changed (e.g., you previously relied solely on your former husband's income to get credit), a change in your marital status should not result in a change in your credit status on previously established accounts.

A creditor may not deny you credit simply because you receive financial aid from Social Security or other public assistance. Of course, a creditor may inquire about the age of your dependents, because you may lose some of your assistance when they reach a certain age. And a creditor may also consider whether you will continue to meet residency requirements for receiving benefits and whether it can reach those benefits by legal process if you do not pay. But your creditor may not deny you credit just because you receive public assistance.

A creditor may not deny you credit on the basis of your age alone unless you are too young to sign contracts (which is usually under age eighteen in most states). However, a creditor may consider your age in determining other elements of creditworthiness. For example, a creditor could consider whether you're close to retirement age and a lower income. Or a lender might be justifiably concerned if you take out a twenty-year home loan at the age of seventy. However, if you apply for a shorter-term loan, increase your down payment, or do both, you might satisfy the creditor's concerns.

In addition, the federal consumer protection laws give you the right to:

- Have someone other than your husband cosign a loan for you if a cosigner is required
- Have your credit records reflect any changes in your name
- Receive an answer to a credit application within thirty days of applying for credit
- Receive the specific reasons why credit is denied to you within sixty days after being denied credit
- Receive an explanation if you are given less favorable terms than for which you applied

STEPS TO TAKE IF YOU SUSPECT DISCRIMINATION

The ECOA requires that if you are denied credit, your creditor must tell you the specific reason why you were denied credit, or at a minimum tell you that you have a right to learn the reasons why you were denied credit if you ask your creditor in writing within sixty days. It is not good enough for your creditor to tell you things like "you don't meet our standards" or "your credit report doesn't show that you have enough points for our scoring system." Such vague and indefinite responses are illegal. Acceptable responses would be something more like "you have not been employed long enough" or "your income is too low."

If you are denied credit based on information that was supplied to your creditor from a credit-reporting agency, the federal law requires your creditor to give you (in writing) the name, address, and phone number of the credit agency that supplied the information. You should check with that agency to find out what is in your credit report. This information is free if you request it in writing within sixty days of being denied credit.

( ) ASK A LAWYER

Q. Does the ECOA prohibit creditors from discriminating against me on the grounds of sexual orientation?

A. The ECOA does not provide protection to those denied credit because of sexual orientation. However, courts can take a broad look at sex discrimination. Consider *Rosa v. Park West Bank & Trust Co.*, a federal case that arose out of Massachusetts.

A bank customer alleged that the bank refused to provide him with a loan application because he dressed in feminine clothes. He alleged that the loan officer told him to go home and change clothes. The cross-dresser sued, claiming gender discrimination under the ECOA. The bank argued that it did not violate the ECOA because its employee legitimately could not identify the cross-dresser because his forms of identification showed him in traditional male attire.

A federal trial court dismissed the lawsuit, determining that the ECOA does not prohibit discrimination based on how someone dresses. A federal appeals court, however, reinstated the lawsuit. According to the appeals court, the bank may have violated the ECOA: "Whatever facts emerge, and they may turn out to have nothing to do with sex-based discrimination, we cannot say at this point that the plaintiff has no viable theory of sex discrimination consistent with the facts developed."

—Answer by David Hudson
Attorney, Smyrna, Tennessee

Q. When I was a student, I forgot to pay a couple of phone bills, and I still owe the phone company $300. I recently tried to apply for a loan and found out that my credit history is in bad shape. Will it help matters if I pay off the $300? What other steps can I take to repair my credit history?

A. It will not help your credit history if you pay off the debt, at least not now. First, you should always dispute information like this on your credit report. You state you forgot to pay the phone bill, but are you sure? It could just be a mistake made by the creditor. If you are going to pay it, ask the phone company to indicate on your credit record that it was paid in full on time. If it will not do so, ask the credit-reporting agency to add a statement from you next to the information that it was overlooked by you or it would have been paid long ago.

—Answer by Denice Patrick
The Law Office of Denice L. Patrick, Lynnwood, Washington

It is also not a bad idea if you are denied credit to ask your creditor what factors it relied on and what are the best ways to improve your application with that creditor. And if you get credit, it is also a good idea to ask your creditor if you are getting the best rate and terms available and, if you are not, why not. If you are not getting better terms because of misinformation in your credit report, then make sure you dispute the accuracy of that information and contact the reporting agency to get it corrected.

If you suspect that one of your creditors has violated the law either because you were denied credit for no good reason or you were required to pay a higher interest rate than someone else with similar finances, you should remember that the law is on your side. Neither you nor any other woman should be denied credit based solely on your sex. If you suspect discrimination, you need to be confident and assert your rights.

First, you should inform the creditor that you suspect it has violated the law. This is important for two reasons: it shows the creditor that you know the law, and it gives the creditor an opportunity to discover and correct an error. You can do this in a letter addressed to the credit department. State your position clearly and without emotion or exaggeration. You might even suggest that the company discuss the matter with its legal department. Ask for a response.

If contacting the company directly does not work, contact the proper state or federal agency. By law, all lending institutions are supposed to have this information posted in their offices, but many do not. You may have to do a little legwork to find the appropriate authority to contact. On the state level, you should contact your state attorney general to see if the creditor violated one of your state's equal-credit-opportunity laws. Your state may decide to prosecute. On the federal level, you can find the proper federal agency to address your complaint to by contacting: Division of Consumer Affairs, Federal Reserve Board, 20th and Constitution Ave., N.W., Washington, D.C. 20511, or by visiting the website at www.federalreserve.gov/consumers.htm.

If state and federal agency action does not satisfy you, you can always consult an attorney and file a civil lawsuit against the creditor. If you win a discrimination lawsuit under the ECOA, you can recover damages, including punitive damages. You can also obtain compensation for attorney's fees and court costs. Check to see if your lawyer will handle the case on a contingency-fee basis. Under this type of fee arrangement, you pay your lawyer only if you recover monies in the lawsuit (the lawyer may get up to one-third of anything you win, plus expenses).

If you do have an issue with your creditor, make sure you keep good records and create a "paper trail." You should keep copies of all the forms that you fill out and any correspondence you send or receive. You might even consider sending your letters by certified mail to avoid an evasive "we did not receive your letter" response when you follow up. If you speak to anyone over

ⓘ WOMEN, BUSINESS, AND CREDIT

If you are a female business owner, your access to credit for your business is just as important as your access to consumer credit is for your personal accounts. Credit laws ensuring equal access to credit apply to business loans as well as to consumer loans. If you are starting your own business, you might also benefit from networking support resources and financial programs for women in business.

the phone, make sure you take notes—write down the time and date, the person's name and title, the gist of what he or she said, and any promises he or she made. If you keep careful records like this, then you're likely to be able to document your complaint more thoroughly and you may get a more favorable response from your creditor.

THE WORLD AT YOUR FINGERTIPS

• Nancy King, whose story appears at the beginning of this chapter, wrote a book with Morgan King that provides useful information on protecting your credit report. The book, *How to Rebuild Your Credit,* appears online at http://www.kingspressonline.com/credit%20book/rebuildcredit.html#Anchor17.

• You might want to consider contacting your local Consumer Counseling Office to find a course in money management to help you better understand credit. The AARP supports a Women's Financial Information Program for middle-aged and older women, which includes a seven-week course offered through local community groups such as the YMCA. Find out more at the AARP website at www.aarp.com.

• *The Consumer Handbook to Credit Protection Laws* contains detailed information about the federal laws that protect credit, as well as information about credit histories and records and making a complaint about a creditor. You can find the handbook online at www.pueblo.gsa.gov/cic_text/money/protection-laws/ccredit.htm.

• The Online Women's Business Center, which is a part of the Small Business Association (SBA), contains detailed information about loans and financing, including information about SBA loans, for women running a business at www.onlinewbc.gov/index.html.

• The Federal Trade Commission (FTC) offers information about federal laws and credit for consumers and businesses at www.ftc.gov/bcp/menu-credit.htm. The FTC also has a guide to the ECOA at www.ftc.gov/bcp/conline/pubs/credit/ecoa.pdf.

REMEMBER THIS

• If you have a joint account with another person, you will both be responsible for the payments, and details of the account will appear on both of your credit histories. An individual account is the best way to establish credit in your own name.

• Federal law prevents creditors from discriminating against you just because you're a woman and prohibits creditors from asking you certain types of personal questions. Federal law does not, however, guarantee that you will be granted credit.

• If you suspect that you have been denied credit or charged higher rates because of your sex, do not take it lying down. You can complain to the creditor, to the relevant agency in your state, or to the Consumer Affairs Division of the Federal Reserve Board. And if it's a serious matter, then you might consider filing a lawsuit against the discriminating creditor.

CHAPTER 18

Welfare, Poverty, and Government Benefits: A Simple Guide to the Complex World of Welfare

Karen and Kevin have been married for seven years and have two kids. They have received cash assistance off and on for the past six years—ever since Kevin was laid off from his job. Karen has a year to go before she will graduate from nursing school, and she is pregnant with her third child. Kevin was recently diagnosed with a learning disability and is working on getting retrained.

In a few months, the family may no longer be eligible for federal cash benefits, because the family will have used up its five-year lifetime limit on federal cash assistance. But they may be able to receive assistance in other forms—from food stamps to Medicaid.

Laws governing government public benefit programs are so complex and change so frequently that people can be surprised to discover that they are eligible for a public benefit program, or shocked and dismayed if they receive welfare and find out that they are no longer eligible. Public assistance programs for low-income individuals and families can include cash assistance (often referred to as a "welfare check"), food stamps or other nutrition programs, and Medicaid or other government health insurance programs. This chapter describes these basic benefits and provides some entitlement information. This is a good place to start if you are on public benefits or if you think you or a friend may be eligible for public assistance.

GETTING STARTED

Some basic principles apply to most public benefit programs. Common to all programs is an application process during which you may be asked to provide a number of documents. You may have to supply proof of your identity, which means your driver's license, Social Security card number, possibly your birth certificate, and any marriage and divorce certificates. Some programs require you to show evidence of your income and assets, which may include pay stubs, bank statements, tax returns, and appraisals of any property you own. You will need to fill out some forms and do some paperwork for all the different types of public assistance, but this is usually fairly straightforward and you can always ask a person at the agency to help you.

The start of benefits is linked to your date of application, so it is important to establish an application date as soon as you need assistance. For example, if you apply for food stamps on August 1, and are granted eligibility on September 1, then you will be given food stamps to cover the whole month of August. Almost any written request with your signature may be enough to establish your application date, even if you have not yet completed the full application form. Many benefit programs require your eligibility to be reassessed periodically—typically every six months or every year for most benefits in most states.

If you apply and are denied benefits, or if your benefits are terminated or reduced, then you have a right to appeal. In most cases, if your benefits are being terminated or reduced, you will receive a notice and it will explain how you can appeal the decision. If you request an appeal quickly, you may have a right to continue to receive aid at your current level pending the outcome of your appeal process. Your request must also usually be in writing. In such cases, you should consider seeking legal help from a local or state legal-aid or legal-services office.

One important tip: When you're applying for any kind of public benefit, you should always make photocopies of every

---

ⓘ WHAT IS THE POVERTY LEVEL?

The poverty level is often used to measure the amount of assistance you can receive under a benefit program. The U.S. government sets the poverty level every year. In 2004, it was $9,310 for one person and $15,020 for a family of three.

Some critics believe that the poverty level is an inadequate and unrealistic measure of basic living expenses. A self-sufficiency standard that considers different costs for different family needs has been proposed as a possible alternative. A comparison example noted by Voices for Virginia's Children   (www.vakids.org/Publications/self-sufficiencystandardarticle. htm) shows that a single parent raising an infant and a preschool-age child in Richmond, Virginia, would need an income of at least $34,510—more than twice the federal poverty level—to be fully self-sufficient. That same family would need to earn $35,695 in Charlottesville, $49,636 in Fairfax County, $32,724 in Virginia Beach, and $21,826 in Abingdon to be financially independent.

---

document you send in with your application, including any correspondence, any forms you fill out, any financial information about your income or assets, and any personal information. You should also keep the originals of any correspondence you receive from any benefits office—just keep it in a safe place all together, such as in a manila envelope. This will be useful to you if something goes astray at the benefits office (which happens more often than you might think) and will also help you if you have to lodge an appeal on your benefits.

FOOD STAMPS

The food stamp program allows low-income individuals and families to buy nutritious food using coupons or a special electronic benefits card. The social service agency takes several factors into account when deciding who is eligible, including your income, housing costs, and medical costs. You do not have to have children to be eligible for food stamps—you can be young or old, disabled or able-bodied, as long as you meet the income requirements. Most programs will require you to attend an interview with the social service agency. If you are eligible for food stamps, you'll probably receive an average of about $80 in food stamps every month for one adult, or around $190 each month for a family of four.

Traditionally, states issued paper food stamp coupons, but today all states offer the equivalent of food stamps on plastic benefit cards. These cards work like a bank debit card—when you use the card to pay for groceries, the cost of the groceries is deducted from your food stamp account, and it is not obvious to other customers that you are using food stamps. Another advantage is that you don't need to visit your local food stamp office to pick up stamps; instead, benefits are automatically loaded into your account each month on a designated date.

You cannot use food stamps to buy any kind of food you want. The food stamp program is designed to provide you with basic foodstuffs, such as

(i) FIND OUT YOUR ELIGIBILITY ONLINE

If you think you may be eligible for food stamps, you can save yourself a trip to the local food stamp office by checking your eligibility online. The Food and Nutrition website (http://209.48.219.49/fns/) offers a prescreening eligibility tool to help you work out whether you are eligible to receive food stamp benefits. The prescreening tool is not an application, but it can help you estimate how much assistance you might get. Remember that only your local food stamp office can tell you for sure whether you're eligible, and you still have to fill out the appropriate forms.

- breads and cereals,
- fruits and vegetables,
- meat, fish, and poultry,
- dairy products, and
- seeds and plants that produce food for your household.

You can't use food stamps to buy highly processed junk foods, food that you'll eat in the store, or hot foods. One exception is that some restaurants are authorized to accept food stamps in exchange for low-cost meals for qualified homeless, elderly, or disabled people. It is self-evident that you can't use food stamps to buy nonfood items, such as alcohol, tobacco, pet foods, soaps, vitamins, medicines, paper products, and household supplies. And it is against the law to redeem food stamps for cash.

MEDICAID

Medicaid is a government health insurance program that pays for basic health and long-term medical care for over 40 million very low-income Americans, 12 million of whom are low-income women. Because women are more likely to have low incomes and have children in the household, and because women generally live longer, they are more likely than men to qualify for Medicaid.

Congress created the Medicaid program in 1965 and makes the general rules, but the states have some discretion in determining which groups their Medicaid programs will cover, the financial criteria for Medicaid eligibility, and the types of medical services that are covered. Federal rules mean that the following groups must be eligible for Medicaid:

- Pregnant women whose family incomes are at or below 133 percent of the federal poverty level
- Infants born to Medicaid-eligible pregnant women. Medicaid eligibility must continue throughout the first year of life so long as the infant remains in the mother's household
- Children under age six in low-income families

ⓘ WILL I LOSE MY MEDICAID COVERAGE IF I MOVE TO ANOTHER STATE?

You will be required to follow the Medicaid rules in your new state if you move. You must be a resident of the state to qualify for Medicaid, which basically means that you must live in the state and intend to stay there permanently or indefinitely, or have come there to work.

- Low-income families with children
- Seniors (aged over sixty-five) and persons with disabilities who receive Supplemental Security Income (SSI; see chapter 19, "Issues for Senior Women," for more information about SSI)

States also have the option to provide Medicaid coverage for other "categorically needy" groups, which are defined by each state. People who are eligible for Temporary Assistance for Needy Families (discussed later in this chapter) are usually eligible, as are people transitioning off welfare benefits.

When assessing whether you qualify for Medicaid, an agency will consider your income and assets. In most states, you will not be eligible for Medicaid if the fair market value of your "countable resources" is more than $2,000 (for an individual), even if you have a very low income. But states do not add up the value of all of your assets to reach that figure—they exclude some major assets, like your home.

There is no in-person interview required when you apply for Medicaid, so you can apply by mail and do not even have to go to the office. Don't be afraid of the paperwork; some categories have short forms or streamlined eligibility processes, and the Medicaid agency can help you complete your application. If you are housebound, a Medicaid worker can be sent to your home to help you apply. If you are in a hospital or other institution, a staff social worker should be made available to help you apply. Don't let your inability to get to the public agency keep you from seeking assistance. Call your social services office and ask it to mail you an application.

The Medicaid office must decide if you qualify for coverage within forty-five days of your application for most Medicaid categories. If you must establish a medical disability to qualify, the state may take up to ninety days to make a decision. If the office asks for more information from you, then the clock stops ticking until you provide the information. It is in your best interests to provide the information the Medicaid office needs as soon as you can.

If you fill in the forms and provide all the paperwork and eventually qualify for Medicaid, then it will cover the full cost of most of your medical care. You must show proof of your Medicaid coverage to your medical provider and request that the provider bill the Medicaid program. Most Medicaid programs will pay for

- hospital stays,
- laboratory and x-ray services,

ⓘ MEDICAID SERVICES FOR WOMEN

Medicaid covers a broad range of services that are vital to women. Many states have broadened their Medicaid programs to provide additional benefits of importance to women, while others have placed greater limits on the scope of their coverage.

- Sixteen states have special Medicaid-funded family planning programs for women who otherwise would not qualify for Medicaid.

- All states participate in the federal Breast and Cervical Cancer Prevention and Treatment Act (which allows states to extend Medicaid to uninsured women diagnosed with breast or cervical cancer).

- Nineteen states use their own funds to cover all "medically necessary" abortions (the other states are more restrictive and only use Medicaid funds to pay for abortions in limited circumstances).

Source: The Henry J. Kaiser Family Foundation, www.kaisernetwork.org/health_cast/uploaded_files/3358.pdf

---

- outpatient hospital services and some clinic services,
- some dental care,
- some care by podiatrists, chiropractors, and optometrists,
- home health services,
- physical therapy,
- medications,
- dentures,
- prosthetic devices,
- eyeglasses,
- some hospice care, and
- some nursing home care.

MEDICALLY NEEDY SPEND-DOWN ELIGIBILITY

If your income is too high for you to be eligible for regular Medicaid, you may still qualify for some assistance with medical costs in the form of medically needy spend-down eligibility for Medicaid. Children, persons with disabilities, pregnant women, and the elderly are eligible.

This is the one Medicaid eligibility group that has no income limit—your eligibility depends on the cost of your medical care, rather than on your income. It's easiest to illustrate how this benefit works by using an example. Imagine eight-year-old Jane is hospitalized in June. The bill is $10,000. Jane lives with her mother, whose income is $4,000 a month—much too high for Jane and her mom to qualify for Medicaid. Therefore, Jane's mother seeks Medically Needy Spend-Down for Pregnant Women, Infants, and Children. After allowed deductions, the family's monthly "countable income" for June is $3,017. The Medically Needy Income Level for two people is $317, so the family's countable income is $2,700 over the $317 limit. This means that Jane's mother must pay $2,700 of the medical bills to "spend down" her income to the $317 limit. Medicaid will then pay for the rest of the bill—a substantial $7,300. To be eligible for Medicaid, you must "spend down" your income by pay-

( ) ASK A LAWYER

Q. I just applied for Medicaid but was turned down. As far as I can tell, I met their requirements and they should have taken me. What can I do?

A. First, try to get advice from your local legal-services or legal-aid office, which may be able to provide you with no-cost legal advice and even representation at a hearing if you are low income. Contact your state or local bar association to find a legal-aid or legal-services office near you, or look under "Attorneys" in the yellow pages of your phone book.

Read your denial notice carefully. You may be eligible but the agency may not have received all of the verifications of eligibility that it needed to award you Medicaid. Provide any missing information right away, and reapply if necessary. You may want to appeal the denial *and* reapply to protect your rights.

Even if you do not have legal representation, you can appeal the Medicaid denial by requesting a fair hearing. The denial notice you received should explain your hearing rights and how to ask for a hearing. Most denial notices include a simple hearing request form that you can use, or just write your own hearing request on a piece of paper. All it needs to say is something like "I want a hearing on the Medicaid denial dated [fill in date]. I believe that I qualify." You should date and sign the hearing request and include any case number that was assigned by the state agency or your Social Security number. Mail or take the original hearing request to the state agency office. Keep a copy for your records. Usually, a hearing request must be received by the agency within ninety days of the date on your denial notice. Read your denial notice carefully to find out what the time limit is in your state.

You will get a notice of the hearing date. Be sure to show up on time. You can bring witnesses and a representative, who does not have to be a lawyer. You have the right to review your Medicaid file. You can question any agency workers or witnesses that are at the hearing and you can present your own information showing why you qualify for Medicaid. You will receive a written decision a few days or weeks after the hearing. You may be able to appeal the hearing decision if you lose. Seek legal advice.

—Answer by Jacqueline Doig
Staff Attorney, Center for Civil Justice, Saginaw, Michigan

ing medical bills, and when you have spent enough of your monthly income to qualify, Medicaid will pay the rest of the cost of your medical care.

You can use bills from doctors, pharmacies, hospitals, and even travel to and from care to meet the "spend-down" requirement. Bills paid by health insurance or other private third-party payers may not be applied to the spend down. Eligibility is calculated on a month-by-month basis, using your income and medical costs in any one month.

WHAT'S THE DIFFERENCE BETWEEN MEDICAID AND MEDICARE?

Medicaid and Medicare both provide health insurance coverage that is jointly funded by the state and federal governments. The difference between them is that Medicaid is health insurance for low-income people—it is based on your income and assets—and Medicare is based only on your age or disability, not on your income or whether you can afford health care. Medicare is part of the Social Security Act and originally it only covered people aged sixty-five or older. However, Medicare has been expanded to include people with long-term disabilities and people with permanent kidney failure who need dialysis or a transplant. Medicare offers different types of health plans (hospital insurance and supplementary medical insurance), and your coverage will depend on the plan or plans you choose. Chapter 19 contains more information about Medicare.

There are some benefits available to **dual eligibles**, those people who are entitled to both Medicare and some type of Medicaid benefit. For example, if you are a dual eligible, you can use Medicaid to cover services that Medicare does not cover, such as prescription drugs, eyeglasses, and hearing aids. In some cases, Medicaid will pay your premiums and deductibles for your Medicare or Medical Supplemental Insurance policies. If your employer offers a group health plan, Medicaid may pay for you to be enrolled in that program. Essentially, Medicaid will decide if it is most cost-effective for you to be on Medicaid or for Medicaid to pay your premiums for you to get coverage elsewhere.

TEMPORARY ASSISTANCE TO NEEDY FAMILIES

In the past, people were able to depend on receiving cash assistance, or "welfare," from the government when they needed it, for as long as they needed it. Welfare used to be an entitlement program with no lifetime limits. All that changed when traditional welfare underwent sweeping changes in the 1990s. It started with a federal law called the Personal Responsibility and Work Opportunity Reconciliation Act of 1996. This comprehensive law transformed the nation's welfare system into a work-oriented system with a five-year lifetime limit for individual recipients of cash assistance.

The primary mission of today's public benefits system is to move people from welfare to work and reduce low-income families' dependence on cash assistance. Moving off of a cash assistance benefit program does not mean a family will lose all benefits under noncash programs, such as food stamps and Medicaid. In fact, many working families that work their way off welfare still have income below the poverty level. Additional goals of welfare reform include promoting job preparation, promoting work and marriage, preventing and reducing the number of out-of-wedlock pregnancies, and encouraging the formation and maintenance of two-parent families.

The 1996 welfare reform law created the Temporary Assistance for Needy Families (TANF) program. TANF marked the end of federal entitlement assistance that gave public benefits to every eligible person for as long as necessary. Congress sets only a certain amount of money aside for cash assistance each year, which means that states cannot necessarily provide benefits to every eligible person for as long as he or she needs it.

States have lots of flexibility to design their own TANF programs—the law specifically says that states may use TANF funds in any manner "reasonably calculated to accomplish the purposes of TANF." States use their TANF funds to provide a variety of benefits, including cash assistance, child care, education and job training, transportation, and other services that help families transition to work. States are required to share the cost of providing benefits—each year, a state must spend a certain amount of its own money to help eligible families.

Eligibility for TANF benefits varies by state, and you will have to check with your state or local benefits office to learn about your state's specific eligibility requirements. The kind of benefit you receive will depend on your particular circumstances. For example, a state could choose to limit TANF cash assistance to very low-income families, but provide TANF-funded child care or transportation assistance to working families with somewhat higher incomes.

However, some features are common to TANF programs in every state:

• Federal law currently allows states to exempt victims of domestic violence from certain requirements for TANF eligibility. This is called the "Family Violence Option," and it allows states to waive federal requirements that make escaping domestic and sexual violence more difficult or that unfairly penalize victims.

• With few exceptions, work requirements for TANF benefits provide that you must start work or **qualifying work** (see the "Qualifying Work Activities" sidebar below) as soon as you are able to do so, no later than two years after starting in an assistance program. States have discretion not to require single parents caring for children under age one to engage in work or work

activities. A single parent with a child under six cannot be punished for not engaging in work activities if adequate, affordable
child care is not available.

• There is a five-year lifetime limit for cash assistance funded
by TANF. This means that if you or anyone in your family has
received federally funded public benefits for five years, you are
no longer eligible for cash aid under TANF. States are allowed to
exempt up to 20 percent of their caseloads for various hardships,
so it is possible that in your state you could qualify for a longer
period of benefits. Your state may also provide you with noncash
TANF services that are not subject to the five-year limit or may
provide you with state-funded cash assistance after your eligibility for federal assistance ends.

• Under the teen parent live-at-home and stay-in-school
requirement, unmarried parents under age eighteen must participate in educational and training activities and live with a
responsible adult or in an adult-supervised setting before they
are eligible for TANF assistance. If you are a teenage mother and
you live with one or both of your parents, then you will qualify. If
you cannot live at home, then states must help you find adult-
supervised living settings.

• Finally, the federal law makes most legal immigrants ineligible for most TANF-funded programs until they have been in the

---

(i) QUALIFYING WORK ACTIVITIES

Qualifying work activities generally include subsidized or unsubsidized
employment, on-the-job training, work experience, community service,
satisfactory secondary school attendance, and up to twelve months of
state-approved vocational training. But caring for your own child, literacy
training, enrollment in English as a Second Language programs, and
postsecondary education may not be qualifying work activities. For
example, in most states, college coursework does not count toward
work requirements except in limited situations and for a limited number
of hours.

United States for at least five years, unless they were in the United States before July 16, 1996.

There are various exemptions and exceptions to many of these rules, which you can find out about by contacting your local legal services organizations, your local or state child and family advocates, your local or state social services offices, or even your local or state elected official.

WOMEN, INFANTS, AND CHILDREN NUTRITION PROGRAM

The Special Supplemental Nutrition Program for Women, Infants, and Children—more commonly known as WIC—is a federal benefits program that provides grants to states to fund nutrition programs. You may be eligible to receive WIC benefits if you are pregnant or have recently given birth, and your children may be eligible if they are under five years old. To qualify for WIC, you must be low-income and you must also be at "nutritional risk" according to a health professional.

There are two types of nutritional risk that might make you eligible for WIC. The first is medically based risk, which gets high priority. You may be in this category if you have anemia, you're underweight, you're a very young mother, or you have a history of pregnancy complications or poor pregnancy outcomes. The second type of nutritional risk is diet-based risk—you could fall into this category if you have a nutritionally inadequate diet.

(i) A BREAK ON INCOME REQUIREMENTS

If you or a member of your immediate family participate in benefits programs such as the Food Stamp Program, Medicaid, or TANF, then you don't need to pull together the voluminous paperwork to show your income all over again—you automatically meet the income eligibility requirement for WIC.

If you are applying for WIC, a doctor, nutritionist, or nurse will examine you and apply federal guidelines to determine whether you are at nutritional risk. Your health screening is free.

If you are eligible for WIC, there are several forms your benefits might take, depending on which state you live in. You may receive checks or vouchers to purchase specific foods each month that are designed to supplement your diet, or you may be given actual food. You may be able to get food delivered to your home, or you may have to pick it up from a warehouse. Food packages may vary depending on your needs, as identified by your doctor or nutritionist. Foods provided by WIC are high in the nutrients most lacking in the diets of the program's targeted population: protein, calcium, iron, and vitamins A and C.

WIC services are provided on a local level at many different places, including

- county health departments,
- hospitals,
- mobile clinics,
- community centers,
- schools,
- public housing sites,
- migrant health centers and camps, and
- Indian Health Service facilities.

Just as it does for the TANF program, Congress authorizes a specific amount of federal funds each year for grants to states to run WIC programs. Unfortunately, funding is always tight, and state programs cannot provide assistance to all eligible people. Keep in mind that you may not receive WIC benefits even if you are eligible—it depends on how many others have applied and on the order of priority.

OTHER PROGRAMS PROVIDING FOOD

There are many benefit programs that provide food—check with your social services office to find out whether you or your child may be eligible for any of the following:

• School meals, under the National School Lunch Program, the School Breakfast Program, or the Special Milk Program

• Summer Food Service Program

• Child and Adult Care Food Program, which may provide food at your child's day care center or child care provider

• Food Assistance for Disaster Relief

• Food Distribution, under the Schools/Child Nutrition Commodity Programs, the Food Distribution Program on Indian Reservations, the Nutrition Services Incentive Program, the Commodity Supplemental Food Program, or the Emergency Food Assistance Program

THE WORLD AT YOUR FINGERTIPS

• The following websites provide screening tools to help you see if you may be eligible for a variety of governmental programs: www.govbenefits.gov and www.benefitscheckup.org.

• If you think you may qualify for TANF benefits, contact your state or local public benefits or social services office. You can find a list of each state's TANF program names at www.acf.dhhs. gov/programs/ofa/tnfnames.htm.

• The U.S. Department of Agriculture's Food and Nutrition Service website offers program fact sheets, a WIC resource center, program data, links, and information on how to contact the national office at www.fns.usda.gov.

• To find your local food stamp office, look in your local phonebook under "Food Stamps," "Social Services," "Public Assistance," or a similar title. You can also call your state's food stamp hotline (you can find the number at www.fns.usda.gov/ fsp/contact_info/hotlines.htm).

• The Centers for Medicare and Medicaid Services website provides fact sheets, FAQs, a prescreening tool, and other useful resources on Medicaid at www.cms.hhs.gov. You can find the agency that administers Medicaid in your state by visiting http://cms.hhs.gov/medicaid/statemap.asp.

REMEMBER THIS

• If you are eligible for one form of public benefit, you may be eligible for other kinds of public benefits (e.g., Medicaid or the WIC program) automatically. Ask your social services office to give you more information—it could help you save a lot of time and effort in filling out forms.

• Make sure you keep a copy of every form and letter you send when you are applying for public benefits. It doesn't take much time and it could make it much easier for you if a document goes missing or there is a problem.

• Applying for public benefits can be a bewildering process, with so many forms to fill out and so much documentation to provide. You can ask many people for help: your local social services office, your local or state child and family advocate, or even your local or state elected official.

PART SEVEN

Planning Ahead

CHAPTER 19

Issues for Senior Women: Plan Now to Ensure Prosperity in Your Golden Years

Janet started work when she finished high school. She worked for much of the next forty years, taking a few years off to have her kids, and working part time through her forties. She retired five years ago, at the age of sixty. Her husband, Bob, was the main breadwinner for their household. He had a higher-paying job than Janet, and a larger pension, and he also took care of most of the financial details of their planned retirement.

But Bob died last month, and Janet has had to start thinking about finances and the future for herself. She has dozens of questions that need to be answered: Is she eligible for Bob's pension? Will she still receive Bob's pension if she remarries some time in the future? Is she eligible for Medicaid? Should she invest in insurance for long-term care?

These are important legal issues for all elder Americans, but if you're a woman, the stakes seem to be higher for you. As a woman, you will probably live longer than most men—according to the Working Woman's Guide to Financial Security, your average life expectancy at age sixty is eighty-three if you are female, but just seventy-eight if you're male. Given the additional fact that women are more likely to marry men older than they, married women tend to outlive their husbands. Women are also likely to have more chronic health problems than men, which results in higher health care costs during their retirement years.

These statistics assume added significance given that working women generally earn less than working men, and probably have fewer pension benefits, less entitlement to Social Security, and fewer assets than their male coworkers. Women live longer and save less, which means that women are more likely than men to outlive their savings. The result is that older women are more than twice as likely to be poor as older men.

This chapter will survey just a couple of the legal issues that you might face as you grow older and retire. We cannot cover all of the issues or tell you everything you will need to know to plan for your retirement in one chapter, but we can give you a good place to start. This chapter will look at pensions, medical issues, and federal benefits. As with most legal matters, we recommend you consult an experienced elder law attorney for specific advice about your particular situation. And remember, you are never too young to start planning for your golden years.

PENSIONS

If you are a working woman, you need to find the answers to several important questions. First, does your employer have a pension plan? If so, are you included in the plan? Has your pension vested? What happens to your pension if you retire early or change jobs? If you do not have a pension in your own name, you may still be entitled to one through a spouse or former spouse and will need to know the conditions that apply to your entitlement.

A **pension** is defined in most dictionaries as a "payment to you that is intended to allow you to subsist without working." About half the employees working for private companies are covered by private retirement plans. There are two basic types of pension plans:

- Defined-benefit plans
- Defined-contribution plans

Defined-benefit plans promise you a specified pension benefit when you retire that is based on the years that you worked and your salary. For example, a defined-benefit plan might pay you $10 a month for every year that you worked. Thus, if you retire after ten years of service, you would receive $100 per month in pension benefits. Under **defined-contribution plans**, you and/or your employer contribute a certain amount per month during the years you work. These contributions are made to a separate account in your name, and your retirement benefits are based on the amount in your account when you retire. Under either type of plan, the amount contributed by your employer will be determined by a formula that considers your age, how long you worked for your employer, and how much you were paid.

The law does not require your employer to set up a pension plan. It can have no plan, a defined-benefit plan, a defined-contribution plan, or, if you're lucky, both. If there is a plan, your employer decides who may qualify—pension plans do not have to include every worker. Some jobs may be excluded from the plan, and part-time workers are rarely covered. This has the

---

( ) ASK A LAWYER

Q. Which is better—a defined-benefit plan or a defined-contribution plan?

A. The answer to this could vary depending on your age, assets, health, cash flow, and other factors. If you are thinking about investing in one or the other, you should consult with your tax advisor or a financial planner. Additionally, the plans are quite different. A defined-benefit plan provides a fixed monthly benefit, generally from the earliest retirement age (usually 59$\frac{1}{2}$) until death. Examples of defined-benefit plans are things such as pensions or pure retirement. A defined-contribution plan has a value that is readily discernable at any given time. Examples of defined-contribution plans are 401(k)s, IRAs, and profit-sharing accounts.

—Answer by Sharon L. Corbitt
Sneed Lang, P.C., Tulsa, Oklahoma

---

effect that women—who are more likely to work part-time jobs than men—are more likely to be excluded. It's a good first step to check with the person running the plan at your workplace (the plan administrator), your personnel office, or your union representative to find out whether you are a plan member and how you can become one.

Many plans require you to work for one year before you can join. Once you are eligible to join, you can start accruing benefits immediately. However, you must work a specified number of years before your pension **vests** and you have the right to receive a pension at retirement age. Your employer can choose one of two vesting methods specified by federal law:

1. your plan might vest completely after five years—this is called cliff vesting, or

2. your plan might vest gradually—20 percent after three years, another 20 percent after four years, and so on, until it's completely vested after seven years.

If you leave your job before your pension has fully vested, you will not be entitled to any nonvested funds that your employer contributed to the plan (although you will still be entitled to any contributions that you made). If you leave your job after your pension has vested, then you are entitled to all the benefits. You can transfer the funds into your new employer's account or into a private account (e.g., an Individual Retirement Account), without paying income tax on the funds. You can also elect to receive the content of your account in a lump sum, but you will then probably have to pay income tax.

When can you start collecting your pension benefits? Most plans set a "normal" retirement age, often sixty-five. Your plan will probably have a minimum retirement age as well, perhaps, fifty-five, sixty, or sixty-two. Check with your plan administrator. You may be able to collect benefits early or you may have to wait until you are older. Keep in mind that because your benefits will be calculated based partly on your age, the younger you are when you retire, the smaller your benefits will be, though presumably you will get them for a longer time.

(i) INDIVIDUAL RETIREMENT ACCOUNTS

If your employer does not offer a pension plan, then you may want to put money into an Individual Retirement Account (IRA). A traditional IRA is a retirement plan for individual investors. You can open one if the funds you contribute come from taxable earned income made during the year of the contribution. However, the limits on contributions are comparatively low—you could only contribute $3,000 per year to an IRA in 2004 if you were under fifty, or $3,500 if you were over fifty. The advantage of traditional IRAs is that your contributions are not taxed at the time you invest or annually, but only at the time you withdraw money. At that point, you'll pay income tax on whatever you withdraw, but presumably at a lower rate because your income will be less at retirement. You must start making withdrawals after you reach the age of $70\frac{1}{2}$. The amount you must withdraw each year depends on your age and is calculated so that you will use up your retirement income by the time you die. You can name someone as the beneficiary of the account when you open the IRA. The beneficiary will inherit the balance of the account on your death, without the need for a will or probate. If your spouse is a beneficiary, he can roll the money over into his own IRA, without paying tax.

Roth IRAs do not offer a tax deduction for contributions, but do provide for tax-free withdrawals. They may be suitable for you if you'll be in the fortunate position of having a higher income after you retire.

401(K) PLANS

401(k) plans are a type of defined-contribution plan. They are very popular and many companies have elected to set up 401(k) plans rather than provide traditional pensions as an employee benefit. A 401(k) plan involves individual accounts and is funded by contributions you elect to make, which are deducted from your salary before taxes. They are also referred to as

deferred-compensation plans, because you do not pay taxes until you take the money out of your fund after you have retired. Some employers may match all or part of your contributions. There are limits on the amount that you may contribute each year, and they increase annually. In 2004, the individual limit was $13,000.

There are several advantages to using a 401(k) plan: it lowers your taxable income, it allows your employer to match all or part of your contributions, and most plans allow you to choose how to invest your contributions—you can be as aggressive or as conservative as you wish in selecting your investment options.

Of course, there are also disadvantages. First, the ability of a 401(k) to provide for your retirement depends on your personal investing skills and on the amount you have been able to contribute. And it is not the best method for passing wealth on to your beneficiaries because it is a "wasting asset" that requires you to withdraw a certain percentage of your account each year once you reach age 70½, which may deplete most of its assets. You may want to consult a financial advisor about whether a 401(k) plan is right for you.

PENSIONS AND ANNUITIES

If you are married, federal law entitles you to a share of your husband's pension; your husband may similarly be entitled to a share of your pension. The Retirement Equity Act of 1984 requires all private pension plans to provide benefits to surviving spouses. The most common type of payment is called the **joint and survivor annuity**. This pays the full benefit to a married person up until his or her death, and then pays a fraction of the full benefit to the surviving spouse. So if your husband receives a pension, you will be entitled to a fraction of that pension after his death. The amount to which you're entitled will depend on the pension plan and how much he paid—it may be as much as two-thirds of his pension. Depending on the pension, you may be entitled to a survivor's benefit for a few years or for the rest of your life. Different rules apply to certain other retirement savings plans, such as 401(k)s and IRAs. Death benefits from a 401(k) are generally paid out to a specified beneficiary in a lump sum, which a surviving spouse can roll over—tax-free—into an IRA.

Federal law protects your rights to this survivor's benefit, unless you sign a waiver to relinquish survivor rights. Why would you ever consider doing this? There are several possible reasons. You might not wish to pay income tax on the distributions from the plan after your husband dies, or perhaps the money might be better used by another beneficiary. If you do waive the right, then the plan should allow your spouse to name another beneficiary, such as a child or a trust. Or your spouse might be able to waive survivor rights entirely, in exchange for receiving a higher pension during his lifetime.

You must sign a consent form in the presence of a notary or a pension plan administrator in order to waive survivor rights. Although this system is not foolproof, this "in-person" signature requirement has been credited with deterring fraud and undue influence. This law has been especially important for elderly widows, who are three times more likely than men to depend on their spouses' pension benefits. Proposed legislation would do away with the in-person signature requirement for waiver of survivor annuities in favor of "paperless technology" (so that you could waive the right to survivor payments online). Critics have suggested that this would be an unfortunate setback for spousal pension rights.

Pensions are important to think about if you divorce. As part of your divorce or legal separation, you may be awarded rights to a portion of your spouse's pension benefit (or he may be awarded rights to a portion of yours). Generally, you must have been married for at least one year before a court will award you rights to a portion of your spouse's pension. State law will govern your pension rights in a divorce, and in most states, pension benefits are part of the marital property that gets divided upon divorce. If you are awarded a share of your spouse's pension benefits, you can collect benefits

(i) PENSIONS FOR UNMARRIED COUPLES

If you are single or are one half of an unmarried couple, you should still be able to nominate someone to receive benefits from your IRA after you die. Usually, this is as simple as filling out a form and nominating a beneficiary. One word of warning—the bank will do what you tell it to do, so it's up to you to make sure that you keep it up-to-date regarding your intentions. If your relationship ends, for example, then you should notify the plan and change the beneficiary designation. If your wishes are more complex—for example, if you want to name a contingent beneficiary— then you can name a trust as your beneficiary, or direct the funds to your estate to be distributed via your will.

Company pensions and 401(k) plans are another story. Some company pension plans bar employees from naming anyone other than a spouse as a beneficiary of survivor benefits. Check with your plan administrator and your state laws on whether your plan will recognize survivor benefits for your partner before you contribute to your plan. You may want to consider other estate-planning options discussed in the next chapter to provide for your partner.

If you are a nonspouse beneficiary of a 401(k) or an IRA, then you cannot roll over benefits into your own IRA. Same-sex partners, children, siblings, or other friends or relatives who are beneficiaries must begin taking distributions from the account in the year after the account holder's death. This requirement means that they have to pay more tax on what they receive than spouses, who can defer benefits until they are over seventy. The good news is that nonspouse beneficiaries may be able to spread out distributions over their remaining life expectancies, which may reduce the income tax they have to pay. Check the details of your plan—plans may impose different requirements on (and impose administrative costs for) small distributions.

• when your former spouse stops working and becomes eligible to start collecting the pension, or

• when your former spouse has reached the earliest age for collecting benefits under the plan and is at least age fifty.

For private plans, a court can do this through a **qualified domestic relations order** (**QDRO**) that requires your spouse's pension administrator to split the benefits as the court directs. To be eligible for a QDRO, a private plan must be one that is "qualified" under the Internal Revenue Code. You or your attorney will need to check with the plan's administrator to find out what requirements your plan needs to meet.

MEDICAL ISSUES

As you grow older, you are likely to have to deal with specific medical issues. Perhaps you are contemplating the possibility of long-term care, perhaps you are trying to navigate your way through the finer points of Medicare, or perhaps you want to identify the person who will make decisions about your health care if you are not able to do so. This section will look at some of these issues and give you some important information about your options.

Making Decisions about Health Care

With few exceptions, you have the right to control decisions about what happens to your body, including the option to refuse suggested medical treatment. If you are unable to make decisions about your health care in an emergency, the law presumes your consent to treatment. But if it is not an emergency and you are too sick to make a decision yourself, then someone else must make decisions about your health care on your behalf. The best way to make sure that health care decisions are made the way you would want and by the person you would want is to make an advance directive for health care, to be used in the event that you become incapacitated. In many states, spouses are automatically given the right to make such decisions. But most states' laws do not authorize other people, including unmarried partners, to make health care decisions on your behalf. Thus, it is particularly crucial for single women and women in unmarried relationships, including same-sex couples, to execute advance directives.

An **advance directive** is a written statement, which you complete in advance of serious illness or emergency, about how you want your medical decisions made. The two most common forms of advance health care directives are a living will and a durable power of attorney for health care.

A **living will** (also called a medical directive or declaration) is a written instruction spelling out any treatments you want if you are unable to speak for yourself. A living will differs from a power of attorney for health care in that a living will does not appoint another person to speak for you. It speaks for you in writing. Your living will simply says: "Whoever is deciding, please follow these instructions." It is called a living will because it takes effect while you are still alive.

As discussed in chapter 5, a **power of attorney** is simply a written document in which you (the **principal**) give certain authority to another person (your **agent** or **agent in fact**) to act on your behalf. A **health care power of attorney** allows you to appoint someone else to make health care decisions for you in the event that you become incapacitated—including, if you wish, the decision to refuse intravenous fluids or to turn off the respirator if you're brain-dead. You can also use a health care power of attorney to allow your agent to make decisions about things like nursing homes, surgeries, and artificial feeding.

Though state law requirements may vary, to properly fill out a health care power of attorney form, you must
- understand the form you are signing, and
- have your signature witnessed by at least two other adults (usually, your doctors and close relatives who may have a conflict of interest are not allowed to act as witnesses).

Many hospitals provide health care power of attorney forms and booklets with helpful information at no charge. You may also be able to get such forms and information from state senators and representatives.

Who should you name as your agent for your health care power of attorney? Your spouse is always a good candidate, but for elder women who may outlive their husbands, a child or close friend are good alternatives. Your state's laws may place some limitations on who you can name (some prohibit health care providers or facility employees from acting as your agent). It is important to discuss your preferences and options with whomever you choose and make sure that person is willing to serve as your agent. It is okay to have an alternate or successor agent named if your primary agent is not available, but it is not a good idea to name coagents, because it creates the possibility for disagreement among your agents. You may also expressly disqualify anyone whom you absolutely want to keep from playing any role in your health care decisions.

If you do not have an advanced directive, many states have family consent (or health surrogate) laws that authorize someone else, typically a family member, to make some or all health care decisions on your behalf. At a minimum, telling your doctor and others what you want provides evidence of your wishes if you later become incapacitated—especially if your doctor writes your wishes down in your medical record. However, written advance medical directives are more likely to be followed.

Medicare

Medicare was started in 1965 as a way to provide medical care services to all Americans who were elderly (over sixty-five) or disabled. But as the population has aged, chronic disease has become more prevalent, the elderly require more long-term care, and Medicare, which was never intended to cover chronic care, no longer fits the bill. If you are a woman, the stakes are especially high for you, because not only are you more likely to live longer than most men, you are also more likely to have more chronic-care needs and to rely on Medicare when you turn sixty-five. The shortfall of Medicare has spawned many debates and reform efforts—especially in the area of prescription drug coverage. As you read this, it is likely that Medicare reform will be in the headlines and still the subject of much debate.

Medicare is administered at the federal level by the Centers for Medicare and Medicaid Services, which is a branch of the U.S. Department of Health and Human Services. Medicare has two main parts:

• **Part A** (the hospital insurance part) covers your medically necessary care in a hospital, skilled nursing facility, or psychiatric hospital, some home health care, and hospice care. This coverage is free to you at age sixty-five if you are also eligible for Social Security. If you are not eligible for Social Security, you can still enroll, but you will pay a sizeable monthly premium.

• **Part B** (the medical insurance benefits part) covers your medically necessary physician's services no matter where you receive them—outpatient hospital care, diagnostic tests, rehabilitation services, and a variety of other medical services and supplies not covered by part A. Part B coverage is available to all part A enrollees for a monthly premium that changes yearly. You will most likely also pay deductibles and copays for most services unless you are enrolled in a managed-care organization.

The exact coverage rules and limitations are complex. Your actual coverage determinations and payments to your care providers are handled by insurance companies under contract with Medicare. These insurance companies are referred to as "fiscal intermediaries" under part A and "carriers" under part B. They determine the appropriate fee for each service. This is why original Medicare is referred to as a "fee-for-service" program.

Medicare provides you with basic health care coverage but leaves many gaps in coverage, for which you have to pay. Some people have supplemental coverage from former employers; others are enrolled in a Medicare health maintenance organization or are eligible for Medicaid (discussed in chapter 18). But those who do not fit into any of these categories may need to purchase a supplemental (or "Medigap") insurance policy to cover some of the costs not covered by Medicare.

If you are not eligible for Medicaid, but your income is low and you cannot afford private Medigap insurance, you may be eligible for help in paying for uncovered costs under the Qualified Medicare Beneficiary (QMB) program. For example, under QMB, the government will pay your Medicare part B premiums and provide supplemental coverage equivalent to a Medigap policy if your income and assets fall below a qualification amount (which is more generous than Medicaid's).

You may also have the option to join a **managed-care organization** (MCO) or other care option permitted under Medicare+Choice. MCOs provide or arrange for all Medicare-covered services and generally charge a fixed monthly premium and small or no copayments. You may also be offered benefits not covered by Medicare, such as preventive care and prescription drugs. However, Medicare+Choice plans are not available in all parts of the country, and like other problematic parts of Medicare are subject to reform efforts. Thus, you need to make

ⓘ MEDICARE AND PRESCRIPTION DRUG COVERAGE

The Medicare Prescription Drug Improvement and Modernization Act, signed into law by President George W. Bush on December 8, 2003, means that Medicare now offers you some assistance with your prescription drugs if you are over sixty-five or have a disability. Beginning in June 2004, the law allows you to apply for a drug discount card with a Medicare-approved seal, which entitles you to save from 10 to 15 percent on prescription drug costs. Medicare contracts with private companies to offer these cards, and discounts vary depending on the type of card. Some cards can only be used at designated pharmacies, so it's worth doing some comparison shopping before you buy a card. These cards will cost no more that $30 per year, and they are optional: You do not have to get one if you do not want one.

In 2006, Medicare will phase out the use of drug discount cards and replace the system with an optional prescription drug plan, which will cover a large portion of the costs of prescription drugs. For more information, visit the Medicare website at www.medicare.gov/ or call toll-free 1-800-MEDICARE (633-4227) or TTY 1-877-486-2408.

▶ ## HOW AND WHEN DO I APPLY FOR MEDICARE BENEFITS?

It is best to apply for Medicare as soon as you become eligible, either after you become disabled or when you turn sixty-five. Your initial enrollment period begins three months before your sixty-fifth birthday and extends three months beyond your birthday month. You can enroll at any time during this seven-month period. Your benefits will begin to run on the first day of the month in which you turn sixty-five. Enrollment for Medicare is automatic for both parts when you begin to receive Social Security. You can also enroll during the general enrollment period, which runs from January 1 to March 31 of each year.

If you continue to work after you turn sixty-five and are covered by your employer's health insurance program or if you are covered under your spouse's plan, then Medicare will be the secondary payer after your other insurance pays.

Always talk to your employer's benefits office, the Centers for Medicare and Medicaid Services, or your local Social Security Administration office to make sure you receive maximum coverage without penalty.

sure you are always getting current benefit information when you inquire about any of your Medicare benefits or want to coordinate supplemental coverage.

Medicaid

Medicare does not pay for most long-term or nursing home care (**long-term care** is for people with chronic health care needs that necessitate ongoing assistance with the activities of daily living). Medicaid, on the other hand, will pay for long-term care if your income is under a certain amount. Many people have to "spend down" their assets in order to qualify for Medicaid.

You've heard the horror stories: Your best friend, aunt, or neighbor is living in poverty because she and her husband had to sell all of their assets to pay for his long-term care when he could no longer live at home. There is nothing left for her to live on, let alone to pass on to their children after she dies. Or maybe she divorced her husband—whom she still loves and is devoted to—just to avoid bankruptcy and welfare and get him on Medicaid to cover his long-term care. You may be able to avoid having to take such desperate measures if you plan ahead.

There are several legal strategies you can pursue under Medicaid to preserve assets and try to ensure your survivor some financial security. You may be able to transfer assets, although such a transfer will make you ineligible for Medicaid for three years or longer, depending on your state of residence. It's important to be aware of the risks associated with giving your property away. For example, if you give your house to your daughter and your daughter dies and her estate goes to your son-in-law, he may sell your house and make you move out. You may also be able to set up a trust and reduce your income to become eligible. Unfortunately, most of the self-help advice regarding Medicaid planning is fraught with danger. Congress periodically changes the rules, so your strategy may have to change, and even with competent advice tailored to your needs, Medicaid planning is not easy. Each state administers its program differently and state rules change periodically, too. Thus, be sure to check with an experienced estate planning attorney or advisor before taking any action that could impact your Medicaid eligibility.

SOCIAL SECURITY

Social Security is the United States' most extensive program to provide income for older and disabled Americans. It is paid for by a tax on workers and their employers. The program is complicated, and like Medicare and Medicaid, the laws and regulations change from time to time.

If you visit the Social Security website (www.socialsecurity. gov), you'll see that Social Security is gender neutral, and that individuals with identical earning histories are treated the same

ⓘ PRIVATE LONG-TERM CARE INSURANCE

It costs a lot to die today if your last few months or years of life are spent in a care facility. If you are not eligible for Medicaid, then you may want to consider purchasing long-term care insurance. Long-term care insurance plans can cover services for you if have a disability or chronic illness, and may include

- help at home with daily personal care such as dressing and bathing,
- assisted-living services such as providing meals, monitoring your health, and providing some medical care, and even
- full-scale nursing home care.

Long-term care insurance can help you avoid the huge expenses of a nursing home or attendant care if you want to stay in your own home as long as possible. Depending on your policy, long-term care coverage can help to protect your assets, reduce your dependence on your loved ones, and ensure that you receive whatever long-term care you need. The downside is that such policies can be expensive, ranging from nearly $1,000 per year if you buy before you're fifty, to more than $6,000 per year at age seventy-five. These plans will impact your estate plan, because the more you spend on your policy, the less you will have to leave to your heirs—but if you wind up needing long-term care, you may well end up saving money.

in terms of benefits. However, women earn less during their working lives, tend to have fewer pension benefits and fewer assets, live longer, and need more income for retirement. Thus, women are likely to be more dependent on a lesser amount of Social Security. More than 40 percent of older women living alone depend on Social Security for almost all of their incomes.

Women who are or have been married may also be entitled to spouse and survivor benefits. When a person who has worked and paid Social Security taxes dies, the following family members qualify for benefits:

- A spouse who is at least sixty years old and has not remarried
- A disabled spouse who is at least fifty and has not remarried
- Children who are under eighteen (or under nineteen if attending elementary or high school full time) or are disabled
- Parents who are sixty-two or older and who received at least half of their support from the worker at the time of his or her death

You can qualify for survivor's benefits based on your husband's work and contribution to Social Security, even if you never worked yourself. If you are a widow, your ability to collect benefits and the amount of benefits you will collect will depend on your age and your deceased husband's work record. You will not have to prove that you were dependent on your husband's income. The amount you will get is usually only half of what would have been paid to your husband. But if you are entitled to benefits based on your own work record, you will get the higher of the two benefit amounts.

Social Security also protects you if you are divorced, provided your marriage lasted at least ten years and you have not remarried. Your husband will be able to collect his full benefit, but you will be entitled to an amount equal to half of his benefit while he is alive. When he dies, you are entitled to the widow's benefit you would have received if you had stayed married.

Note that women in unmarried relationships, even long-term relationships, are not entitled to spouse or survivor benefits. Even if a woman in an unmarried relationship has stayed home to take care of the children, she will not be eligible for Social Security on the basis of her partner's work record.

SUPPLEMENTAL SECURITY INCOME

You may be entitled to financial assistance from the Social Security Administration even if you do not have a record of employment. The **Supplemental Security Income (SSI)** program pays you monthly benefits if you are

1. sixty-five or older, disabled, or blind, and
2. have very little income and personal property.

SSI benefits are not large. (In 2004, the maximum benefit for an individual was $564 per month, and it was $846 per month for a married couple. These figures are adjusted each January for cost-of-living increases.) The assets tests for SSI mean that you will only be eligible if you have very few assets—a total of $3,000 for a married couple. However, in assessing your assets, the Social Security Administration will not include your home, your car, your life insurance, and some other assets.

It is not uncommon for those on SSI to receive Social Security benefits at the same time. This is especially true for women,

---

ⓘ CAN YOU AFFORD TO GET MARRIED?

Many pension and benefit programs favor married people over single people and unmarried couples, but in an odd twist, some older couples are finding that they cannot afford to get or stay married. Some seniors are divorcing so they can qualify for Medicaid, while other seniors are living together instead of marrying to avoid losing their surviving-spouse pensions or health benefits.

The story of sixty-four-year-old Darlene Davis and her boyfriend of nineteen years, Cary Cohen, is illustrative. Darlene and Cary chose to live together, because marrying would mean that Darlene would lose her deceased husband's health benefits. As a heart-attack survivor with three stents, this was not an option for Darlene. When the state of Virginia learned of her living arrangement, it refused to renew her day-care license because of old state laws that were still on the books that classified cohabitation as illegal. "Sometimes you have to break the rules to make a living," said Darlene. The American Civil Liberties Union took up her case and the state relented. "In the spiritual sense, we are husband and wife," she said. "'But the law just doesn't see it that way.'"

Source: Michelle Conlin, "Unmarried America," Business Week (October 20, 2003).

---

who account for 60 percent of all SSI benefit recipients. In addition, if you receive even $1 per month in SSI benefits, then in most states you will also be eligible for free medical care through Medicaid. If you think you may qualify, check with your local Social Security Administration office or its website at www.ssa.gov/OP_Home/handbook/handbook.21/handbook-toc21.html. You will need to prove your age and provide a great deal of information about your financial situation. If you are applying because of disability or blindness, you will also need copies of your medical records.

WHEN DO I APPLY FOR SOCIAL SECURITY?

You should apply for social security two to three months before your retirement date. Your first Social Security check should arrive soon after you quit working. It is important not to file late for either retirement or survivor benefits, because even if you have been eligible for years, you can only be paid retroactive benefits for the six months prior to the month you file your application. Disability benefits can be paid up to a year before the date of filing, if you were disabled during that year.

Retirement and survivor benefit applications take two to three months to process. Disability benefit applications take longer.

You may apply for benefits online (www.ssa.gov), by calling the toll-free number (1-800-772-1213), or by visiting your local benefits office. Documents that you may need to support your application for benefits include

- your Social Security card or proof of your number,
- your birth certificate or proof of your age,
- your W-2 forms for the past two years (or if you are self-employed, your last two federal income tax returns),
- your marriage certificate if you are a spouse of a worker entitled to benefits,
- your divorce decree if you are a former spouse of a worker entitled to benefits,

- your spouse's death certificate (if you are a surviving spouse), and
- proof of your military service (if applicable).

Depending on your particular circumstances, you may also want to prepare

- a list, with addresses and phone numbers, of the doctors, hospitals, or institutions that have treated you for your disability,
- a summary of all of the jobs you have had for the last fifteen years, listing the type of work you performed, and
- information about any other checks or payments you receive for your disability.

THE WORLD AT YOUR FINGERTIPS

- Older women may be in need of a wide range of legal services. A comparatively small but growing area of specialization among lawyers has become known as elder law. The National Academy of Elder Law Attorneys (NAELA) can give you more information about lawyers who specialize in elder law in your area. You can contact NAELA at 1604 N. Country Club, Tucson, AZ 85716, 1-602-881-4005, or at www.naela.org.
- State and local bar associations may also have information about programs for older persons that provide referrals or legal services on a pro bono basis. These programs, along with other sources of legal assistance, are listed on the website of the American Bar Association's Commission on Law and Aging at www.abanet.org/aging (click on "Law and Aging Resource Guide," then select your state).
- You can get more information about pensions from the U.S. Department of Labor's publication "Women and Pensions: What Women Need to Know and Do," at www.pueblo.gsa.gov/cic_text/money/women-pensions/women.htm.
- The Women's Institute for a Secure Retirement has more detailed information for women about pensions and links to other valuable resources on the web at www.wiser.heinz.org/pensions.html.

• There's a lot of easy-to-understand information on the government Medicare site at www.medicare.gov. You can find more information about eligibility for Medicaid on the website of the Centers for Medicaid and Medicare Services, at www.cms.hhs.gov.

• If you want more detailed information about elder law, check out the *ABA Legal Guide for Older Americans* (1998). The book includes complete chapters on age discrimination in employment, Medicare and Medicaid, grandparents' rights, and other important issues.

REMEMBER THIS

• Women earn less, have fewer assets, and live longer than men, so it is particularly important for women to plan well for their retirements.

• It's never too early to start planning for retirement—find out what kind of pension plan your workplace offers and think about increasing your contributions if you have the opportunity.

• Most pensions vest after five years. If you leave your job before your pension has vested, you will lose any contributions made by your employer.

• If you're married, you may have a right to a fraction of your spouse's pension after his death.

• You will be eligible for Medicare after you turn sixty-five, but you will have to pay some premiums and will probably need to pay for Medigap insurance to cover other costs. Medicare does not pay for long-term nursing care.

• Medicaid does pay for long-term care, but you will only qualify if your income is below a certain amount. Talk to your lawyer if you want to plan to reduce your income to qualify for Medicaid in the future.

• If you worked in your younger years, then you may be entitled to Social Security. If you are a widow, you may also be entitled to a fraction of your deceased husband's Social Security.

CHAPTER 20

Estate Planning: Save Your Family Time, Money, and Heartache

Jasmine remarried after her husband passed away. She took the money that she and her husband had planned to leave to their children and put it into a joint account with her new husband, James. James moved into Jasmine's family home, and he and Jasmine held the house as joint tenants. Jasmine never wrote a will, but she assumed that James would leave the house, the family heirlooms, and the cash to her daughters when he died.

Unfortunately, James did no such thing. The house went to him automatically when Jasmine died, because of the joint tenancy. And since she didn't have a will, the family heirlooms and the cash went to him through the state's intestacy laws. James wanted to pass the assets on to his own children from his first marriage. He had never much liked Jasmine's kids, so they were left out in the cold.

J asmine's story is all too common. According to a recent survey by Prudential, only 14 percent of women have done some form of detailed estate planning. Are you one of the millions of American women who have not written a will? Perhaps you think that you don't need a will, because you plan to leave everything to your children. Perhaps you think that estate planning is only for rich people. Or maybe you've put off planning your estate because you just don't want to think about dying. There are two very good reasons why you should think about estate planning, rather than letting state law or chance decide who inherits your estate. First, you may want to think carefully about your beneficiaries, given that you are likely to live longer than your husband or male partner. Second, you are more likely to have a large estate subject to estate taxes, because your estate may include assets that both you and your partner accrued during your lifetimes. Federal estate tax rates can run as high as 50 percent; if you fail to plan your estate in such a way as to minimize taxes, your family's wealth can be greatly reduced when you die.

Unfortunately, not making a will could have serious consequences and might mean that your loved ones don't inherit your property in the way you've planned. This chapter will discuss the basics of estate planning and explain why it is so important.

ESTATES AND ESTATE PLANNING

An **estate** is simply your property, and includes:
• Your home and other real estate. Of course, you may not own 100 percent of your home—perhaps you share ownership with another person or you have a mortgage.

⟨⟩ ASK A LAWYER

Q. Is there a minimum estate you have to have before making a will makes sense? In other words, if you're leaving a small amount, is it ever better to just not worry about a will?

A. It is always a good idea to have a will, if only to simplify the process for those who need to deal with your assets after your death—in a will you can simply give authority to a particular person to deal with your assets and provide that he or she does not need to post a bond, which is usually required.

—Answer by Pamela L. Rollins
Attorney, Simpson, Thatcher, and Bartlett LLP,
New York, New York

• Tangible personal property, such as your car, furniture, jewelry, and other valuable items.

• Intangible property, such as your bank accounts, insurance policies, and stocks and bonds, as well as your pension and Social Security benefits.

An **estate plan** is your blueprint for who you want to get your property after you die. Planning your estate is really about caring for your loved ones, seeing that they are provided for, and making sure your hard-earned property is distributed according to your wishes.

In order to plan your estate, you need to know the facts about your family's assets. But lawyers say they find that many clients who come to them for estate-planning advice don't have basic information about their spouse's or partner's income. All too often, the client doesn't know what benefits she is entitled to, where the money is invested, or how much her spouse or partner earns. Whatever the reason for this situation, you need to know this information when planning your estate. It's especially important to find out how property you own—including land and brokerage accounts—is titled.

Many people might be afraid to cause a rift in their relationship by asking their spouse about financial affairs—especially if that spouse is the primary breadwinner in the family. But you might be able to raise the need to share information and plan ahead indirectly—through another family member, an attorney, or other trusted professional. Full knowledge of your family's assets is an essential part of any sound estate plan.

INTESTATE SUCCESSION

If you die **intestate** (without a will), your property must still be distributed. If you haven't made arrangements to transfer your property through a trust or in some other way, then you've in effect left it to state law to write your will for you. This doesn't mean that your money will go to the state. This happens only in very rare cases in which there are no surviving relatives. But the law does make certain assumptions about where you'd like your property to go—assumptions with which you might not agree. In some states, intestate-descent laws prefer "blood" over "marriage" and will give a share of your estate to your children or to your parents, rather than to your surviving spouse. In other states, your surviving spouse inherits your entire estate and your children (and parents) are entitled to nothing. In addition, the intestacy rules in most states give no part of your estate to family members who are not related to you by blood, marriage, or adoption, such as stepparents or life partners. For this reason, it is particularly important for unmarried couples to write wills. You might live with your partner for thirty years, but that makes no difference—if you die without a will, the state intestacy laws will apply, and your partner could be left with nothing.

(i) COMMUNITY PROPERTY STATES

In community property states, most property acquired by each spouse is held equally by both of them as community property. When one spouse dies, his or her half of the community property passes according to either the will or intestacy laws. Community property does not automatically pass to the surviving spouse. When your spouse dies, you own only your share of the community property, and if your spouse wants you to have his share, he must give it to you in a will.

This arrangement can affect estate planning in many ways. What if your spouse leaves everything to your grown children? This would mean that the children would own half the car and half the house. The only way they could really benefit from such a will is to sell the property so that they can have their share of the proceeds. Either you'll have to move out and get another car, or they'll have to struggle along until you die. Married people in community property states should think long and hard before leaving property to anyone other than their spouses.

WILLS

A **will** is simply a document in which you specify who gets your property when you die. The people and institutions who inherit your property are called **beneficiaries**. Wills are relatively easy to make, and you can pretty much leave your property to anyone you wish—no one can stop you from leaving property to your partner, lover, or even the local animal welfare center if you wish.

However, there are some limitations on your freedom to give away your property in your will. If you are married, you can't disinherit your spouse. State laws generally entitle a surviving spouse to take a portion of the deceased spouse's estate—regardless of the deceased spouse's will or estate plan. If your husband dies with a will that makes no provision for you, or conveys less than a certain percentage of his assets, then you can take a statutorily defined **elective share of the estate**. This means that you can choose to accept the amount allowed by law, usually one third or one half of the estate. You do not have to take an elective share of the estate—it's your choice. If you do not exercise the choice, the will stands and the property is distributed as stated in the will.

Elective-share provisions are troubling to many people entering into second marriages, particularly late in life. Even if you've only been married a couple of years, your surviving spouse would be eligible to take up to one half of your property at your death, even if you wanted it to go to your children and your will reflected that. Recent revisions to the Uniform Probate Code (which has been adopted by eighteen states) provide a "sliding scale" for surviving spouses who take against the will. Under this approach, the longer the marriage, the higher the elective share. If the marriage lasted only a few years, the elective share could be quite small, minimizing one source of worry for older couples. You or your husband can also voluntarily give up your right to a share of the estate in a pre- or postnuptial agreement.

(i) **MORE PROTECTION FOR**
SURVIVING SPOUSES

If you survive your husband (as most women do), you may have the protection of homestead laws and exempt-property laws. Typically, these protections are in addition to whatever you receive under the will, the elective share that you can choose to take under the will, or the statutory share that you receive if there is no will.

Homestead laws protect certain property from your deceased husband's creditors. Typically, they permit you to shelter a certain value of the family home and some personal property from creditors. In some states, the homestead exemption protects a statutorily specified sum of money from creditors, rather than the deceased's real or personal property. As a general rule, the protection is temporary, extending for your lifetime or until any minor children reach legal adulthood. However, in a few states homestead laws permanently shelter specified property from creditors of the deceased.

Exempt property laws give you certain specified property, provide protection from creditors, and protect against disinheritance.

The situation with children is dramatically the opposite. Except for Louisiana, every state permits you to disinherit your children. However, to be effective it's better if your intent to disinherit is expressed, which usually means it has to be stated in writing.

In addition to using your will to bequeath (give away) your money and property, you can use it to

• set up trusts to benefit your children, partner, a charity, or any combination of people and causes,

   • name a guardian for your minor children,

   • forgive debts owed to you,

• name the person you want to settle your estate and be in charge of distributing your property (usually called an executor/executrix or personal representative), and

• disinherit people (though you cannot completely disinherit your spouse).

You can also use your will to specify how and where you want to be buried (or if you prefer to be cremated and how you want your ashes disposed of), but this provision is probably not binding because the will is usually not probated until after burial. If you have particular wishes about your funeral, burial, or cremation, you should set them out in a separate document, and give a copy to your lawyer, your spouse, and the executor of your will.

If you change your mind about something in your will, you shouldn't write any changes on an existing will. But you can easily make a change in a legal amendment to the original will, called a **codicil**, or you can simply draft a new will in which you revoke all previous wills.

So you may think you have your will all figured out—the house goes to your husband, the money to your kids, and your sister will get mom's antique engagement ring. But when you're talking to your lawyer about drafting your will, there are a few eventualities you will want to think about.

For one thing, who do you want to get the **residuary estate**? "Residuary" estate basically means "everything else." After all the specific gifts have been made, and the house and money distributed, there will probably still be some things that you haven't accounted for in your will, including items you acquire after you drafted your will. If you don't specify where the residuary of your estate is to go, then it will be distributed in accordance with the intestate succession laws in your state.

What if one of the people to whom you leave property dies before you? If your sister dies before you, then the gift you made to her in your will might **lapse**. This would mean that mom's engagement ring will go back into the residuary estate and might end up with someone you hadn't intended. Many states have antilapse statutes, which specify that if a beneficiary who is your child or dependent dies before you, that beneficiary's dependents would receive the gift. But if an asset is particularly important or valuable, then it's a good idea to name a **contingent beneficiary**, who will get the gift if the primary recipient dies before you.

DO YOU NEED A LAWYER?

If you are an adult and of sound mind, you can make your own will. In many states, you can buy a will in a stationery store and simply fill in the blanks. Unfortunately, these wills are very modest. They often assume you want to leave everything to your spouse and children and provide for few other gifts. These days you can also buy computerized will kits, which are a viable alternative to a lawyer if your estate is small and you only want a straightforward distribution of your property. For your will to be valid, you must still follow very strict requirements when signing it, including having a number of witnesses. If you or your spouse

⚠ WHY A JOINT WILL IS A BAD IDEA

A **joint will** is a contract between two people (who are not necessarily married) who agree to leave their property to each other. It generally provides that each partner's property will go to the other, and then it spells out what will happen to the property when the second person dies. If you are married or living with a partner, and you want to use a will to pass on your property, you should execute separate wills and avoid a joint will. Joint wills require the consent of both you and your partner before they can be modified, which means they aren't revised as frequently as they should be—either because of a family dispute or a double dose of inertia. They are also not a good idea because they

- can keep the survivor from using the property as she or he wishes,
- don't allow for circumstances that change after the will was made,
- may be impossible to revoke,
- frequently result in litigation if one person makes a new will after the other one dies, and
- can make for problems in the event of a divorce or separation.

have children from a previous marriage, if you own a business, if your estate is substantial (an estate around the $1.5 million mark will make estate tax an issue), or if you anticipate a challenge to the will from a disgruntled relative, then you should consult with an experienced estate-planning attorney.

PROBATE

If you have a will or die intestate, your estate will be administered through probate in a local court. **Probate** is the court-supervised legal procedure that
- determines the validity of your will (if you have one),
- gathers and distributes your assets (according to your will if you have one or according to the laws of intestacy if you do not), and
- provides a process for paying creditors and places a time limit on claims against your estate.

Your will needs to be probated in every state in which you own real estate. If you own property outside the state in which you live, it's a good idea to avoid going through probate in an additional state by owning the real estate through a partnership, corporation, or revocable trust.

Your will should name an **executor**, who will administer the will during probate. The executor just has to be sure to complete the various forms, appraisals, and inventories required and may need to obtain court approval before selling and distributing certain assets or paying debts. If your estate is relatively modest, a level-headed relative can probably handle probate.

Probate used to be a slow, cumbersome, and expensive process, but it has been greatly improved in recent years and may well be quick and inexpensive in your jurisdiction. **Family allowance laws** make probate less of a burden on family members. Under these laws, the family is entitled to a certain amount of money from the estate while the estate is being probated, regardless of the claims of creditors. Many people still think that probate should be avoided at all costs and go to some trouble to create a trust or another will substitute to circumvent the process. But for many families, especially those of moderate means, it can be more trouble to avoid probate than to go through with it.

WILL SUBSTITUTES AND PROBATE AVOIDANCE

A will is usually the most important part of an estate plan, but it's not the only part. There may well be advantages—including avoiding probate—in passing some property outside of the will, through **will substitutes**. Will substitutes include everything from pensions, life insurance, and gifts, to that staple of the probate-avoider, the trust. One word of warning—all of your property must be in the trust or other will substitute for you to be able to avoid probate. If you leave any property outside the trust, then it will have to go through probate.

Trust Property

A **trust** is a legal relationship in which a trustee (which can be one person or a qualified trust company) holds property for the benefit of another (the beneficiary). The **grantor** creates the trust, the **trustee** holds or manages the property, and the **beneficiaries** are entitled to the benefits.

Putting property in trust transfers it from your personal ownership to the trustee who holds the property for you. The trustee has **legal title** to the trust property. For most purposes, the law looks at these assets as if the trustee now owned them. For example, many (but not all) trusts have separate taxpayer identification numbers.

But trustees are not the full owners of the property. Trustees have a legal duty to use the property as provided in the trust agreement and permitted by law. The beneficiaries retain what is known as **equitable title** or **beneficial title**—the right to benefit from the property as specified in the trust.

( ) ASK A LAWYER

Q. My husband named me as the executor of his estate. I have no idea what this means. What do I have to do? What kinds of things have to be taken care of?

A. An executor is in charge of dealing with another person's property after that person dies. The basic duties of an executor are to probate the decedent's will, gather the decedent's probate (nonjoint) assets, pay the creditors, pay any estate and inheritance taxes that may be due, and then distribute the assets to the decedent's beneficiaries or heirs. This process is called estate administration. The executor also needs to protect and invest the assets appropriately during the administration of the estate.

—Answer by Pamela L. Rollins
Attorney, Simpson, Thatcher, and Bartlett LLP,
New York, New York

Q. I understand that if I create a trust, I no longer own the property—the trustee does. I find this very worrying. How can I be sure that the trustee won't take or mismanage the property?

A. For a revocable living trust, you can generally be the sole trustee. If other trustees act during your life or after your death, they are subject to strict rules about what they can and cannot do, both in the trust document you create and under state law. The beneficiaries of the trust, and those authorized to act on their behalf (guardians, and so on), are entitled to enforce these rules against the trustee.

—Answer by Pamela L. Rollins
Attorney, Simpson, Thatcher, and Bartlett LLP,
New York, New York

The grantor may also retain control of the property. A revocable **living trust** is a trust that you set up during your lifetime that you can change or revoke. If you make yourself the trustee, then you retain the rights of ownership you'd have if the assets were still in your name. You can buy anything and add it to the trust, sell anything out of the trust, and give trust property to whomever you wish.

If you set up the trust by your will to take effect at your death—a **testamentary trust**—you retain the title to the property during your lifetime, and on your death it passes to the trustee to be distributed to your beneficiaries as you designate.

Should you have a trust? It depends on the size of your estate and the purpose of the trust. For example, if you mainly want a living trust to protect assets from taxes and probate, but your estate is under the current federal tax floor, you have no out-of-state real estate, and probate is not a problem in your state (or your estate can qualify for quick and inexpensive probate in your state), some lawyers would tell you it isn't worth the cost and administrative hassle. Trusts are impractical for most young people unless they're relatively wealthy.

On the other hand, a trust may be a very desirable solution to many problems. A funded living trust may avoid the need to appoint a guardian of your estate if you should become disabled (although a durable general power of attorney may also avoid a guardianship proceeding). A trust for the benefit of others, such as minor children and grandchildren or disabled relatives, provides a mechanism for managing property and making distributions over the years, without court supervision. A trust can ensure your property is not taxed in future generations and provide ways of maximizing tax credits and exemptions. A trust can also provide protection from creditors for beneficiaries. Here's an example of a situation in which a living trust makes sense. Let's say you're a widow with no children and no close relatives, and you can no longer manage your finances. If you set up a living trust, then you can transfer your property and other assets to a trustee, who can then manage your assets and distribute a regular income to you for the rest of your life. Upon your death,

ⓘ ADVANTAGES OF TRUSTS

- A trust can protect your privacy—unlike a will, a trust is confidential.

- If you have a trust, your trustee can manage assets efficiently if you die and your beneficiaries are minor children or others are not up to the responsibility of handling the estate.

- A trust can protect your assets by maximizing tax credits and reducing the taxes you have to pay. This is a complex area—talk to an estate-planning lawyer about how a trust can help you reduce taxes effectively.

- A living trust can manage property for you while you're alive, providing a way to care for you if you should become disabled. A living trust also avoids probate, lowers estate administration costs, and speeds transfer of your assets to beneficiaries after your death. If you want to avoid probate, however, you must ensure that all of your property is in the trust—including your house.

your trustee can distribute your assets to the people or charitable organizations of your choice. If at any time after you create your trust, you change your mind as to any of your beneficiaries (i.e., you want to add one or eliminate one), you can make a simple amendment to your trust by a written letter or memo signed and dated by you and delivered to your trustee.

Property You Own in Joint Tenancy

Joint tenancy is property you own with someone else. **Joint tenancy** is a legal term that means, essentially, "co-ownership." If you and your partner buy a house or car in both your names, each of you is considered a joint tenant and has co-ownership. When one of you dies, the other joint tenant immediately owns it all, regardless of what either of you says in your will.

Joint tenancy can be a useful way to transfer property at death. Family cars and brokerage accounts often pass this way. Joint tenancy has its advantages. It's inexpensive to create, for example. In some jurisdictions, if one of the tenants dies, jointly held property might defeat the claims of creditors, or at least make collecting against the will a great deal more difficult.

But joint tenancy can also cause problems. It's not a good idea if you're in a shaky marriage, if your intentions might change, or if you want to distribute an asset gradually rather than all at once.

Beneficiary Designations

Your Individual Retirement Account (IRA), your pension, and your life insurance may be among your most valuable assets. At your death, such plans are usually passed to beneficiaries directly and are not disposed of in your will. However, the benefit is included in your estate for estate tax purposes. You should be able to name someone as a beneficiary for your life insurance, IRA, or similar individual retirement plan on a beneficiary designation form when you open the account. This is simple enough if you want to leave the balance of the account to one beneficiary. If your wishes are more complicated, you may want to leave the fund to a trust, to be distributed in accordance with the rules of the trust. There may be income tax implications for the beneficiary.

Employer pension plans are a little different from IRAs—whether you can designate a beneficiary depends on the rules of the plan. Contact your plan administrator for more information.

Gifts

You can make an unlimited number of gifts each year while you are alive—referred to as **inter vivos gifts**—to anyone you please and avoid tax, as long as the annual gift to each person is worth $11,000 or less (or $22,000 or less if you and your husband make a gift).

( ) ASK A LAWYER

Q. I was separated from my husband for ten years; we never got a divorce. He died a couple of months ago and I assumed that I'd be able to claim a part of his estate under state law. But the sneak didn't have a will or an estate—everything is in a trust. Is there anything I can do to get to my fair share of his money?

A. In most states, a surviving spouse has rights to collect her elective share against "will substitutes" under certain conditions. You will need to consult with an estate attorney in your state to determine what rights you may have in the property.

—Answer by Pamela L. Rollins
Attorney, Simpson, Thatcher, and Bartlett LLP,
New York, New York

An inter vivos gift can help reduce your estate in order to avoid high death taxes or avoid probate. Such gifts can also give you the pleasure of seeing the recipient enjoy your generosity.

PROTECTING YOUR ESTATE AFTER A DIVORCE OR SEPARATION

It might seem pretty easy to name beneficiaries for trusts, retirement vehicles, and insurance policies, but life has a way of making things difficult. If you get divorced, remarry, or have another child, it's up to you to make sure that the paperwork keeps up with your life and that your beneficiary designations reflect your current intentions. If you divorce or separate, your trusts may also need to be specifically amended and you may need to replace trustees if they were members of your husband's family. If your husband is the beneficiary on your employer's retirement plan, federal law prohibits you from removing him until the divorce is final. But be sure to make this change (if permitted by the divorce settlement) as soon as things have been finalized. Under recent revisions of the Uniform Probate Code, your state may automatically revoke provisions of some estate documents if you divorce. But few states have adopted all the provisions of the code. So to be on the safe side, it's best to change these documents yourself.

Obviously, it's hard to agree on anything at this stage, but perhaps through negotiation you and your soon-to-be-former spouse can convert any jointly held assets (bank accounts, living trusts, property, and so on) into separate holdings.

One final thing to keep in mind: Patchwork families are a prime category for will contests, as children from different marriages may be more likely to disagree about the distribution of estate assets. People in this category should be especially careful that their wills, prenuptial and postnuptial agreements, and trusts are properly prepared.

THE WORLD AT YOUR FINGERTIPS

- The American Bar Association (ABA) offers a new edition of its *Guide to Wills and Estates* (2004), which contains a wealth of detailed information on all the areas covered in this chapter and more.

- The ABA's Section of Real Property, Probate, and Trust Law has information for the public on its website at www.abanet.org/rppt/public/home.html.

- The AARP site (www.aarp.org/estate-planning) has a wide range of good information about wills and estates.

- Who Gets Grandma's Yellow Pie Plate (www.yellowpieplate.umn.edu/07-lm.html) is an excellent website that will help you think about inheritance planning.

- *Beyond the Grave: The Right Way and the Wrong Way of Leaving Money to Your Children (and Others)* (2001), by Gerald M. Condon and Jeffrey L. Condon, is a good resource. The Condons, who are father and son and both lawyers, look at traditional estate planning but also consider the psychological and emotional aspects of leaving money.

REMEMBER THIS

- If you die without a will, your property will be distributed according to the state's intestacy laws. This may mean that your property is not distributed in the way you'd like.
- It's particularly important to draft a will and think about estate planning if you have minor children and need to make arrangements for guardianship of a child, if you're married but have children from another relationship, or if you're unmarried and living with a partner.
- If you're married, state laws entitle you to a percentage of your spouse's estate.
- If you have a large estate, then you may want to avoid probate and minimize taxes by setting up a trust. Talk to your lawyer about the details of setting up a trust.
- Property that you own in joint tenancy does not go through probate on the death of the co-owner. Regardless of what your will says, joint property passes directly to your joint tenant.
- Don't forget about beneficiary designations on valuable assets like life insurance, IRAs, and pensions when planning your estate. And don't forget to change these designations when your life changes—if your relationship ends or you get divorced.

Where Do You Go From Here?

RESOURCES

As the old saying goes, "A woman's work is never done," and neither is ours. Throughout this book, we've provided you with resources for finding more information on a variety of legal topics, and we still have more to give you. Some of these may have been mentioned in previous chapters, and others are all-new recommendations. Also included are some suggestions you can use to go about getting more information.

10 WEBSITES TO GET YOU STARTED

Many of the sites below are general—they cover everything from sexual harassment to family care—so be sure to explore them fully to see what they have to offer. In some cases, we've also pointed out more specific areas of interest housed within the site.

National Women's Law Center
www.nwlc.org

Gender Issues Research Center
www.gendercenter.org
www.gendercenter.org/importantleg.htm

Institute for Women's Policy Research
www.iwpr.org

National Collegiate Athletic Association's (NCAA) Gender Equity/Title IX section
www1.ncaa.org/membership/ed_outreach/gender_equity/index.html

Feminist Majority Foundation
www.feminist.org/fmf_default.asp; www.feminist.org/911/

National Organization for Women's Key Issues
www.now.org/issues/

Legal Momentum
www.legalmomentum.org

Equal Employment Opportunity Commission
www.eeoc.gov

National Partnership for Women & Families
www.nationalpartnership.org

National Center for Lesbian Rights
www.nclrights.org

Don't forget that many websites offer posting boards, user groups, mailing lists, and chatrooms where you can ask questions, exchange information, and sign up for e-newsletters on topics that are important to you. You can also search the web for specific lists or groups that are more tailored to your needs.

If and when you tire of surfing the Internet for more information, consider these other possibilities for learning more about legal issues women face.

WHAT? MORE READING?

Yes, more reading. Visit your local library for a plethora of books on your topic(s) of choice. If you're not sure where to start, here are a few suggestions:

Women's Legal Guide, edited by Barbara Hauser, (Fulcrum Publishing, 1996)

"Just Sign Here, Honey": Women's 10 Biggest Legal Mistakes and How to Avoid Them, by Marilyn Barrett (Capital Books, Inc., revised edition, 2003)

Living Together: A Legal Guide for Unmarried Couples, 12th edition, by Toni Lynne Ihara, Ralph E. Warner, Frederick Hertz, (Nolo Press, 2004)

IT'S A COMMUNITY THING. . .

Public events such as meetings, lectures, and support groups are a great way to get and share information. They're also good places to make new contacts and meet people who may have similar questions or be facing the same issues that you are. To find these events, check your local media outlets (newspapers, TV, radio) or call your area's community centers and libraries. Colleges, universities, hospitals, and churches may also sponsor programs or lecture series.

If no events are scheduled and you think your community might benefit from a question-and-answer session on women and credit, for example, get in touch with your state or local bar association to engage a speaker for the occasion. You might also contact your chamber of commerce.

We hope we've provided you with enough information to get you started, and we welcome your comments and suggestions for future editions of this book. Please visit us on the Web at www.abanet.org/publiced/ or drop us a line via e-mail at abapubed@abanet.org. We'd like to hear from you!

INDEX

cosigning loans, 94, 95, 96,
264, 268
credit, 260–77
for business owners, 275
defined, 261–62
discrimination laws,
269–72
forms of, 261–65
marital status and, 271
payday loans, 261
steps to take against discrimination, 272,
274–76
titles, names, and, 270–71
unmarried status and, 113
widows and, 267–69
credit history, 273–74
credit-reporting agencies, 272
credit union membership,
domestic partnerships
and, 104
creditor, 262
cross-dressers, 273
cruelty, divorce and, 118, 121
custodial parent, 136

date rape, 236–37
dating, 24–25
Davis, Darlene, 313
debtor, 262
Defense of Marriage Act, 82,
108
deferred-compensation plans,
301
defined-benefit pension
plans, 297–98
defined-contribution pension
plans, 298
Delaware, mediation pro-
grams in, 140
delayed discovery or realization, 236
Department of Agriculture,
293
Department of Education,
Office for Civil Rights,
10, 11, 12–15, 18, 21,
27–28, 29
Department of Labor, 59, 66,
315
Dependent Care Assistance
Programs (DCAPs), 74,
76
dependent care issues,
67–79
child care, 67–75
elder care, 75–78
desertion, 121
Diners Club, 262
direct-entry midwives, 203–4
directives, 105, 168
disability leave, 42, 60–62

disparate impact discrimination, 5, 36
disparate treatment discrimination, 4–5, 34–36
District of Columbia
child custody decisions in,
143, 144
domestic violence cases,
253
protection orders in, 245
spousal rape laws in, 241
Division of Consumer Affairs,
275
divorce, 117–33
child custody and visitation
issues, 134–49
defined, 120
embryo ownership issues,
168
estate planning and,
331–32
history of, 117–18
joint credit accounts and,
127, 129, 266–67
joint wills and, 324
pensions and, 302
record-keeping and, 130
same-sex marriages and,
123–24
Social Security and, 312,
314
tips when considering, 129
types of, 120–22
domestic partnerships, 102,
104
domestic violence, 222,
240–58
criminal process for,
249–53
defined, 241
divorce and, 118, 121
filing criminal charges,
246, 248–49
illegal immigrants and,
255–56
legal protections against,
242–49
mediation and, 140
proarrest policies, 256
progress against, 253, 256
reporting, 254–55
safety plans, 246, 254
self-defense and, 247
Domestic Violence Aware-
ness Month, 253
drug use
divorce and, 121
pregnancy and, 196–98
drunkenness, 121
dual eligibility, 288
Dubin, Arlene G., *Prenups for
Lovers,* 115

durable power of attorney, 76
durable power of attorney for
health care, 76, 105–6

early retirement incentive
programs, 43
Earned Income Tax Credits,
74
ectopic pregnancy, 166
education
laws against discrimina-
tion, 17
pregnancy and, 8–9
Title IX and, 1–19
education assistance, domestic partnerships and, 104
education expenses, child
support and, 153
egg donation, 172–73
agreements for, 173–75
eggs ownership issues,
166–68, 170
Eisenstadt v. Baird, 186–87
elder care, 67, 75–78
Eldercare Locator, 79
elective share of the estate,
321
embryo donation, 172–73
agreements for, 173–75
embryo ownership issues,
166–68, 170
emergency contraception
laws, 237
Emergency Food Assistance
Program, 293
employment manuals, 40
Employment Non-
Discrimination Act
(proposed), 37
employment policies, family-
friendly, 62–66
Employment Standards
Administration, 59
endometriosis, 180
Equal Credit Opportunity
Act (ECOA), 113, 269,
272, 273, 275
Equal Educational Opportunities Act of 1974, 17
Equal Employment Opportu-
nity Commission
(EEOC), 40, 44, 46–49,
52, 59, 189–90, 335
Equal Employment Opportu-
nity (EEO) counselor, 51
Equal Pay Act of 1963, 43–44
Equal Pay Day, 53
Equal Protection Clause of
the Fourteenth Amend-
ment of the U.S. Consti-
tution, 17
Equal Rights Advocates, 53